# FREE STUFF

# STUFF

## IF YOU'RE OVER 50

### BY THE EDITORS OF FC&A

# Publisher's Note

The editors of FC&A have taken careful measures to ensure the accuracy and usefulness of the information in this book. While every attempt was made to assure accuracy, some Web sites, addresses, and telephone numbers may have changed since printing.

This book is intended for general information only. It does not constitute medical, legal, or financial advice or practice. We cannot guarantee the safety or effectiveness of any treatment or advice mentioned. Readers are urged to consult with their personal financial advisors, lawyers, and health care professionals.

The publisher and editors disclaim all liability (including any injuries, damages, or losses) resulting from the use of the information in this book.

"Finally, brothers, whatever is true, whatever is noble, whatever is right, whatever is pure, whatever is lovely, whatever is admirable — if anything is excellent or praiseworthy — think about such things. Whatever you have learned or received or heard from me, or seen in me — put into practice. And the God of peace will be with you."

— Phillipians 4:8-9 (NIV)

FC&A
103 Clover Green
Peachtree City, GA 30269

Produced by the staff of FC&A

**First printing July 2001**

ISBN 1-890957-48-8

# TABLE OF CONTENTS

# HOW TO FIND THE BEST DEALS

Pay close attention to this chapter, and you'll rarely pay full price for anything. Whether you prefer surfing the Internet with your computer or digging through boxes at curbside, you'll find searching for free stuff and great deals exciting and challenging.

This chapter gives you the best advice for successful shopping everywhere — from yard sales and thrift stores to malls and government auctions. It will help you find quality as well as low prices.

You'll also learn how to avoid pitfalls — like how to tell a good deal from a scam. And how to be sure something you get second hand is safe. Read on for all that and more.

## How to get goods for little or nothing

"There must be a better way," you say to yourself when you come home from a budget-busting shopping trip. The truth is, with a little creativity — and a bit of boldness in some cases — you can find lots of ways to get things you need for little or nothing.

**Share and share alike.** Be generous in lending your tools to a trustworthy neighbor, and he'll likely do the same for you. You may even find that sharing the cost of something you both use only occasionally — maybe a fishing boat or a chain saw — will save you both money. Just work out in advance such concerns as where you'll store it and what you'll do if one of you moves away.

**Swap, don't shop.** Everybody is a winner if you exchange things you no longer use for things you need. You might trade informally with a friend or hold a neighborhood swap meet. You can sometimes find items you want in "swap" publications or the newspaper's classified ads.

**Practice curbside "shopping."** When people do their spring cleaning, all kinds of furniture, clothing, and household accessories appear along neighborhood streets, free for the taking.

Don't be embarrassed to look through other people's discards. This practice is very popular in some places, especially in Europe where specific days are designated for putting out large items. Those people would find it shameful to let perfectly good items be thrown in the trash.

The end of the school term is a good time to visit the curbs near college campuses. Students will leave books, furniture, lamps — maybe even a computer — as they head home for the summer. Check out yard sales in these areas, too. Those who can't bear to just toss good things out may be willing to practically give them away.

**Dare to dive for freebies.** Maybe hunting through a dumpster for free stuff is where you draw the line. And you really should be cautious if you do it. But a lot of unused merchandise, still in good condition, is thrown away every day by businesses.

---

### Secrets of a successful swap meet

If you are organizing your first swap meet, follow these tips to keep it simple.

*Start small.* Invite interested friends to participate. If you want a larger group, advertise by word-of-mouth, flyers, or bulletin board announcements.

*Set guidelines.* Decide what kinds of items are acceptable. Everything should be in good condition.

*Sort it out.* Display like items together. Place most items on tables where folks have room to easily see everything.

*Keep swapping simple.* For an informal group, have everyone take whatever they wish. Or, to make it more fair, give participants a ticket for each donated item, which they can trade for another item. You can also work out a system for swapping by value.

*Plan for leftovers.* If it's a small meet, ask everyone to take back whatever they bring that no one selects. Or donate all left-over items to a charity thrift store or other worthy organization.

---

Check behind grocery stores for cases of dented canned goods, for example. Find not-quite-perfect roses near flower shops. And for a wide variety of clothing and household items, visit department store dumpsters.

A lot of other perfectly good stuff is thrown away in neighborhood dumpsters as well. If you want to hide your true purpose, you can always pretend you are hunting for boxes.

**Post your "most wanted" list.** Find a bulletin board in your community — at a church, community center, or grocery store, perhaps — where you can put your name, phone number, and a list of the things you are looking for. Encourage others to do the same to form a savings network. If someone has what another wants, or knows where to find it free or at a bargain price, they can call and let them know.

## The wealth of junk mail

If you are looking for free stuff, just open your mailbox. You'll find a constant stream of freebies. Advertisers use them to draw your attention to what they want to sell you. Some come as trial offers — like a free issue of a magazine. You pay nothing if you cancel when the bill arrives.

You may receive the offer of a pre-paid telephone card if you sign up for a credit card. A charitable organization may offer you a free tote bag if you make a donation to their cause. And a music company will send you a selection of free CDs or tapes if you join their music club.

In some cases the item really is free. But they'll also send you the products or sign you up for trial services they want you to pay for. If you don't want them, just return the products — usually at the sender's expense — or cancel the services. You get to keep the gift.

In other cases, like with the free CDs, you have to agree to a minimum number of purchases within one year. This is still a good idea if you select music you would have bought anyhow.

Just be sure you understand what you are agreeing to when you accept any free offer. It's not really free if you wind up paying for something you don't need or can get at a better price elsewhere.

# Put money in your pocket with coupons and rebates

**Clip your way to savings.** Are you a compulsive coupon clipper? If you are, you know that you can save money on things you need every week. You are probably already getting coupons from the Sunday newspaper circulars and clipping cents-off deals from products you buy.

In addition, be sure to check mailers that are delivered to your home. Local businesses use these coupons to get you into their stores. Often restaurants will have a buy-one, get-one-free dinner special on certain nights of the week, usually Sunday through Thursday.

If you're retired, why not make Thursday your night out instead of Friday or Saturday? You'll be able to take advantage of these specials with your special someone and have money left for something else.

Coupon mailers are also good ways to save on things like dry cleaning, fast food, pet supplies, and lots of other products. Look through them carefully when you receive them, and put the ones you'll use in your wallet or purse. That way, they'll be there when you need them.

**Click on these deals.** Did you know that you can use the Internet to get the exact coupons you need? Web sites like Third Age have free member services, like their "e-centives," which are special offers and digital online coupons that you can print out or have mailed to you.

Membership is free, and Third Age will give you an organizer to keep track of all the offers you're interested in. You'll only get coupons you want, so you don't have to worry about being flooded with junk mail. The site also has free recipes from manufacturers and famous people. Go to <www.thirdage.com> to find out more.

**Get back those hard-earned greenbacks.** Occasionally you'll buy a product that offers a rebate, and if you're lucky you'll get $5 back from the store or manufacturer. If you like deals like this that put money back in your pocket, you'll love the Web site called Cyber Rebate. This site keeps track of dozens of rebate offers, many so good that the product ends up being free.

For example, a Godzilla Handheld Electronic Game that was listed at $23.99 had a mail-in rebate of $23.99, making it a potentially free Christmas present for a grandchild. The book *Pride and Prejudice* was listed for $13.99 with a mail-in rebate of $13.99 — another possibility for a free present.

These are just two of dozens of items listed. If you want to be on their mailing list, they'll send you a free newsletter with all the latest rebates. For more information, go to their Web site at <www.cyberrebate.com>.

## Free shopping-mall services

As a rule, shopping malls are not the place to find your best bargains. But they are convenient, offer good places for a quick lunch with friends, and serve as a free indoor track when the weather is less than perfect. If you are going to be there anyway, you might as well take advantage of any free or bargain products and services they offer.

Some shopping centers, for example, have frequent shopper programs. They give gifts or discounts after you spend a certain amount in their stores. The people at the information desk can tell you about any special deals they offer.

And while some people pay a lot of money for the services of a personal shopper, you may get this kind of help for free at your favorite department store. A person who knows the stock, has a good eye for the colors and styles that work for you, and is good at putting several outfits together can save you a lot of time and money. And you'll probably be more pleased with how you look in your new clothes than you would be if you shopped on your own.

Ask for help with other purchases, too, like finding the perfect gift for a hard-to-please loved one.

## How to get the best bargains

A big "sale" sign catches your attention as you pass a store window. You go inside, pick up an item, and wonder, "Is this really a bargain? What did I pay last time? What was the price in that ad I saw recently? I think this is cheaper, but is the quality the same?"

The key to effective comparison shopping is to keep a notebook of items you buy frequently. Add anything you expect to be needing in the near future as well. When you find the items in stores, see ads for them, or overhear someone bragging about the bargains they found, jot down the prices and locations.

Also note the dates of sales. This will let you know how long the current prices will be available. And you can refer to your notes to see what time of year you are likely to find similar items on sale again.

Make notes of the quality, size, brand name, and any other important information. For things sold by weight or volume, note the unit pricing on the store shelf. If it's not available, use a calculator, and divide the cost by the number of pounds or ounces.

For some items, you might find a Web site like the one at <www.shop pinglist.com> helpful as well. It uses your zip code to help you locate specific items on sale in stores near you.

Keep the notebook handy at home, and take it along whenever you go out, even if you aren't expecting to shop. You never know when someone might tell you about a terrific sale.

## Comparison shop to save big bucks

Some people are born to shop. They love to look around and compare items and prices. Others prefer to dash in, grab what they need and dash back out. You may not be a natural-born shopper, but you should know that sometimes a little comparison shopping can save you a lot.

One shopping trip to several stores revealed the following price comparisons. Not surprisingly, the thrift store usually had the best prices, with the consignment shop a close second. If you don't mind buying used items, and have the time and patience to sift through them, you can find some great deals.

Otherwise, take time to note what types of items sell for less at different stores. Newspaper circulars can save you some legwork, and many stores will match their competitors' advertised prices, so bring those circulars along when you shop.

Check out the following charts for examples of how much you can save when you shop around.

## Woman's long-sleeve blouse, button front

| Store | Condition | Price |
|---|---|---|
| Value Village Thrift | Used but good | $.99 |
| Cat's Pajamas, Ltd. (consignment shop) | Used but good | $4 |
| J.C. Penney Outlet | New | $4.99 (orig. $20) |
| Cat's Pajamas, Ltd. | Like new | $7 |
| Wal-Mart | New | $7 (reg. $14.96) |
| J.C. Penney Online | New | $16.99 |
| J.C. Penney Catalog | New | $28 (tall, $31) |
| Macy's | New | $34.98-$39.98 |

## Navy skirt

| Store | Condition | Price |
|---|---|---|
| Value Village Thrift | Like new | $6.99 |
| Cat's Pajamas, Ltd. | Like new | $8 |
| Wal-Mart | New | $11.96 |
| J.C. Penney Outlet | New | $19.99 (orig. $40) |
| Macy's | New | $59 |

## Woman's sweater

| Store | Condition | Price |
|---|---|---|
| Value Village Thrift | Used but good | $2.99 |
| Wal-Mart | New | $12.94 |
| Sam's Club | New | $12.91 |
| J.C. Penney Outlet | New | $14.99 (orig. $32) |
| J.C. Penney Catalog | New | $24.99 |
| Macy's | New | $29.98 |
| J.C. Penney Online | New | $30 |

## Woman's jacket/blazer (wool or wool blend)

| Store | Condition | Price |
| --- | --- | --- |
| Value Village Thrift | Like new | $2.99 |
| Value Village Thrift | Used but good | $4.91 (orig. about $100) |
| Cat's Pajamas, Ltd. | Like new | $25 |
| Wal-Mart | New | $32.96 |
| J.C. Penney Outlet | New | $39.99 (orig. $79) |
| Macy's | New | $70 |

## Electric toaster (2-slice, wide-slot)

| Store | Condition | Price |
| --- | --- | --- |
| Value Village Thrift | Used, somewhat older | $3.83 |
| J.C. Penney Outlet | New | $14.99 |
| Macy's | New | $24.99 |
| Sam's Club | New | $39.96 |

## Man's white shirt (cotton or cotton/polyester blend)

| Store | Condition | Price |
| --- | --- | --- |
| Value Village Thrift | Like new | $2.99 |
| J.C. Penney Outlet | New | $6.99 |
| Wal-Mart | New | $12.96 |
| J.C. Penney Outlet | New | $12.99 |
| Sam's Club | New | $17.94 |
| J.C. Penney Catalog | New | $24.50 |
| J.C. Penney Online | New | $26 |
| Macy's | New | $29.99 |

## Man's sweater

| Store | Condition | Price |
|---|---|---|
| Value Village Thrift | Probably never worn (still had tag) | $4.99 |
| J.C. Penney Outlet | New | $9.99 (orig. $30) |
| Wal-Mart | New | $17.94 |
| Sam's Club | New | $19.98 |
| J.C. Penney Online | New | $27.99 (reg. $40) |
| J.C. Penney Catalog | New | $40 |
| Sam's Club | New | $49.87 |
| Macy's | New | $55 |

## Man's khaki pants (cotton or cotton/polyester blend)

| Store | Condition | Price |
|---|---|---|
| Value Village Thrift | Used but good | $2.99-$4.99 |
| Sam's Club | New | $17.81-$24.99 |
| J.C. Penney Outlet | New | $16.99 (orig. $32) |
| Wal-Mart | New | $19.94 |
| Macy's | New | $39.99 |
| J.C. Penney Catalog | New | $42 |
| J.C. Penney Online | New | $48 |

# No-sweat exchanges and refunds

You find a printer at a terrific price that looks like a perfect match for your computer. But when you get home, you discover it's the wrong color. You haul the printer back, only to discover the store has a no-refund policy. What are your rights?

By law, a business is not required to make an exchange or give a refund if an item performs as advertised. In some states, however, businesses are required to make their policies known to customers. Here are a few tips for ensuring hassle-free refunds and exchanges.

★ Learn each store's policy for returns and refunds before you shop. It is often posted in a prominent place like the cash register or behind the courtesy desk. If you don't find the policy posted, ask an employee.

★ If the return policy isn't posted, ask the manager to put it in writing for you.

★ Keep receipts for at least 30 days after purchase. Few stores will allow returns without receipts.

★ Purchase with plastic. The Fair Credit Billing Act allows you to withhold payment for unsatisfactory goods over $50 if you bought them in your home state or within 100 miles of your home, and you can show you tried to resolve your dispute with the seller.

★ If you're unsuccessful at getting a refund from the store, check with the manufacturer. The government requires that clothing items have a registered number (RN) or wool products label (WPL) number. You can find a list of manufacturers through RN and WPL numbers online at <http://www.ftc.gov/bcp/rn/rn.htm>.

★ If a store has a strict return policy, decide if you like the store enough to continue shopping there. If so, make your opinion about their policies known by talking to the manager or writing letters to corporate headquarters. If enough customers complain, they might just change their policies.

## Mail-order resources for less than a cent apiece

There's a lot to be said for shopping from home. You don't have to get dressed, fight the traffic, or stand in long lines. The Direct Marketing Association wants to make it even easier for you by sending you a guide that lists more than 350 catalogs and their Web sites. To order it, send a $3 check or money order to:

Consumer Services Department
Direct Marketing Association
P.O. Box 33033
Washington, DC 20033-0033

## Join the club for super savings

When you look for good deals, don't overlook membership in warehouse clubs — like Sam's Club, Costco, and B.J.'s Wholesale Club. They can offer you lower prices because they sell in bulk, require fewer employees, operate in frills-free buildings, and generally do less advertising than the supermarkets, discount drugstores, and other businesses with whom they compete.

On the other hand, there are some drawbacks. They may not take coupons, offer generic brands, or have "loss-leader" sales like supermarkets do. But they can still offer a lot of savings for the careful shopper.

**Best buys in bulk.** You'll find a lot of different kinds of goods at warehouse clubs, although not a lot of choices of brands within each category. Here are some things that are almost always good bargains when you buy in large amounts.

★ Office supply products like paper, pens, and cellophane tape.

★ Food items such as pasta, rice, canned foods, dried spices, and long-lasting bottled products like soy sauce, vinegar, ketchup, and vegetable oil.

★ Household goods, including paper napkins, paper towels, wax paper, and plastic trash bags.

★ Club-brand laundry detergent — as much as 50- to 70-percent cheaper than supermarket prices.

★ Pet food, both dried and canned.

Warehouse clubs also offer a variety of services. Ask how they can save you money on travel, long-distance telephone service, eye examinations and glasses, car buying and renting, and real-estate transactions.

**When membership is a good deal.** Warehouse clubs generally require you to have an association with some organization, but most people qualify in one way or another. You can call the club that interests you to find out about their policies.

But joining isn't a good idea for everybody. It's a wise investment only if you use it enough to save more than the $25-$40 cost of membership.

Ask if they'll first give you a free trial membership. That way you can get a feel for how much you'll use it before you have to pay. If a special promotion is underway, you may get as much as 60 days to see how it works for you.

Some clubs offer a one-day pass as often as you wish but add 5 percent to the cost of your purchases. Unless you spend more than $500 to $800 a year, depending on the cost of the card, you'll come out ahead using these passes.

---

## Is this a deal for you?

Membership warehouses may have great prices overall, but a terrific buy for one person isn't necessarily a good deal for another. It helps to ask yourself these questions as you shop.

- *Can I use that much?* Items offered only in large amounts are not always wise buys. Cheese and butter, for example, may be 30 to 50 percent cheaper than in grocery stores. But that's no bargain if you don't use it before it goes bad.

- *Is this the lowest price around?* It may not be easy to comparison shop because warehouse stores usually don't provide unit pricing. Be sure to carry along a calculator so you can do your own figuring.

- *Do I really need this?* When prices are low, you may be tempted to buy things you wind up not using. Shopping with a list — and sticking to it — will help. Also, carry only cash so you won't be tempted to pick up more "bargains" than you can afford.

---

# Cash in on resale

You may love shopping the big sales in fancy department stores, but if you really want quality bargains, try a consignment shop. Diane Moore did, and today her love of pretty clothes and a good bargain has turned into a full-time job as the owner of Cat's Pajamas Ltd., a consignment shop in Fayetteville, Georgia.

Buying resale is becoming more popular, a trend that pleases Moore. "People who can well afford to buy expensive clothes retail," she says, "are now shopping at consignment shops. It makes sense. They can get expensive, quality clothing for a fraction of their retail cost and save their money for other things they want."

If you hate being wasteful, you have another good reason to buy at consignment shops. You'll help to recycle perfectly good clothing and other useful items. They won't wind up in a rag bag or a landfill somewhere while they are still in good condition.

And in consignment shops, unlike in most retail stores, you can shop with the seasons. "You can actually buy a sweater in December or January — not just in July," says Moore.

**How to get the best bargains.** Shop often. Merchandise turns over frequently, sometimes daily. And when you find something you like, buy it. There won't be another like it if you come back later and that one is gone.

It's a good idea, too, to get to know the shop owner. Tell her what you like, and she'll probably give you a call when something comes in that suits your taste.

**How to profit from your own resale.** Not only can you save money when buying at a consignment shop, it's a great place to make money on items you'd like to sell. Here are some tips to help you get the most with the least amount of hassle.

★ Visit a few shops in your area to see which ones handle items similar to those you wish to sell. It's easier to deal with the folks at just one shop. You get to know them and vice versa, which leads to a better business relationship.

★ Select a shop that's well established — one that has been in business for at least three years, if possible. Go back to visit it a few times to see how much traffic comes through.

★ Ask what types of merchandise they are looking for. Do they need more jewelry? Do they accept men's, women's, and children's clothing? What sizes and styles? Are they taking items for the current or the upcoming season?

★ Ask to see their contracts and policies. At her shop, Diane takes in clothing items on a 90-day consignment. The owner gets 40 percent of the sales price, the store 60 percent. Articles must be in like-new condition, no more than two years old, cleaned, and on hangers. At the end of 90 days the owner may reclaim unsold items. Remaining clothes are donated to a thrift store where sales help support a children's hospice.

★ Make sure everything you wish to take in is clean, pressed and in good repair — no stains, tears, or missing buttons. Set up an appointment with the owner so you can look over everything carefully together. This way there will be no question later about the condition of any item.

★ Remember this is a business relationship. Be sure to get the terms in writing, and get a receipt for the items you leave. Later, at the time of payment, ask for a statement listing what was sold.

Want to make even more money? Buy cheap at yard sales or thrift stores — only the quality stuff, of course — and take them to a consignment shop to sell at a profit.

## Thrifty shoppers save hundreds of $$$

Do you have to pay high retail prices for classy clothes and fine furnishings? Not necessarily. If you have the time and patience to shop in second-hand thrift stores, you can often find them at bargain-basement prices.

And if you are like at least one avid thrift-store shopper, you'll be proud to tell your friends about the treasures you've uncovered. "I have been called a reverse snob," says Bill McMillan of Galveston, Texas, "because of bragging about how cheap I have bought something."

**Where to dig out the best deals.** While you can usually find good bargains in any thrift store, you may have to do some hunting to get the best buys. Prices vary from shop to shop, even from one geographic area to another.

McMillan, who calls himself a "junking addict," travels across the United States and Canada searching out great deals on high-quality goods. He finds the best prices, however, close to home. "I visit thrift stores in every town that I come to," he says, "but Houston remains the best for junking."

Prices are generally twice as high on the West and East Coasts, according to McMillan. Second-hand shopping is more popular in those areas, not just with people who can't afford new things. Stores are more picked over so the bargains are harder to find.

Goodwill, Salvation Army, and Family Thrifts are among the charity thrift stores where McMillan does most of his junking. But he says, "The best and by far the cheapest are the Value Village stores. They have prices less than half those at most other thrift stores."

There are more than 160 Value Village locations in the United States, according to their Web site at <www.valuevillage.com>. Check your phone book, or go online to find a store near you.

**Top-of-the-line for less.** You may be surprised at the upscale name-brand products — still in good condition — you can buy on a thrift-store budget. McMillan, who prefers high-quality clothing that does not go out of style, lists the following in his current wardrobe:

★ 2 Burberry Trench Coats, $1,000 items that he bought for approximately $8 each.

★ 10 pairs of western boots that retail for $150 to $350 per pair. He paid from $6 to $30 for each pair. His favorites are by Nocona, Luchese, and Rios of Mercedes.

★ Sport coats made of cashmere, loden, and Harris tweed with brand names like Dunhill and Orvis. His cost, $4 to $6 each.

★ Pants, shirts, and jackets with Patagonia, Polo, L.L. Bean, Brooks Brothers, and similar labels. He rarely pays more than $7 for these — often considerably less.

McMillan also purchases ties, belts, suspenders, and socks at give-away prices. "I buy everything but underwear," he says.

---

### Tips on tackling the thrifts

Policies vary from one store to another. But these tips should help make your thrift-shopping adventure more successful.

- *Shop often.* Merchandise turns over frequently so shop the best thrift stores regularly. Ask if there are certain days when they put out newly arrived items, and shop as soon as possible after that time.

- *Don't rush it.* Be willing to take your time and dig through unwanted items until you uncover the best stuff.

- *Accept a little inconvenience.* If there's no dressing room, you may take something home and find it doesn't fit. But it's a risk worth taking when prices are so low.

- *Check out special discounts.* Senior citizens may get a 10- to 20-percent discount all the time or on certain days. Prices may be reduced for everybody one day a week. A certain colored tag can indicate a price cut. Some stores even give discount certificates to frequent shoppers.

Retail shopping may be faster and more convenient. But think of your thrift-store shopping as a hunt for hidden treasure, and it will become more fun.

---

You may wonder how he can get such terrific deals on those expensive items. "It depends on what the person doing the pricing thinks about a specific garment," explains McMillan. "In many stores, the workers price a K-Mart jacket the same as one made in England by Burberry."

If you, too, want the finest, be patient. "You will not find all those great things the first time you go," says McMillan. "But if you just want plain old ordinary clothing, you will find loads on your first trip."

Most thrift stores carry all kinds of household items — from plastic cups to televisions and living room furniture. And everything isn't second hand. New things are often donated by merchants, especially in the charity-sponsored stores.

In recent years, a great effort has been made to upgrade thrift stores, making them look roomier and more attractive. Some even have "designer racks." That has led to higher prices, which doesn't particularly please bargain hunters like McMillan. "Us addicts," he says, "prefer the old ways with cheaper prices, as it is really more of a treasure hunt than satisfying a need."

## Bargains by the yard

Where can you find a like-new silk blouse for $2? Or a set of four kitchen chairs for $12? At a yard sale, of course!

You can't find yard sales every day, however. They tend to be seasonal and held on the weekend when more people are free to shop. These tips will help you find them fast, uncover the best deals, and enjoy your search.

**Plan ahead to save time.** Watch for yard-sale signs a few days in advance, and make note of them. Check, too, for any sales listed in the classified ads in your local newspaper. Map out a route, beginning with the one closest to your house. Plot a circular course, if possible, so no time is wasted backtracking.

**Limit your liquid intake.** Drink as little as possible, and go to the bathroom before you leave home. Unless it's an emergency, don't ask to use the bathroom at the yard-sale location.

**Dress for comfort.** Wear clothes in which you can easily bend and stretch, if necessary. Don't carry a purse. It gets in the way when you pick things up to examine them. Keep your money loose or in a wallet in your pocket, or wear a pouch around your waist.

**Carry cash, but not too much.** Take $1 bills and coins. Sellers will appreciate not having to make change. But don't make it too easy to buy things you may not really want or need. Consider limiting how much cash you take, and leave your checkbook at home.

If you don't have enough for something that's too good to pass up, you can ask the seller to hold it for 30 minutes or so while you get more cash or a checkbook — if a check is acceptable.

**Arrive early — or late.** Serious shoppers will scoop up many of the best bargains as soon as the yard sale starts. On the other hand, by waiting until the end of the day, you can bargain for lower prices. (Most folks really don't want to take all the leftover stuff back inside their homes.)

**Ask for what you want.** If you are in the market for something specific and you don't see it, tell the seller what you are looking for. There's a chance he has what you want and didn't put it out but is willing to sell it. Or another shopper may hear you ask and tell you about another sale where you can find it.

**Shop for now and later.** Keep in mind both what you need right now and what you are likely to need later. Holiday items can be found year round, and picking up party invitations for a birthday six months away is smart planning. What are the chances they'll show up again just when you need them?

**Take your time.** You may miss the best treasures — often hidden among piles of stuff you don't want — if you rush. And take time to check items carefully for broken parts or stains that may not come out.

**Hold on to what you like.** If something really catches your eye but you aren't sure you want it, pick it up anyhow. Otherwise someone may take it, and you'll be disappointed. You can always put it back if you decide you don't want it after all.

**Bargain for a lower price.** The seller can say no, but chances are good your offer will be accepted. Put the dollars you save into your pocket to spend at the next stop.

**Ask for a phone call.** If you find a really good yard sale — perhaps one with clothes in your size that really suit your taste — tell the seller you'd like to know when she has another. Leave a card with your name, phone number, and the words "yard sale." Chances are you'll get a call about the next one.

---

### Three generations save at yard sales

Hardly a Saturday goes by that Mary Beth Vick of Tuscaloosa, Alabama, doesn't go to a few yard sales. That's where she buys all her clothes and most of those for her kids.

Vick had never shopped at yard sales until a few years ago. She was trying to find a way, in the midst of her busy life, to spend more time with her grandmother who, she knew, loved yard sales. So Vick got herself and the kids up early one Saturday morning, picked up her grandmother, and took her out to enjoy her favorite pastime.

They had such a good time and found such impressive bargains that Vick decided to make it a regular Saturday morning outing. Now on Friday afternoons grandmother Clara Cork checks the yard sale advertisements in the newspaper and has a route all mapped out when Vick arrives the next day.

Vick says she has convinced her kids — who are learning the value of a dollar — that they can get anything at a yard sale. One night 5-year-old Joseph dreamed he was a doctor. When he told his mother about it, she teasingly said, "That's great, Joseph. And where did you get your medical degree?"

"At a yard sale," he responded.

---

## How to hold a succe$$ful yard sale

You are a little short of cash, and your closets are overflowing. That means just one thing — it's time for a yard sale. And with the proper planning, you'll not only make money and clean out your storage space, you'll have some fun, too.

**Plan ahead.** This may be the most important factor in whether your sale is a headache or a success. Here are some things to consider.

★ **Date and time.** People are most likely to come on weekend days in warm weather. Set it far enough in the future that you'll have plenty of time to get ready and at a time when you can give full attention to the sale.

★ **Individual or multi-family sale?** Decide if you should go it alone or involve others. You'll attract more buyers to a multi-family sale. Plus you can share the advertising costs and the work involved. It may, however, call for more planning.

★ **The best location.** It's certainly easier to set things up in your own yard or garage. But it may be worth the effort to box things up and cart them to a location where you'll get more attention — perhaps a park or shopping center. Check with your town first to see if you need permission.

**Sell anything and everything.** If you have something you no longer use, chances are good someone else will want it. This is a good time to really clean house. Don't throw anything away until after the sale. People are often quickest to buy the very things you thought were junk.

Buyers will likely be looking for clothing for men, women, and children. Toys, too, are big sellers, especially Barbie and Ken dolls and their accessories. Other popular items include dishes, tools, games, jewelry, and books — comic books in particular.

Homemade items like needlework and other crafts usually sell well. And fresh produce from your garden is likely to be snapped up. Children may also find this a good time to sell lemonade.

**Advertise and make it easy to find.** The more people who know about your sale the better. Prepare flyers and start telling people about it a couple of weeks beforehand. Newspaper ads and signs should appear for several days including the day of the sale. There are even Internet sites where you can list it for free. One example is <www.GarageSaleHunter.com>.

Be sure to include the dates, hours, and address. Consider providing a map on flyers and precise directions in the newspaper. Mention some of what you have for sale, especially things you have a lot of.

Post big, colorful signs that drivers can read easily on every busy traffic corner within a two-mile radius. Make sure you follow any sign ordinances your town may have. Put a big sign in front of your house and, on the day of the sale, tie some balloons on the mailbox so it can't be missed.

**Stick to your schedule.** Be ready to start at the advertised time, but don't sell in advance. That isn't fair to the customers who respect your schedule.

**Make your display inviting.** Be sure all items are clean and polished. Provide plenty of room for shoppers to move around easily to view all the items. Group similar items together — toys near children's clothes, for example.

---

## Don't sacrifice safety for savings

You've found some neat stuff — old, but in great condition — at yard sales, thrift stores, and junk shops. But look it over carefully. The U.S. Consumer Product Safety Commission (CPSC) warns that some things you buy at these locations may not meet current safety standards. Here are a few examples:

- *Children's clothing with drawstrings.* These can catch on something — like playground equipment — and cause strangulation. If you buy something that has one, be sure to remove it before you put it on a child.

- *Hair dryers made before 1990.* Since they may not have the required devices to prevent electrocution, think twice before you use one.

- *Cribs or playpens.* A child could be strangled if he gets his head caught between the slats. Measure carefully before you put a child in one of these.

If you aren't sure about the safety of an item you've bought, call the CPSC at 800-638-2772 (800-638-8270 for hearing and speech impaired). Or check the CPSC's Web site at <www.cpsc.gov>.

---

Use tables so people don't have to do too much bending. A few large items, however, can be placed in the space under tables. You may even put a few boxes of items there to attract the attention of those who enjoy digging for hidden treasures.

People will pay more for items in their original boxes. And you'll sell more clothes if you string up clothes lines and hang them rather than pile them on tables.

**Price every item.** If prices are clearly marked — a heavy black marking pen works best — you'll save yourself a lot of time answering questions. If money for individuals or families needs to be kept separate, mark price tags with a code such as B$.25 or W$3.50.

People at yard sales are looking for bargains, and you are getting rid of things you no longer want. So price items to sell. You'll wind up with more cash in the long run and have less to dispose of afterwards.

Have plenty of coins and small bills on hand to make change.

**Clean up after the sale.** Don't put leftover items in the trash. Instead, donate them to a charity thrift store or a homeless shelter. And don't forget to go around the neighborhood and gather up all the signs.

## Shop Uncle Sam's garage sales and save

Have you ever heard of someone buying a car for a dollar at a government auction? It's a great story, but it's probably not true. Uncle Sam tries to get the best price he can at auction, just like anyone else. After all, it's your tax dollars being recycled. But even if you can't get a car for pocket change at these auctions, you can get a smorgasbord of things at discount prices.

**Pocket savings on mailing mishaps.** Every few months, the U.S. Postal Service has auctions of damaged and unclaimed items at three Mail Recovery Centers. If it can be mailed, it could be there. They have auctioned jewelry, electronic equipment, clothing, toys, and almost every item you could imagine someone mailing — and some you couldn't.

The merchandise can only be seen one hour before the bidding starts, so there is no risk of an early bird beating you out of a deal. In addition, the items are sold in lots, not individually, so you are bound to get a mixed bag of treasures.

To find out when and where the next auction will be, contact one of the following Recovery Centers for information:

Atlanta Mail Recovery Center
P.O. Box 44161
Atlanta, GA 30336-9590

St. Paul Mail Recovery Center
443 Fillmore Ave. E
St. Paul, MN 55107-9607

San Francisco Mail Recovery Center
P.O. Box 7872
San Francisco, CA 94120-7872

**Marshal your forces for money-saving auctions.** The U.S. Marshal Service takes charge of things that have been seized by the Federal Bureau of Investigation, Drug Enforcement Administration, and Immigration and Naturalization Service.

Each year they sell more than 20,000 items of real estate and personal property taken from people who found themselves on the wrong side of the law. And from the list of things for sale, it appears that law breakers are living much cushier lives than the rest of us. Besides real estate, there are boats, jewelry, art, antiques, and even airplanes for sale.

The auctions are held in almost every state, and you'll find things that were seized in or near that state. If you're looking for a boat, your best bet is to check coastal and Great Lakes states, as you're more likely to find them there. You could get a super deal on something you were planning to pay retail for. For a list of all auction locations, send a check or money order for 50 cents to:

Consumer Information Center
Dept. 321G
Pueblo, CO 81009
888-878-3256 (request item 321G)

**Buy government surplus for less.** The General Services Administration (GSA) is the agency in charge of buying supplies, equipment, and vehicles for federal workers. When these items are no longer needed — or in the case of cars, when they've reached an allotted mileage — the GSA sells them to the public.

Typically, this agency sells cars, trucks, boats, and airplanes; computers, printers, and copiers; food service equipment; hardware, plumbing, heating, and electrical equipment; jewelry and collectibles; medical and lab equipment; office and household furniture; recreational and athletic equipment. These items are sold through auction, spot bid (you write down a bid after viewing the item), fixed price, and sealed bid.

When the sale items are in many different locations, the GSA conducts sealed bids. Everyone on their mailing list gets a description of the items for sale and the deadline for bids. You make an offer by the deadline, and the highest bidder gets the merchandise. Usually there is a minimum acceptable bid established, and if no bids above that amount are received, the GSA will simply keep the merchandise for a future auction. That's why the story of the $1 car is pretty unlikely.

For information on future offerings and getting on the GSA mailing list, visit the GSA's Web site at <www.gsa.gov/regions.htm> or watch your local newspaper for announcements of upcoming sales.

## Do your homework and save at online auctions

If you've ever been to an auction, you know how easy it is to get caught up in the excitement of buying. It's a thrill to outbid someone else and get something you want for a fraction of its worth.

Online auctions can have the same effect on people. You can find almost anything, from antiques to zoological equipment, and you can usually bid any time, day or night. Just looking through all the stuff on one site can be an afternoon's worth of entertainment. Web sites like e-Bay and AuctionUniverse are multiplying like rabbits and are one of the biggest draws of Internet activity.

Unfortunately, online auctions are also one of the biggest sources of Internet complaints. As the ancient Romans were fond of saying, let the buyer beware. You might find the deal of a lifetime, or you could get scammed. For a safe, successful online auction experience, you should consider the following advice.

★ **Investigate the seller.** The Internet can be a shady place. That's because it's hard to check up on so many people in so many places. Ask for a business address, then call the Better Business Bureau in that city. Usually the Better Business Bureau can only tell you if there have been any complaints filed against a certain company or individual. It's not as good as knowing the seller's reputation, but it's a start.

★ **Set a limit and stick with it.** If you find something you just have to have, you can enter a bid through e-mail. Usually the sites tell you how many days bids will be accepted and what the highest bid is so far. You can check back and raise your bid if you like, but don't get carried away. Decide before you start bidding just how much the item is worth to you, and stick to that figure. And don't forget that you'll have to pay shipping charges unless the seller offers to take care of it for you.

★ **Pay with a credit card.** When you've found what you believe is a legitimate deal, be sure to protect your payment. Many online auctions offer an escrow system for expensive items. This system works by having a third party hold your money until you get your merchandise. In theory, both the buyer and seller are protected. But for smaller purchases, credit cards are a better bet. Most major credit card companies will let you dispute the bill if you feel you've been cheated, something you won't be able to do if you write a check. If you prefer not to use credit cards, ask for a cash-on-delivery deal, where you pay when you receive the goods. Whatever you do, don't mail cash or a money order. Someone who asks for that type of payment is probably not reliable.

Now that you know a little more about online auctions, visit some of these Web sites and have fun. Just remember to do your homework.

★ <www.eBay.com>
★ <www.Ubid.com>

★ <www.WebAuction.com>

★ <www.AuctionUniverse.com>

# 7 steps to safe online shopping

Convenience and selection make Internet shopping almost impossible to resist. With thousands of sites offering a seemingly limitless variety of merchandise, you can find almost any item you're looking for. And you don't have to fight traffic, find a parking space, or stand in the checkout line.

You can find great deals on the Internet, but just be aware that the Internet is also a convenient way for dishonest people to get your money. The Federal Trade Commission offers these tips for safe shopping online.

★ **Stick with familiar companies.** After you've shopped online for a while, you'll probably have a few favorites, and the big names are probably the most reliable. If you've never heard of a particular site, check out its reputation with the Better Business Bureau or your state attorney general's office.

★ **Protect your privacy.** Be careful about providing personal information. Make sure you only give out information if you know how it's going to be used.

★ **Vary your passwords.** Don't use the same password all the time. If a criminal obtained that password, he would have access to all your accounts and information. It may help to keep track of your passwords in your Rolodex or address book. Just make sure you then keep those passwords in a safe place.

★ **Charge it.** Using a credit card protects you more than checks, money orders, or debit cards.

★ **Make sure it's secure.** Order only from sites that offer a secure server. Your browser should have an unbroken key or padlock that lights up when you're on a secure page.

★ **Don't forget shipping and handling.** The great prices you find on some Web sites might not be such a bargain after you add in shipping and handling charges. Make sure these charges are reasonable, and remember to add them into the price of the items you're ordering.

★ **Keep records of transactions.** Print out the page with details about your transaction to keep as a receipt. Make sure you also print the page that describes return policies in case the Web site changes after you place your order.

The top Internet scam involves online auctions. Auction sites like eBay are among the most popular on the Internet and usually provide a great way to connect individual buyers and sellers. Typically, the top bidder on an item sends a check to the seller and then receives the merchandise. Sometimes, however, the merchandise never shows up, or when it does, the quality isn't as high as the seller reported.

One way to protect yourself from losing out in an online auction is to use an escrow service, such as i-Escrow <www.iescrow.com> or Secure-Trades <www.securetrades.com>. If you use one of these services, you send the payment to them instead of the seller. When the money arrives, the escrow service notifies the seller, who then ships the item. You then have the opportunity to look at the merchandise and decide if you're going to keep it or return it. If you decide to keep it, you notify the escrow service, and they send the money to the seller. If you return the item, the escrow service refunds your money.

If you're ever the victim of Internet fraud, you can call the National Consumers League's Internet Fraud Watch at 800-876-7060, or visit their Web site at <www.fraud.org>.

# Protect yourself from telephone scams

Your telephone makes it easy to stay in touch with faraway friends and family. It also provides a convenient way for crooks to try to bilk you out of your money. Unbelievably, fraudulent telemarketers pocket an estimated $40 billion a year.

How do you separate a legitimate telemarketer from a convincing con artist? And how do you protect yourself from the dishonest ones? The following tips may help.

★ Ask for written literature about the company or a telephone number so you can call them back. Legitimate companies will be happy to provide you with that information.

★ Call your Better Business Bureau to see if any complaints have been filed against the company. But just because there have been no complaints doesn't mean a company is reputable. Try contacting the National Fraud Information Center at 800-876-7060. They have professional counselors who will tell you if an opportunity seems to be a typical telemarketing scam.

★ Never give out personal information (Social Security number, credit card number, etc.) unless you're sure the company is a reputable one, and it really needs the information to complete the transaction.

★ Don't let a telemarketer pressure you into making a decision right away. High-pressure tactics are a warning signal for fraud.

★ Never wire money or use a courier service to send a payment to a telemarketing company. That's a common way for con artists to avoid the legal consequences of using the U.S. Postal Service to defraud people.

★ Be aware that it is illegal for a company to require money for you to enter a contest or claim a prize.

★ Remember, if it sounds too good to be true, it probably is.

★ Hang up! Don't worry about being impolite. Even if it's a legitimate business, if someone is calling your home and making you uncomfortable, you have the right to end the call. They're invading your privacy.

The most common type of telephone fraud is a work-at-home kit you buy with promises of big profits that never materialize. Other common scams include sweepstakes that require a fee to claim your "prize," magazine sales for subscriptions that never arrive, and phony credit card offers that require upfront fees.

By taking the time to learn how these swindlers operate, you and your loved ones can avoid falling victim to their scams.

# Ax annoying phone calls

You know the scenario. You're expecting an important call so you rush to the phone when it rings, stubbing your toe on the way, and dripping bath water all over your floor — and it's a telemarketer on the other end.

Telemarketing calls can be annoying, and sometimes you may get several each day. Fortunately, you can take action. Telemarketing companies are required by law to keep "do not call" lists. (Nonprofit organizations are exempt from this law.)

Whenever a telemarketer calls, tell them politely to put you on their "do not call" list. Keep a pen and paper near your phone so you can make note of the date, the company's name, phone number, and address. They are required to give you this information.

If a company calls you after you've requested that they put you on their "do not call" list, you can sue them in small claims court for your actual monetary damages or $500, whichever is greater.

You can also take advantage of the Direct Marketing Association's (DMA) Telephone Preference Service. Just send a letter to the following address, and you'll be put on the "do not call" list of all companies that belong to the DMA.

Telephone Preference Service
PO Box 9014
Farmingdale, NY 11735-9014

# Slash phone bills by dialing toll-free

When you have to call to order something from a company, be sure to check for a toll-free number. Many companies, and most mail-order businesses, have toll-free numbers for your convenience. If you call them on their regular business line you're wasting money. A call during the day could cost you several dollars depending on the distance.

Don't know if a company has a toll-free number? There's an easy way to find out. Simply call information at 800-555-1212 and ask if the company has a toll-free number. If you have the Internet, you can check AT&T's directory at <www.att.com/directory>.

If you prefer to have a printed directory at your fingertips, you can send for a government publication called *The Consumer Action Handbook*. This free handbook is full of all kinds of useful information such as a listing of toll-free numbers, Better Business Bureau addresses and phone numbers, and the phone numbers of each state's Attorney General. You can get it by contacting:

Handbook
Federal Consumer Information Center
Pueblo, CO 81009
800-688-9889

# CURES FOR HIGH-COST HEALTH CARE

Are you interested in lowering — even doing away with — dental charges and hospital bills? Want the number to call for a free over-the-phone hearing test? Wonder who gives away free contact lenses and how to save on braces?

If you want the answers to these questions, as well as to learn how to get free samples of over-the-counter medicines, who has the best drug prices, or how to qualify for free prescriptions, read on. You'll find a wealth of information about these and other ways to save money on healthcare.

# MEDICAL

## Heal body and budget with free hospital care

Don't put off surgery or other hospital care because you can't afford it. You may be able to get free care or reduced charges under the Hill-Burton Program.

Certain hospitals, nursing homes, and other health facilities are required by the federal government to provide some services at no charge or at a reduced rate to those who qualify.

You may be eligible for this program with an income twice that of the poverty level — or three times the poverty level for nursing home care. It does not, however, cover the cost of private pharmacy, laboratory, and physician fees.

For a copy of the guidelines and a list of participating facilities in your area, call 800-638-0742. Maryland residents should call 800-492-0359. Or you may write:

Office of the Director
Division of Facilities Compliance and Recovery
Room 10C-16
Parklawn Building
5600 Fishers Lane
Rockville, MD 20857

You will also find information and regular updates to the listings at the Web site <www.hrsa.dhhs.gov/osp/dfcr/>. To apply for this assistance, you must go to the admissions office of the participating medical facility.

## Profit from others' billing mistakes

You have good insurance coverage and don't owe any money for a recent hospital stay. So why should you even bother looking at the bill? Because there may be a reward for you hiding in those pages.

You may find an error on your bill that, if corrected, could save your insurance company a lot of money. Chances are, if you do, they'll be happy to split the savings with you. Some companies make this a policy to encourage patients to catch errors their auditors might not find.

So go over that bill with a fine-tooth comb. Are there charges for procedures you didn't have? Or is the same service listed twice by mistake?

If you find an error, call the insurance company and point it out. They'll work it out with the hospital. And you may receive a pleasant bonus for a little bit of your time.

## Raise your hand for free medical care

You may get free medications, checkups, and other health services if you volunteer to take part in a medical research project to test a new health treatment. For general information about these clinical trials, check the Food and Drug Administration's Web site at <www.fda.gov/oashi/home.html> or contact:

Office of Special Health Issues
Food and Drug Administration
Parklawn Building, HF-12
5600 Fishers Lane
Rockville, MD
888-463-6332
Fax: 301-443-4555
E-mail: oshi@oc.fda.gov

A lot of studies sponsored by the National Institutes of Health (NIH) take place at the Warren Grant Magnuson Clinical Center in Maryland. For information about those that might be appropriate for you, contact:

Patient Recruitment and Public Liaison Office
Warren Grant Magnuson Clinical Center
National Institutes of Health
Bethesda, MD 20892-4754
800-411-1222
Fax: 301-480-9793
E-mail: prpl@mail.cc.nih.gov

You can find more information about this clinical research center at the Web site <www.cc.nih.gov>.

To learn about research studies available in other locations, go to the Web site <http://clinicaltrials.gov>. There you'll find a searchable database provided by the National Library of Medicine. Just click on diabetes or arthritis, for example, and you'll find information about the clinical trials related to that condition.

Eventually, you will be able to search this database by telephone, but for now you'll need a computer. If you don't have one, you can probably use one at your public library. Or you might ask for help with your search from your community health center or perhaps your doctor's office.

Once you locate a specific clinical trial, you'll find what you need — the mailing address, phone number, and maybe the e-mail address — to make direct contact with those doing the study.

# Delicious desserts for diabetics

Having diabetes doesn't mean you have to give up delicious desserts. Not when you have specially designed recipes like those in the *B-D Delicious Desserts Cook Booklet*. You'll be sent a copy as a free gift when you register at the BD Diabetes Village Web site at <www.bd.com/diabetes>.

And for more recipes, you can call the BD Consumer Services Department at 800-237-4554 and request copies of *Graham Kerr's Healthy Entrees* and *Graham Kerr's Healthy Holiday Recipes*.

At that same number you can ask questions and order brochures on diabetes-related topics. Titles include:

★ *Controlling Low Blood Sugar Reactions*
★ *Dining Out Made Simple*
★ *Fast Food Guide*
★ *Exercise and Its Benefits*
★ *Vacations, Travel, and Diabetes*
★ *How to Handle Stress*

If you wish to write the company, the address is:

BD
1 Becton Drive
Franklin Lakes, NJ 07417

# Free info for graceful aging

Your chances of living a long life are greater today than ever before. And the National Institute on Aging (NIA) has a number of free publications to help answer your questions about how to stay sharp, healthy, and active into what may be the best years of your life.

**Just how long can modern humans expect to live?** Read *In Search of the Secrets of Aging* for fascinating insights about longevity.

**Am I likely to find a medical fountain of youth?** Order *Pills, Patches, and Shots: Can Hormones Prevent Aging?* and find out.

**Does passion have to go?** Learn what to expect in the romance department as time goes by. Send for *Sexuality Later in Life.*

**How does a woman's body change?** Check out her health issues in *The Women's Health and Aging Study.*

**What kind of exercise do I need? How often?** Get expert advice in *Exercise: A Guide from the National Institute on Aging.*

To order one or more of these, or for a list of other publications on topics like skin care, the prostate, depression, and Alzheimer's disease, write or call:

The National Institute on Aging Information Center
P.O. Box 8057
Gaithersburg, MD 20898-8057
800-222-2225
800-222-4225 (TTY)
E-mail: NIAIC@JBS1.com

You can also go to the NIA publications database at the Web site <www.nih.gov/nia/site-index.htm> and read the publications directly or print copies.

## Don't let springtime take your breath away

Spring may not be your favorite season if you suffer with asthma or allergies. It may, in fact, leave you gasping for breath. If this is the case, the following free resources may be like a breath of fresh air.

**NAB a pollen count report.** Maybe it's one of those days when it's best to stay indoors. Find out from the National Allergy Bureau (NAB). Each Tuesday, Wednesday, and Friday, NAB releases a new report of the pollen and spore counts in your area.

Listen to radio or television broadcasts, or get the counts from the newspaper. You can also make free phone calls to 800-9-POLLEN (800-976-5536) and 877-9-ACHOOO (877-922-4666), or go to the Web site at <www.aaaai.org/nab> for this information.

**Get the facts with a free phone call.** The folks on the Asthma and Allergy Foundation's free help line are well-informed and ready to answer your questions. They'll talk with you, for example, about what foods or other substances may be triggering your symptoms. All you have to do is call 800-7-ASTHMA (800-727-8462) and ask.

**May you get a free screening.** May is National Asthma Month. With the extra attention focused on this condition during this "merry month," the chances are good you can get a free asthma screening. So watch your local media for announcements of health fairs and other opportunities for help from asthma experts.

**Go Gazoontite.** The prices on air purifiers, anti-allergy bedding, and other products at the Gazoontite Web site are nothing to sneeze at. But you can find great bargains in the "basement." You'll find deals like the Dri Dome — a small dehumidifier, just right for a damp closet or pantry — originally $10, on sale for $6.99.

And Gazoontite has more than good prices. Each day, between 9 a.m. and noon Pacific time, an online registered nurse will answer your questions for free.

You'll also find helpful articles — everything from how to get a good night's sleep to controlling allergens in your home. And Gazoontite even has a free online calculator to use with your peak flow meter to help you see how well you're controlling your asthma. Check all this out at <www.gazoontite.com>.

## Free help for headaches

Don't suffer from a lack of information about headaches. Learn what causes them and how to treat them. Send for the brochure *Headache: Hope Through Research* from:

National Institute of Neurological Disorders and Stroke
Office of Communications and Public Liaison
P.O. Box 5801
Bethesda, MD 20824

Or, to read it online, go to the Web site <www.ninds.nih.gov> and click on "disorders" and "headache." You'll find a wealth of information on different types of headaches along with the best ways to treat them.

# Easy relief from itches, pains, and sprains

Would you like to know how to tell the difference between poison oak and poison ivy? Or are you just looking for relief from that awful itching, no matter which is to blame?

Perhaps you have sore muscles, or maybe you need to bandage a sprain. The free offers below can soothe your discomforts and help you avoid them in the future.

**Ease the itching.** Be prepared in case you brush against one of those plants that makes you break out in a rash. Tec Labs will send you free samples of CortiCool anti-itch gel and Tecnu outdoor skin cleaner. And they'll enclose a helpful free pamphlet called *Fact and Fiction about Poison Oak and Ivy*. Fill out the order form online at <www.teclabsinc.com>. You can also contact Tec Labs at:

P.O. Box 1958
Albany, OR 97321
800-482-4464 or 541-926-4577
Fax: 541-926-0218
E-mail: sales@teclabsinc.com

**Roll on relief.** Absorbine Jr., a remedy for muscle aches and arthritis pain, is a popular freebie. They sometimes run out of samples, so don't be disappointed if you can't find it on their Web site at <http://absorbine.com>.

If you miss the offer, though, you should still be able to register to win $100 worth of free Absorbine Jr. products. And you can order a free catalog to see what they have — for your horse as well as for yourself.

**ACE that sprain.** Enjoy those healthy exercises like hiking and playing tennis. But be ready with $1 and $2 rebate coupons for ACE brand products in case you twist an ankle or sprain a wrist. Or, better yet, avoid getting hurt in the first place with a free copy of the *Sports Injury Prevention Guide*.

You can order these at the Becton, Dickinson, and Co. Web site at <www.bd.com>. Write or call them at:

BD
1 Becton Drive
Franklin Lakes, NJ 07417
201-847-6800
E-mail: ace@bd.com

## Wheels and other deals for special needs

The right wheelchair — or even a particular walking cane — can make a big difference in how well you get around if you have a disability. And every day new products are appearing that can make your life more manageable.

But where do you go to find the latest rehabilitation technology? If you have a computer, go to ABLEDATA at <www.abledata.com>. This searchable Internet database contains more than 17,000 products from more than 2,000 different companies. It even has some non-commercial customized and do-it-yourself items.

You'll find a detailed description of each product and its price. Plus, you'll see the name and contact information for the manufacturer and distributor.

You can search the database for free or have someone do it for you. There's a charge of $5 for each 50 entries if you order a printed list by mail. But if you have a simple request — for example, you want to know how to reach the manufacturer of a specific communications device — you can get that information at no charge. Just call 800-227-0216, 301-608-8998, or 301-608-8912 (TTY); or send a fax to 301-608-8958.

You can get other helpful information from ABLEDATA as well, such as the publication *Informed Consumer's Guide to Wheelchair Selection*. If you need your first wheelchair, or wonder if there is a better choice than the one you are using, read this online, or order a print copy.

And if you are looking for financial help with buying your wheelchair, see the document *Informed Consumer's Guide to Funding Assistive Tech-nology*. It includes a list of sources, including technology assistance programs by state.

You can read these documents online for free and print a copy if you'd like. To get a print copy by mail, send $4.25 to:

ABLEDATA
8401 Colesville Road, Suite 200
Silver Spring, MD 20910

## Minimal-cost medical care

Don't add to your health woes with worries over high medical bills. Here are some low-stress ways to bring down costs.

**Go to med school.** If you live near a University with a medical school, call to see what services they offer the general public. Since students — supervised by licensed professionals — do most of the work, you can save a lot of money.

**Take a free shot.** If you are a parent or guardian, you know how expensive it is to keep kids healthy. Call your local health department to see if they provide vaccinations and other services at little or no charge.

**Get a "fair" chance at good health.** Health fairs offer free or low-cost tests and screenings for things like diabetes and high blood pressure. And they give you a chance to get free information — maybe even specific answers to questions about your health. You can learn about local fairs through newspaper, radio, or television announcements.

**Don't pay twice for the same test.** Your doctor may send you to a specialist, or you may go to another doctor for a second opinion. Ask your primary doctor to send along any X-rays, test results, or other records the second doctor will need.

## Free help with cancer concerns

Are you concerned about cancer — preventing it, getting the best treatment for yourself, or perhaps providing support for someone else who has it? These free sources should be helpful.

**Get the facts with a free phone call.** News reports of the latest cancer research can leave you more confused than informed. But with a free call to the Cancer Information Service (CIS) at 800-4-CANCER (800-422-6237) you'll get clear, understandable answers to your cancer-related questions.

No matter where you live in the United States, Puerto Rico, or the U.S. Virgin Islands, you can call Monday through Friday from 9 a.m. to 4:30 p.m., your local time.

Dial the same number anytime — 24 hours a day, 7 days a week — and you can listen to recorded information about cancer. The hearing disabled with TTY equipment can call 800-332-8615.

You can also get answers to your questions about cancer by writing CIS, which is part of the National Cancer Institute, at:

NCI Public Inquiries Office
Building 31, Room 10A03
31 Center Drive, MSC 2580
Bethesda, MD 20892-2580

**Dial up no-charge nutrition news.** A healthy diet is important in preventing and treating cancer. The American Institute for Cancer Research (AICR) offers a free nutrition hotline. Call 800-843-8114 Monday through Friday between 9 a.m. and 5 p.m. Eastern time. An operator will take your question, your phone number, and the best time to return your call. A registered dietitian will then research your question and call you back, usually within 48 hours.

The AICR also has lots of nutritious, delicious, easy to prepare — and free — recipes. You are sure to enjoy dishes like Very Berry Shortcake, made with both strawberries and blueberries. You can print the recipes from the Web site at <www.aicr.org>.

**Turn to a source of support.** If you or someone close to you has recently been diagnosed with cancer, you may be wondering where to turn with all your questions.

Through the CancerResource program, sponsored by the AICR, you can talk with someone who understands the emotional, physical, and psychological aspects of cancer and its treatment.

Call them at 800-843-8114, ext. 80, Monday through Friday between 9 a.m. and 5 p.m. Eastern time. This resource is available to people in the U.S. and Canada.

# VISION AND HEARING

## The 'eyes' have it for free vision care

Are you putting off important eye care because of the high costs of examinations and treatments? If so, see what these organizations have to offer. You may be able to protect your precious eyesight for free.

**March right up for free eye care.** During March — Save Your Vision Month — many eye doctors who are members of the American Optometric Association (AOA) provide free services as part of Vision USA. If you qualify, you can get an eye exam and a prescription for eyeglasses if you need them. In some states, Vision USA provides glasses as well.

You may be eligible if you have not had an eye exam within two years, and you have no vision insurance. And while at least one person in your household must have a job, your income has to fall below a certain level, based on how many people are living in your home.

Applications become available in November for the following March. To get one, contact:

Vision USA National Coordinator
243 N. Lindbergh Blvd.
St. Louis, MO 63141
314-991-4100, ext. 261

You can find more information at the AOA Web site at <www.aoanet.org>.

**Get a hand from LensCrafters.** The folks at LensCrafters have several programs that might help you get free eye care. For example, each December, on Hometown Day, they open their stores early and give free eye exams to those who have been approved in advance.

Through another program, called Gift of Sight OutReach, LensCrafters sends doctors and other workers to nursing homes, shelters, and health fairs. They give free vision tests and make eyeglass adjustments and repairs.

To find out more about these and other programs, contact the Gift of Sight Captain at your local LensCrafters. Or go to the Web site <www. lenscrafters.com>.

**See for free with NECP.** If you are at least 65 years old and have not had an eye examination in three years, you may qualify for free eye care through the National Eye Care Project (NECP). Call 800-222-EYES (800-222-3937) and get the name of a volunteer ophthalmologist, or eye doctor, near you.

The ophthalmologist will give you an examination, and for one year he will treat you for any eye problem he finds — even serious ones like cataracts or glaucoma. If you have Medicare or other insurance, the eye doctor will accept that as full payment. If you have no insurance, it's free.

**Look for a Lion.** Your local Lions Club may offer financial assistance for vision care. Services vary from club to club, so find the number in your telephone directory and give them a call.

If you have an eye test and it shows you need glasses, the Lions may help pay for them. Apply for this assistance through the international headquarters at:

Lions Clubs International
Program Development Department
300 W. 22nd Street
Oak Brook, IL 60523-8842
630-571-5466, ext. 318
Fax: 630-571-1692

They will need your name, mailing address, phone number, and some financial information.

**Find more aid for your eyes.** For a list of other organizations that may be able to help you, send for the free National Eye Institute (NEI) publication *Financial Aid for Eye Care* (#872). Write or call:

National Eye Institute
2020 Vision Place
Bethesda, MD 20892-3655
301-496-5248
E-mail: 2020@nei.nih.gov

Or get it online at <www.nei.nih.gov>.

**Volunteer for vision care.** Be a participant in a government-sponsored clinical trial of a medicine or other treatment for your eyes, and you'll receive the very best care. And some of it, if not all, may be provided for free.

To find out if you are eligible for any upcoming research, you or your doctor can get in touch with the NEI. See the contact information given above.

To learn more about what is involved in vision-related clinical trials, order NEI publication #99, *Clinical Trials in Vision Research — Information for Patients.*

## See your way clear with no-cost contacts

Don't pay for soft contact lenses — with most major brands the first pair is free. If you're trying them for the first time or simply switching brands, you shouldn't have to pay to find out if you like them.

Ask your local vision center about free offers they can handle for you. For a free trial certificate, you can also call or visit the Web site for these contact lens manufacturers:

★ **Acuvue by Johnson and Johnson:** <www.acuvue.com> ; 800-876-4596

★ **CIBA Vision:** <www.cibavision.com> ; 770-734-5959

★ **Bausch and Lomb:** <www.bausch.com/products/contacts/free trial.jsp> ; 800-553-5340

Perhaps you'll find money-saving certificates or personalized rebates as well. Bausch & Lomb, for instance, had a $50 rebate form online good for a 4-box purchase of PureVision contact lenses.

If there is another brand you'd like to check for free offers, try typing the name into your Internet search engine or calling their customer service department.

## Read about eyes through free sunglasses

Want the latest news about eye-care products as well as tips about how to save money when you buy them? How about insights about eyesight from health experts? You'll get this kind of free info in AllAboutVision.com's monthly e-mail newsletter.

Go to <www.allaboutvision.com> to enroll. And if luck is with you, they'll throw in a free pair of sun shades. Every 50th subscriber gets a pair of Timberland Eyewear high-performance sunglasses at no charge.

And while you are at the Web site, check out the coupons for discounts and rebates on purchases. A recent offer was for a $50 rebate on a purchase of four boxes of PureVision contact lenses from Bausch & Lomb.

## Recycle so others may see

May is a good month for spring cleaning. And it's also the International Association of Lions Clubs Recycle For Sight Month. So that's a good time to pull out those old eyeglasses cluttering up your drawers and donate them to a good cause.

Lions Clubs are part of the world's largest service club organization, best known for their sight-related programs. They take used eyeglasses, clean and repair them, and distribute them to needy individuals in developing countries. There, a pair of glasses can cost a month's salary. And poor eyesight can mean losing your job or failing in school.

Look for a collection box or call your local Lions Club for more information. Better yet, if you belong to a service club, ask your group to assist the Lions with this worthwhile project.

To find out how to help, visit their Web site at <www10.lionsclubs.org/Lion/English/FRecycl.html>, or contact them by mail, phone or fax:

Public Relations Department
Lions Clubs International Headquarters
300 W. 22nd Street
Oak Brook, IL 60523-8842
630-571-5466, ext. 358
Fax: 630-571-8890
E-mail: pr@lionsclubs.org

Don't forget to recycle old sunglasses as well. They are especially important to people with cataracts and those living near the equator where the sun's rays are most damaging.

## Turn up the volume for free

Is it difficult to hear voices clearly on the telephone? Do you turn the television volume so high it blasts your family out of the room? Go to the American Speech-Language-Hearing Association (ASHA) for free information about the different kinds of assistive listening devices (ALDs) and where to find them.

Even if you wear a hearing aid, you can still have problems in certain situations. An ALD helps by making it easier to hear sounds from a specific source. Unlike a hearing aid, which makes everything in the environment louder, an ALD works without turning up those distracting background noises.

ASHA can also provide a list of certified audiologists in your area to run hearing tests and give advice on correcting your hearing problems.

Request a free copy of the ALD information packet from:

American Speech-Language-Hearing Association
10801 Rockville Pike
Rockville, MD 20852
800-638-8255 (voice or TTY)
301-897-8682 (voice or TTY)
E-mail: actioncenter@asha.org

You can also go online for more information at <www.asha.org>.

If your hearing exam shows you need help hearing on the telephone, look in the front of your local phone directory for free services and devices available for the hearing impaired.

## Mark your place, protect your hearing

When you want to read a book, you probably go to a quiet location. But it's important to protect your ears from loud noises at other times as well.

Check out two free bookmarks and a fact sheet — designed to help you safeguard your hearing — from the National Institute on Deafness and Other Communication Disorders.

*How Loud Is Too Loud* (DC-104; Spanish Version, DC-104S) gives the actual decibel levels of some of the most damaging noises around you.

*Ten Ways To Recognize Hearing Loss* (DC-106; Spanish version, DC-106S) lists questions to ask yourself to help you decide if you need a hearing test.

The fact sheet *Noise-Induced Hearing Loss* (DC-148) explains how we hear and how noise can lead to hearing loss. Request these from:

NIDCD Information Clearinghouse
1 Communication Ave.
Bethesda, MD 20892-3456
800-241-1044
TTY: 800-241-1055jk
E-mail: nidcdinfo@nidcd.nih.gov

You can also log on to the Web site <www.nih.gov/nidcd> to place your order and to get other information about hearing.

---

### Help others hear

If you have an old or broken hearing aid, consider sending it to the Hear Now organization for recycling. It will be refurbished or repaired and given to a hearing-disabled person in a developing country. This is a tax-deductible donation, so if you include your name and address, a receipt will be mailed to you. The address is:

Hear Now
The Starkey Hearing Foundation
4248 Park Glen Road
Minneapolis, MN 55416

---

# Listen up! Here's how to get a free hearing aid

Being deaf or hard of hearing can be isolating, even dangerous. So if you or someone you know needs a hearing aid but can't afford it, don't despair.

First check to see if your insurance will pay all or part of the cost. Or maybe you qualify for government assistance through Medicare, Medicaid, Vocational Rehabilitation, or the Veterans Administration. If those options are not available to you, check these out.

**Hear ye now.** If you qualify, you may be able to get free hearing aids from Hear Now. This organization was recently taken over by Hearing Aide Of Minnesota, a division of the Starkey Hearing Foundation. So if you have their phone number, check to be sure it's the new one, 800-328-8602.

You'll hear a recorded message when you call, but if you leave your name and address, they'll send you an application packet. If you prefer, you may e-mail a request to mnproj@hearingaid.org. The regular mailing address is:

Hear Now
The Starkey Hearing Foundation
4248 Park Glen Road
Minneapolis, MN 55416

Pay close attention to the guidelines for qualifying. There is an application fee of $30, which will not be refunded if you don't meet the financial eligibility requirements.

**"Lion" up for better hearing.** Most people know the Lions Club helps provide eyeglasses for those who need them but can't afford them. But did you know the Lions Clubs International Foundation sponsors a hearing-aid program as well?

Apply directly to the international headquarters. They must have your name, mailing address, and phone number. They will want to know if your hearing has been tested and if hearing aids are necessary. And they will need your age and some financial information. Here's where to reach them:

Lions Clubs International
Program Development Department
300 W. 22nd Street
Oak Brook, IL 60523-8842
630-571-5466, ext. 318
Fax: 630-571-1692
E-mail: lcif@lionsclubs.org

**Seal a deal.** Of the 410 Easter Seals sites in the United States, 59 sites have a program to help folks get hearing aids. Call the one nearest you to see if they provide this service. If you have access to a computer, you can e-mail the national headquarters and ask for a list. Send your request to info@easter-seals.org.

## Phone for a free hearing test

If you are thinking about having your hearing tested, why not have it done over the telephone for free? The test itself takes only two minutes, but you'll need to make two phone calls.

First dial 800-222-EARS on a weekday between 9 a.m. and 5 p.m. Eastern time. The person answering the phone — no numbers to punch — will tell you the number of an organization in your area that gives the test.

Call that local number and take the test. If you need further testing or treatment, the organization providing the test can advise you about it.

## Lend an ear to a free magazine

If you or someone close to you has a hearing problem, you might want to order a free copy of the magazine *Hearing Health*. Each issue contains human interest stories, coping strategies, research developments, and legislative news. The publishers even promise you'll find a bit of humor in their pages.

To request a complimentary copy, contact:

Hearing Health Magazine
P.O. Drawer V
Ingleside, TX 78362
361-776-7240
Fax: 361-776-3278
E-mail: ears2u@hearinghealthmag.com

# DRUGS AND SUPPLEMENTS

## Beat the prescription blues with free drugs

Are expensive medicines draining your budget? Don't despair. There may be a way to get them for free.

Most drug manufacturers offer free medications to people who can't afford to buy them. You may qualify if you don't meet requirements for government programs like Medicaid and if you don't have insurance — or if you have already reached your maximum drug coverage.

To make it simpler for you, a nonprofit volunteer organization called "The Medicine Program" will work with your doctor to help find the programs that are appropriate for you.

You may apply no matter what your age or income. Each program has its own requirements. If you need extremely expensive medications — like for AIDS and cancer, for example — you may be more likely to qualify, even with a higher income. In 1999, the annual family incomes of recipients ranged from below the national poverty level up to $50,000.

You can find more information at the Web site <www.themedicine program.com> where you can also print an application. Or call 573-996-7300, Monday through Friday, 8 a.m. to 5 p.m. CST. Or write to:

The Medicine Program
P.O. Box 515
Doniphan, MO 63935-0515
E-mail: help@themedicineprogram.com

Send a $5 processing fee for each drug with your application. If you haven't been approved within 120 days, you can ask for a refund.

If you are approved, a three-month supply of each medication will be sent to your doctor, and he will dispense them to you. Keep copies of the forms to apply for refills.

## Money saving pills delivered to your door

Mail-order pharmacies, because they have low overhead, can help you reduce your high medicine bills. Medi-Mail, Inc. is one that delivers good deals. And they make it simpler by including the shipping costs in the prices they quote. Call 800-331-1458 between 6 a.m. and 5 p.m. Pacific time. Or write:

Medi-Mail, Inc.
P.O. Box 98520
Las Vegas, NV 89193-8520

Your doctor may call in your prescription at 800-648-6834. Calls to this number go straight to the pharmacy and should be used by doctors only.

If you request it, Medi-Mail will provide an itemized receipt to keep with your records or to submit to your insurance company. They also offer a free catalog of their over-the-counter health products.

## Do a 'bust' on drug bills

Prescription drugs can take a big bite out of your budget. But you'll get more medicine for your money when you follow these tips.

**Sample and save.** There are good reasons to ask your doctor for free samples of the medications he prescribes. For example, having these pills gives you extra time to comparison shop for the best price on the prescription.

Also, it gives you a chance to see if the drug will work for you without undesirable side effects. There's no need to waste money on medicines you may not be able to tolerate.

And, hey, every free pill saves you cash. So why not ask? There's no cost to your doctor. He gets lots of free samples of prescription and non-prescription medications from the drug companies — especially the newest, which are often the most expensive.

**Pay up to 50 percent less on generic drugs.** Name-brand drugs are expensive. So talk to your doctor about prescribing the lower-priced generic equivalent whenever possible. The two may not have exactly the same content, but it's usually the bases and fillers that are different, not the active ingredients. The price difference, however, can be great.

**Make sure the prescription is necessary.** Sometimes an over-the-counter drug will work about as well as a prescription medication. Since they are usually a lot cheaper, check with your doctor about trying one as a substitute. But take into consideration the out-of-pocket cost, since your insurance probably doesn't pay for non-prescription drugs.

**Divide and conquer costs.** Some pills have been scored so they can more easily be cut in half. This comes in handy if you have a hard time swallowing the bigger pills.

And if you need a smaller dose, it may still be a good idea to buy the bigger ones and cut them in half. A 10-milligram size, for example, may cost little more than the 5-milligram size.

You can probably buy an inexpensive pill splitter at the drugstore. So ask your doctor about prescribing the larger tablets that can be cut in half. This won't work, however, with capsules or pills with a shiny coating.

**Buy more, pay less.** For any medication you take for a chronic condition — once you are sure you will be continuing it long-term — try to buy a three- to six-month supply at a time. The price per pill is usually lower when you buy in bulk. And since the pharmacist charges a fee each time he fills a prescription, you'll save by avoiding refills.

**Pack your own meds.** If you are facing a stay in the hospital, ask your doctor if you can bring your prescription and non-prescription drugs from home. If the hospital supplies them, they're likely to be a lot more expensive.

---

## Take your medicine — at a discount

It may be convenient, but is your neighborhood pharmacy the best place to get your prescription filled? Make a few phone calls to compare costs. You may be amazed at the wide range of prices you'll find.

The discount drugstore chains — like Drug Emporium, Phar-Mor, Wal-Mart, and K-Mart — are likely to have prices up to 35 percent lower than those of regular pharmacies. And mail-order and online pharmacies can save you money as well.

But what if you'd really prefer to support your neighborhood pharmacy? Chances are, if you ask, they'll match the best deal you found.

---

## Members save money on meds

You can save up to 65 percent on prescription drugs by joining one of the FFI Health Services programs — femScript, aVidaRx, MatureRx, or MatureRx Plus.

Find out which of these programs best suits your needs by going to the Web site <www.femscript.com> or calling 800-511-1314. You may even get free membership — regularly $9.95 — for simply completing a health survey.

Present your membership card to get low prices at any of the 35,000 participating pharmacies. You can also place your membership order through Wal-Mart Pharmacy Mail Services. Call them at 800-273-3455, or write to:

WMS
P.O. Box 115112
Carrollton, TX 75011-5112
E-mail: wmsrx@wal-mart.com

## Where to find good deals on drugs

You can depend on AARP Pharmacy Service, Inc., to give you good prices on brand name drugs. You'll get even bigger savings — 30 to 50 percent — on the generic brands.

To check their prices, place an order, or request a catalog, call 800-456-2277. Or, if you want to order by mail, send your original prescription, the doctor's name and phone number, and your name, address, date of birth, and phone number to:

AARP Pharmacy Service, Inc.
Dept. #258390
P.O. Box 40011
Roanoke, VA 24022

You can also send the information and prescription by fax to 800-456-7631. Or order at the Web site <www.rpspharmacy.com>. For your first telephone or online order, be ready to give your doctor's telephone number so the pharmacist can call to verify the prescription.

You don't have to be a member of the AARP senior citizens' organization to order from this well-known pharmacy. But they do have a special program — called Member Choice — for AARP members.

If you enroll in this program, you can order medicines by mail or use the card for discounts in pharmacies across the country. You pay an annual fee of $15, but you should save an average of $8.49 on each prescription.

To get more details, or to enroll, call 800-439-4457. Or go to the Web site where you'll find an application to print, fill out, sign, and mail to:

AARP Member Choice Program
WS01 P.O. Box 40019
Roanoke, VA 24022-9921

At the Web site, you can also find specials on non-prescription items like vitamins and herbs. And look for important health information, such as updates about dangerous drug interactions, withdrawals and recalls of products, and other drug-related news.

## Get super savings at safe Internet sites

Going online beats waiting in line for a prescription to be filled. And the prices at Internet pharmacies may be better, too, because they have lower overhead than walk-in drugstores.

Another bonus is the free stuff they often throw in to entice your business. For example, your first prescription from PlanetRx.com may net you a coupon worth $25 off a purchase of non-prescription items. And they always provide free shipping when you order prescription drugs.

Other sites offer free drugstore items like vitamins, shampoo, or shaving cream with your first purchase.

Yes, the savings are good. But be careful. Some online sites don't take the proper steps to protect your health. And getting the wrong medication, or even a fake one, puts you at risk of losing more than your money.

The best way to choose a reliable Internet pharmacy is to check for the VIPPS (Verified Internet Pharmacy Practice Sites) seal displayed on the

Web site. This seal shows that a pharmacy is licensed by the states in which it operates and has passed the National Association of Boards of Pharmacy (NABP) requirements for quality and security. If you click on the seal at a certified site, you will be taken directly to the NAPB Web site.

These 11 online pharmacies have received VIPPS certification:

★ Caremark, Inc. at <www.rxrequest.com>

★ CVS Washington, Inc. at <www.cvs.com>

★ Drug Emporium.com at <www.drugemporium.com>

★ Drugstore.com at <www.drugstore.com>

★ Familymeds.com at <www.familymeds.com>

★ HealthScript Pharmacy Services, Inc. at <www.healthscript.com>

★ Merck-Medco Managed Care LLC at <www.merck-medco.com>

★ PlanetRx.com at <www.planetRx.com>

★ PrescriptionOnline.com at <www.PrescriptionOnline.com>

★ Rx.com Pharmacy at <www.rx.com>

★ Tel-Drug, Inc. at <www.teldrug.com>

To find out if others have been added to the VIPPS certified list, you can go directly to the NABP Web site at <www.nabp.net> or call 847-698-6227.

These Web sites also offer free health and nutrition advice as well as information about the drugs you order. You can check for side effects and possible drug interactions. Phone numbers are available if you need to talk to the pharmacist.

## Prices that are easy to swallow

To get the best deals on herbs, minerals, vitamins, and other nutritional supplements, watch newspapers and magazines for specials. And do some comparison shopping, too. You'll find a wide range of prices at drugstores, supermarkets, specialty shops, and discount stores.

Mail-order companies can also save you money. Most of the ones that sell prescription drugs by mail also sell dietary supplements. (See "Money saving pills delivered to your door") And here are some others with good prices.

**"Supplement" your savings.** Pia Discount Vitamins regularly offers 20 to 40 percent discounts off retail prices. And some of their specials will save you more than 50 percent.

For example, 100 vitamin C tablets — 1000 mg each — selling for $11.50 retail were on sale for $5.74 on the Web site at <www.piavita mins.com>. And 90 multiple-vitamin-and-mineral capsules from Twin-Lab, retailing for $23.49, were on sale for $11.74. To take advantage of these great deals, request a free catalog from:

Pia Discount Vitamins
708 Saw Mill River Road
Ardsley, NY 10502
800-662-8144

**Dig for deep discounts.** At Mother Nature.com, get $10 off your first order of vitamins and other natural health products. And look at their "deep discount" specials for savings of 20 to 67 percent. They also offer other deals, like buy one and get a second free. Do your comparison shopping at the Web site <www.mothernature.com>. Or call 800-517-9020.

**Get a pearl of a deal.** How would you like a free freshwater pearl necklace, valued at $80? It may be yours with your order of $50 or more from Allherb.com. Or you might get a pair of pearl earrings — a $26.50 value — with your order of $30 or more.

Look for these specials at the Web site <www.allherb.com>. And while you are there, check out the "Half-Price Boutique." This is where herbs, books, and other products are sold at a 50-percent discount. You can also contact them at:

AllHerb.com
14900 Sweitzer Lane
Laurel, MD 20707
877-255-4372 (toll free)

**Get the best price or it's free.** Vitamins.com wants your business. So if, while surfing the Internet, you find a lower price (regular, not sale price) on a brand name product listed at their Web site, they'll send that item to you for free. Get the details at <www.vitamins.com>.

You may also find an online special of $15 off your first order. And if you are just getting started using supplements, while you are at the site, you might want to read *Your Beginner's Guide to Choosing Vitamins & Herbs.*

You can also reach them at:

Vitamins.com
2924 Telestar Court
Falls Church, VA 22042
800-741-8273

**Save up to 50 percent off retail.** The folks at eNutrition.com sell brand-name vitamins and other supplements at a big discount. And from time to time they offer specials, like a free bottle of Popeye chewable vitamins with a $25 purchase. Or, for new customers, $10 off your first order of $50 or more plus free shipping.

Check prices or place an order at the Web site <www.eNutrition.com>, or reach them at:

eNutrition
8550 Balboa Blvd., Suite 140
Northridge, CA 91325
800-641-5558
818-775-4550 for calls from outside the United States

**Find steals, deals, and a free catalog.** You can save 30 to 40 percent on most items at The Vitamin Shoppe Web site at <www.vitaminshoppe.com>. You'll find some terrific $5 specials and order a free catalog online as well. You can write, call, or fax them at:

VitaminShoppe.com
4700 Westside Avenue
North Bergen, NJ 07047
888-880-3055
Fax: 800-476-3851

When comparison shopping, don't forget to take shipping charges into consideration. Some of the companies listed above mail your purchases for free. Others offer free mailing on shipments of over $20 or $50. But these may be temporary specials, so check each time you order.

As an additional bonus, some of these Web sites have medical advisory boards that provide free health and fitness information and services. You can ask questions or receive free e-mail newsletters tailored to your specific needs.

# Free tips about taking medicine

It can be confusing to keep track of your medicines — when to take them and how much of each one — especially when you are not feeling your best. But making errors can be dangerous.

A free booklet, *Prescription Medicines and You*, has helpful tips and guidelines to help you take your medications safely. It also suggests questions to ask your doctor about the medicines he prescribes as well as things to mention about your experiences while taking the drugs.

This booklet is available from the Agency for Health Care Policy and Research (AHCPR). You can order a copy by calling 800-358-9295 or writing to:

AHCPR Publications Clearinghouse
P.O. Box 8547
Silver Spring, MD 20907

Or you can read it online at <www.ahcpr.gov/consumer/ncpiebro.htm>.

The AHCPR also publishes free brochures about a variety of other health issues and conditions. They'll send you a free list of the titles if you request it.

# Ease the price of pain relief

Free samples and cents-off coupons for over-the-counter medications can save you headaches as well as money. Here are a few that were recently available by phone or over the Internet.

**Put out the fire of heartburn.** Prelief is a dietary supplement that helps relieve the pain — plus, it's a good source of calcium. For a free sample, call 800-994-4711 or request it online at <www.prelief.com>.

**Feel fit with fiber.** If you don't get enough fruits, vegetables, and whole grains in your diet, you may suffer from constipation. Get relief —

and maybe reduce your risk of heart disease at the same time — with Metamucil, a fiber laxative and dietary supplement.

For two free packets of sugar-free, orange-flavored powder and a pamphlet, *Your Guide to a High Fiber Diet*, go to the Web site <www.metamucil.com>. If you have questions or comments, you can call 800-686-7139.

**Pay less for pain relief.** To get a discount coupon for Motrin IB pain relievers, call McNeil Consumer Healthcare, Consumer Affairs, at 800-962-5357. Chances are, they'll send you a couple of free gelcap samples as well. Learn more about using the different Motrin products at the Web site <www.motrinib.com>.

**Sleep easy.** With Tylenol PM, nighttime pain shouldn't keep you awake. Request a free sample at the Web site <www.Tylenol.com>. They'll probably send you a cents-off coupon as well.

While you are at the Web site, read the helpful suggestions for avoiding and dealing with pain. You can also get information by dialing 800-962-5357.

**Dissolve your distress.** You can receive two free Alka-Seltzer tablets if you fill out an online survey at the Web site <www.alka-seltzer.com>. You may get the lemon-lime flavored tablets for indigestion and heartburn. Or perhaps they'll send the cherry-flavored Alka-Seltzer Plus Cold Medicine.

If you live in Ohio, you'll get an additional bonus of two discount coupons worth 75 cents each to use on future Alka-Seltzer purchases.

**Sip and save.** Get $1 off the purchase of medicinal tea — like Throat Coat or Nighty Night — from Traditional Medicinals. Go to the Web site <www.traditionalmedicinals.com> and print the coupon. For more information you can also call 800-373-3832.

**Help a headache.** Get headache relief by registering with the Excedrin Headache Resource Center. The sponsors of this education and research program will send you free samples of their headache remedies. They'll also include some printed materials to help you manage your pain. Just call 800-580-4455 for the application form, or find it at the Web site <www.excedrin.com>.

# DENTAL

## Put a dent in the cost of dental care

Don't pay a penny the next time you need dental work done. Whether it's fillings, dentures, implants, cleaning, or just a checkup, here's how to lower, even eliminate, your bill.

**Become a volunteer.** The National Institute of Dental and Craniofacial Research (NIDCR) conducts clinical trials to find better ways to prevent or treat all kinds of dental problems. If you take part in one of these trials, you can get free dental care. In some cases you may even be paid for your time and for expenses like transportation costs, child care, meals, and accommodations.

To find out if you qualify for upcoming research, contact:

Patient Recruitment and Public Liaison Office
Building 61
10 Cloister Court
Bethesda, MD 20892-4754
800-411-1222
Fax: 301-480-9793
E-mail: prpl@mail.cc.nih.gov

Or go to the National Institutes of Health Web site at <http://clinical trials.gov> and browse by condition. A recent check of "Mouth and Tooth Diseases" showed 91 studies recruiting volunteers.

**Go back to school.** Routine dental work costs a lot less at a local dental school than in a dentist's office. To find out if there is one in your area, contact the American Dental Education Association (ADEA), a professional organization of all the dental schools in the United States and Canada.

American Dental Education Association
1625 Massachusetts Avenue, NW, Suite 600
Washington, DC 20036-2212
202-667-9433
Fax: 202-667-0642
E-mail: adea@adea.org

**See what your state can do.** Free dentures and free or discounted dental care are available in most areas for certain people with special needs and limited incomes. For services available where you live, check with your local health department. Your state's dental association may also help. Get local contact information from:

American Dental Association
211 E. Chicago Ave.
Chicago, IL 60611
312-440-2500
Fax: 312-440-2800
<www.ada.org>

## Polish those pearly whites for free

Most people would like to try out a new product before buying a large supply. Free samples are a great way to do this — at no cost. If you search the Internet on the brand name of a product you're curious about, chances are you'll find free samples like these.

**Let Rembrandt brush up a masterpiece.** Visit the Rembrandt toothpaste Web site at <www.rembrandt.com> to get freebies and other good deals.

The offers may change, but you could receive trial- and full-size tubes of different dental products simply by writing to the company or filling out request forms. You'll likely get coupons worth over $7 with your samples, as well as an informative leaflet on causes, prevention, and healing of canker sores.

You can also register to receive samples of regular Rembrandt, Age Defying Adult Formula, Canker Relief Gel, and Naturals in exotic flavors like papaya and ginseng or aloe vera and Echinacea.

Perhaps you'll also find the travel bag containing Rembrandt products — 2 kinds of toothpaste, mouthwash, breath drops, and a toothbrush — for only $6.99. It's a $15.99 value you can order online or by calling the company.

Contact Rembrandt at:

2727 Skyway Drive
Santa Maria, CA 93455
800-548-3663

**Win 12 months of whiter teeth.** Just enter your name and e-mail address each month at Floss.com, <www.floss.com>, for a fresh chance to win different prizes — anything from a year's supply of toothpaste to an electric toothbrush.

In addition, this Web site offers all kinds of money-saving specials on breath products, toothbrushes, toothpastes, and new dental products through their online health store. You could save almost $2 on toothpaste and $1.50 on mouthwash. Or purchase a Fresh Breath Kit, regularly $20, on sale for $16. It contains toothpaste, a tongue scraper, breath drops, mouth rinse, and tongue spray.

Contact Floss.com at:

1055 Stewart Avenue
Bethpage, NY 11714
516-877-0509

**Brighten the smile of a friend.** Every day Mentadent provides 100 toothpaste samples for friends of visitors to their Web site. Just go to <www.mentadent.com> and fill out some information. If yours is one of the lucky names chosen, the free sample, with your compliments, will be sent to the person of your choice.

## No-cost info will brighten your smile

Want to make your happy face even happier? Get free information on how to keep your teeth clean and healthy. The online article "Electric Toothbrush Review," written by a dentist and a dental hygienist, gives reasons to use an electric toothbrush, a description of several models, and even a recall notice for one. Go to <www.smiledoc.com/dentist/elctbrs.html> for lots of free, helpful information.

And if you want to know more about the different kinds of electric toothbrushes, they'll send you a free brochure about each brand. Just send a stamped, self-addressed, envelope to:

Candy Akizuki, R.D.H.
Boyden Dental Practice
1565 Hollenbeck Avenue, Suite 114
Sunnyvale, CA 94087

The Web site also has articles about bad breath, candy that's supposed to fight cavities, the most effective toothpaste, and other toothsome topics. Find these at <www.smiledoc.com/dentist/tips.html>.

## Online drugstores offer dental freebies and savings

Online pharmacies are great places to save big on prescriptions, vitamins, and other health care items. But you can also find loads of free offers and giveaways on these sites.

Save money on toothpaste, mouthwash, and other oral care products when you shop at FamilyMeds.com, <www.familymeds.com>. You may even get a free toothbrush travel kit just for registering with them. And while you're there, check out the name brand specials. You'll find bargains like Aim's Gel Tartar Control six-ounce toothpaste for 77 cents. That saves you 70 cents off the regular price. Or look for 108 tablets of Efferdent Denture Cleanser Plus Listerine — regularly $6.49 — on sale for $4.37.

At Drugstore.com, <www.drugstore.com>, you can sign up for a free newsletter, get various free gifts with purchase, buy drugs at low prices, get free shipping, and find super savings on lots of health products. You might find the 4-ounce Colgate Sensitive Toothpaste, regular price $4.19, on sale for $2.77. Or save 40 cents on 54 yards of mint flavored Glide Dental Floss.

Also check for specials at PlanetRx.com at <www.planetRx.com>, CVS Washington, Inc., at <www.cvs.com>, and other online drugstores.

## Free advice for the mature mouth

Seniors can have special dental needs that require special care and information. The National Oral Health Information Clearinghouse (NOHIC) is a free government resource for just this kind of assistance.

*Oral Health Care for Older Adults* (OP-41) is a helpful packet of information dealing with dental issues that may not have concerned you a few years ago.

And the brochure *Dry Mouth* (*Xerostomia*) (OP-14) addresses this problem common to seniors. You'll learn the causes of dry mouth and helpful tips for relieving it.

Order these and other free publications from:

National Oral Health Information Clearinghouse
1 NOHIC Way
Bethesda, MD 20892-3500
301-402-7364
Fax: 301-907-8830
TTY: 301-656-7581
E-mail: nidr@aerie.com

Or go to their Web site at <www.aerie.com/cgi-bin/ohpubgen> to read about all the oral health topics you can get information on for absolutely free.

## Chew on these free no-chew recipes

Sometimes chewing can be difficult or painful like when you have mouth sores, oral surgery, jaw problems, or dentures that don't fit properly. If you have such a problem, try free sample recipes from the *Non-Chew Cookbook* by J. Randy Wilson. The dishes not only taste good, but the nutritional information shows you just how healthy they are.

Find samples online at <www.rof.net/yp/randyw>. If you like the barbecue meat loaf, for example, or maybe the seafood casserole, you can order the entire cookbook for $23.95. Shipping and handling are free. Order it online or contact:

J. Randy Wilson
P.O. Box 2190
Glenwood Springs, CO 81602
800-843-2409
Fax: 970-945-5600
E-mail: randyw@rof.net

## Save at the dentist by snacking smart

If you enjoy munching between meals, do you grab a candy bar or a taco, a bowl of ice cream or a slice of pizza? The answer might surprise you. For a list of healthy snack foods and tips for avoiding tooth decay, read the free pamphlet *Snack Smart for Healthy Teeth*.

Published by the National Institutes of Health, this is one in a series of articles on all kinds of dental health issues. You can read them free online at <www.nidcr.nih.gov/news/publica.htm> or order a printed copy from the National Institutes of Health. Write to:

National Institute of Dental and Craniofacial Research
45 Center Drive MSC 6400
Bethesda, MD 20892-6400

And remember, healthy teeth mean lower dental bills.

## Bite on braces that fit your budget

If you are responsible for a youngster — or a not-so-youngster — who needs braces, you may be bracing for a blow to your budget. These tips should help bring down the cost.

**Get straight second-hand.** Some orthodontists use reconstructed brackets that cost them 50 to 80 percent less than new ones. Part of this savings should be passed along to you.

Are these recycled braces sanitary? After all, they were once in someone else's mouth. The Association of Orthodontists declares them safe since they're carefully cleaned, resurfaced, and sterilized before being used a second time.

**Say yes to youth.** Look for a young orthodontist just starting out. He is more likely to lower his price while getting his practice established. Offer to give him a referral after the work is satisfactorily done.

**Negotiate your bill.** Ask for a discount if you pay cash. The doctor may be willing to give you a cut in price if he saves the costs of billing. Taking off about 5 percent is not unusual.

Or arrange to pay smaller amounts starting immediately. This way you'll already have a few payments made before the billing would ordinarily begin. The smaller payments over a long period will be easier on your budget.

Make your request for any special arrangements directly to the orthodontist. The receptionist or billing clerk may assume the unexpected can't be done.

# FOOD FREEBIES AND MONEY SAVERS

You can save money by putting off some purchases — like a new car or a family vacation. Food, on the other hand, is a daily necessity. Fortunately, you don't have to give up a delicious or nutritious diet to save money on food.

Follow our tips, and eat like a king on a modest budget.

## Never buy a cookbook again!

Mediterranean pasta, low-fat chicken casseroles, hot and spicy Mexican dishes, scrumptious desserts — it's fun to experiment with all kinds of foods. And with these free recipe offers, instead of buying expensive cookbooks, you'll save your cash for the ingredients.

**Make healthy Mediterranean meals.** Olive oil is a healthy, cholesterol-free ingredient in the 25 recipes you can get from the Bertolli company. Send $2, check or money order, to cover shipping and handling to:

Bertolli Nutrition Center
P.O. Box 2001
Grand Rapids, MN 55745-2001

They'll also send you some discount coupons for purchasing the oil. You can call them at 800-908-9789 to find out about other offers as well.

For even quicker access to recipes using olive oil, go to the Web site <www.bertolli.com>. You'll find other useful information as well, like a chart that helps you convert less-healthy oils and fats in other recipes to olive oil.

**Get a taste of the blues.** For seven new and unique blueberry recipes, order *Healthful Treats Made with Blueberries*. Just send a long self-addressed stamped envelope(LSASE) to:

North American Blueberry Council
4995 Golden Foothill Parkway, Suite 2
El Dorado Hills, CA 95762
916-933-9399

For more tasty recipes — like blueberry bars, blueberry dessert pancakes, and blueberry custard — go to the Web site <www.realblueberries.com>.

**Put potatoes in your pot.** Most everybody has a few favorite potato recipes. And you can add more for free. The Idaho Potato Commission has a huge selection of recipes just waiting for you online — everything from potato soup to a dessert called Wet Chocolate L'Orange Pound Cake. Their Web site <www.idahopotato.com> also has helpful tips about how to buy, store, and prepare potatoes.

If you'd like to order recipes by mail, send for a free copy of the *Idaho Potato Microwave Cookbook*. Write:

Microwave Cookbook
Idaho Potato Commission
P.O. Box 1068
Boise, ID 83701

Or get the *Idaho Heart Healthy Recipes* from the same address. Send an LSASE, including two first-class stamps for each booklet requested.

And if you know any youngsters who would like to try some cooking, have them join the free Spuddy Buddy Fan Club online. They'll get kids' recipes and a fuzzy Spuddy Buddy sticker to decorate a school notebook or a skateboard.

**Cook with the Colonel.** Back in the 60s, Kentucky Fried Chicken was the only place to get a full picnic meal — fried chicken, rolls, and potato salad — all ready for fast take-out.

Today you may prefer staying home and preparing some of those famous recipes for yourself. To get a free copy of *The Colonel's Secret Recipes — From Our Table to Yours* recipe booklet, send an SASE to:

Colonel Sanders' Recipe Booklet
200 E. Randolph Dr., 63rd floor
Chicago IL 60601

You can also find some of the recipes online at <www.kfc.com>.

**Ham it up.** Buy a Hormel Cure 81 ham, and you can order a free cookbook with full-color photographs. It contains more than 81 recipes, menu ideas, cooking tips, and helpful information on buying, serving, and carving hams.

Go to their Web site at <www.hormel.com> and print out an order form. Fill it out, and mail it with a check or money order for $2.95 shipping and handling and one Cure 81 ham label to:

"Ham For All Seasons" Cookbook Offer
P.O. Box 5000
Austin, MN 55912

Allow 8 to 10 weeks for delivery.

**Reduce with sugar substitutes.** If you want to reduce the calories in your diet, try some dishes made with the sugar substitute Equal. Just call 800-323-5316 between 8 a.m. and 5 p.m. CST and ask for operator "H." They will send you the recipes and probably some cents-off coupons as well. You can also find sugar-free recipes at the Web site <www.equal.com>.

**Tempt your tastebuds.** Try a delicious, low-fat dish like Citrus Chicken and Rice or Oven-Fried Italian Chicken. To get these and other low-fat recipes, send $1 for postage and handling to:

Diane Trombley
2 Rhonda St.
Hudson, NH 03051

The recipes given here are available while supplies last. In most cases, if they are out of the one you ordered, they will send you another. If you don't want substitutions, especially if you must send money for shipping and handling, write first to see if the offer is still good.

Keep an eye out for free recipe offers like these, and you'll never have to buy a cookbook again.

## Free cooking tips for every taste

No need to take a costly cooking class or subscribe to pricey food magazines. You can find plenty of free information on selecting, preparing, serving, and enjoying the foods and beverages that make your mealtime a treat.

**Make it better with butter.** Land O Lakes has a booklet — yours for the asking — to help you with your baking. To get it, as well as recipes for foods like bread pudding and scones, call 877-221-8255. Or you can send your name and address to:

Land O Lakes Butter
"Baking Basics — Trusted Techniques"
P.O. Box 26341
Shoreview, MN 55126-0341

For menu ideas, cooking tips, nutrition information, and more recipes, log on to the Web site at <www.landolakes.com>.

**Read up on rice.** Want to know the difference between Arborio, Basmati, and Jasmine rice? Or would you like some ideas about how to perk up your bland rice dishes? To learn these things and more, order the free pamphlet *Rice 101: Everything You Need to Know About Cooking With Rice.* Send a long, self-addressed, stamped envelope (LSASE) to:

"Rice 101"
USA Rice Federation
P.O. Box 740121
Houston, TX 77274

In a hurry to get more rice info and recipes? Check out the offerings of the "Have a Rice Day Cafe" Web site at <www.ricecafe.com>.

**Learn to eat a mango.** If mangos are a new treat for you, log on to <http://freshmangos.com> to learn several ways to peel and slice or dice them. You'll find a lot of other interesting information about this nutritious fruit on the Web site as well.

And while you are there, sign up to receive the free monthly newsletter — *Mango News Online* — with health tips, recipes, contests and prizes, and more. You can also register online for the monthly drawing for a free box of gourmet mangos.

**Cook with queso.** If you are interested in learning about Spanish cheeses, write for a copy of the free guide, *The Soul of Spain.* The address is:

Cheese From Spain
Commercial Office of Spain
405 Lexington Ave., 44th Floor
New York, NY 10174-0331

Or go to the Web site <www.cheesefromspain.com>. You'll find recipes, storage tips, and other information.

And if you'd like to learn more about cheeses from other parts of the world, go to the Internet Web site <www.cheese.com>. You can check on your favorite — or something different — by name, by country, or by the kind of milk used.

**Enjoy nutritious citrus.** For recipes and a brochure that tells why oranges, limes, and grapefruits are so important to your diet, send an LSASE to:

TexaSweet Citrus Recipes
901 Business Park Drive, Suite 100
Mission, TX 78572

To get this information and more online, go to the Web site <www.texasweet.com>.

**Discover the benefits of milk.** Go online at <www.whymilk.com> and order some free brochures that will tell you just about everything you ever wanted to know about milk. Or call 800-WHY-MILK (800-949-6455) to request some of these titles:

★ *Cut Calories, Not Calcium*
★ *Reduce Your Risk*
★ *Shape Up Celebrity Style*
★ *Milk 101: Meeting Core Requirements*
★ *Real Men Drink Milk*
★ *Clueless About Calcium*
★ *Drink 3 for the Calcium You Need*
★ *Make it Better with Milk*
★ *Milk on the Training Table*
★ *The Lowdown on Lactose Intolerance: Making the Most of Milk*
★ *Choc It Up!*
★ *Leche, La Mejor Opcion Para Su Familia*

★  *Shake Up Your Shape-Up Plan*

The Web site offers lots of recipes for shakes, smoothies, and other milk-based drinks. Also check out the soup and salad, entree, and dessert recipes.

**Make food safety a priority.** Answer 10 questions about food safety at <www.nppc.org> and the National Pork Producers Council will send you a food safety kit.

In addition to the brochures and leaflets, you'll get a handy refrigerator magnet with food-safety reminders. And they'll also send you a full-color booklet of recipes, nutrition facts, and other useful information about pork.

You can also get this information by writing to:

National Pork Producers Council
P.O. Box 10383
Des Moines, IA 50306

**Become a wine connoisseur.** When you join American Cellars Wine Club, you receive two bottles of wine every four weeks. You have to pay for those, but you get a lot of freebies, too.

They'll send you a wine reference binder filled with interesting and helpful information about wine. You'll also get *The Grapevine* newsletter free with each wine shipment.

You'll become eligible to win a free case of wine — there's a drawing every four weeks. And you'll get discounts on wines you aren't likely to find in stores.

To learn more about these and other member benefits, go to the Web site <www.acwc.com>. You may find a free pair of laser-etched beechwood and natural cork wine stoppers as an additional bonus when you sign up.

## Cook like a gourmet with free, easy recipes

If you enjoy cooking and you like surprises, what could be more fun than free recipes that arrive by e-mail? If you like a recipe, you can print it to use again and again. If not, simply delete it — no wasted paper to throw away or recycle. And no big expensive cookbook taking up shelf space.

**Sample recipes from around the planet.** A family that loves good food gathered recipes while traveling around the world and now shares them with others by e-mail. Go to their Web site at <www.wwrecipes.com> to sign up. Each week you'll receive free recipes for a complete, multiple-course, gourmet menu.

On Mondays, you will get a recipe to start the meal — perhaps an appetizer, canapé, or first course. You'll get a soup recipe each Tuesday, and on Wednesdays, a side dish like vegetables, salads, or pasta.

Thursdays, you receive a recipe for the entrée of the week, usually a meat dish. Be ready for dessert on Friday. You can expect a recipe for an egg dish or other breakfast or brunch food on Saturday. And finally, Sunday is likely to bring an unexpected treat, like a compote, candy, or sauce recipe.

You can save the recipes and prepare them as one meal, or try them separately.

**Send for Campbell's meal-mail.** If you love using Campbell's soup in your recipes, sign up at <www.campbellkitchen.com> to receive their recipes by e-mail. You can get them daily or just once a week from any of six categories, including healthy, one-dish, and meatless meals.

**Get more than recipes.** Another free recipe newsletter, from ArcaMax Inc., includes information about how long it takes to make each recipe and how many it will feed. You'll also get a shopping list and other helpful hints.

Send an e-mail with the subject "subscribe" to recipes@arcamax.com. To see a sample recipe, go to the Web site <http://www.arcamax.com/ezines/recipes.htm>.

# Bake better with free ingredients

Are you looking for ways to make your cooking healthier, tastier, and less expensive? Sample these free products, and see if you like them better than what you are using.

**Bake with a buttermilk blend.** Your recipe calls for half a cup of buttermilk, but the smallest amount you can find is a quart. You probably won't use the rest, so how can you keep from wasting it?

The SACO company has a solution. It's called Cultured Buttermilk Blend, and they'll send you an 8-ounce packet of this dried powder — equal to one cup of liquid buttermilk — for free. You may receive a cents-off coupon, recipes, and nutrition information as well. Contact them at:

Saco Foods
P.O. Box 620707
Middleton, WI 53562
800-373-7226
E-mail: askus@sacofoods.com
<www.sacofoods.com>

**Sample a butter substitute.** Do you like the taste of butter but prefer fewer calories? Butter Buds contains only five calories per serving and no cholesterol. You can use it in place of all the fat in most quick-bread recipes. And you can substitute it for 25 to 50 percent of the fat in cakes and cookies.

Get a free sample online at <www.butterbuds.com>. While you are there, look over their recipes, nutrition information, and the handy fat-converter chart.

**Reach for a rising sample.** E-mail your favorite bread-baking recipe to SAF, and you will receive a free twin pack of Perfect Rise Yeast for your next loaf. Get the details online at <www.safyeast.com>.

And if you are looking for baking tips and recipes, check out the offerings at the SAF Web site as well as at <www.robinhood.ca> and <www.kingarthurflour.com>.

## Cash in on big savings with Web bucks

Some major supermarket chains — like Kroger, Cub Foods, and Winn Dixie — will give you cash back for buying certain name-brand products in their stores. You'll need a computer to take advantage of this great deal. Just go to the Valupage Web site at <www.valupage.com>, enter your zip code, and select the store where you'd like to shop.

You'll then see a Valupage listing the products you can buy to earn Web bucks. For example, you might get $1 in Web bucks for buying

Ocean Spray juice, or 50 cents for Earth Grains bagels. It changes each week, but recently you could find 84 products worth $65.05 in Web bucks, which you could cash in at your favorite store.

Simply print the Valupage from your computer, and take it with you when you shop. You may select as many of the items as you wish from the list. Present the Valupage at the checkout before the cashier begins scanning your groceries. He will scan or key in the code that appears on the Valupage.

When your order is finished, he will give you a certificate for the amount of Web bucks you have earned. The next time you shop at that store, present the certificate when you check out, and the cashier will deduct that amount from your total bill — no matter what you buy.

Check out the Web site and get started saving, or call 888-746-7123 for more information.

## 3 ways to help the hungry

A lot of unfortunate people go hungry every day. If you'd like to help them out, here are some things you can do for little or no cost.

*Plant a row for the needy.* If you are a gardener, how about planting an extra row in your garden so you can share your fresh produce? Find out more about the Plant a Row program by calling 877-GWAA-PAR (toll free) or logging on to <www.gwaa.org>. Or write to: Garden Writers Association of America, 10210 Leatherleaf Court, Manassas, VA 20111.

*Consider a cash donation.* America's Second Harvest operates 190 food banks throughout the 50 states and Puerto Rico. For each $1 you donate, they provide 35 pounds of food for hungry people. To learn more or to locate a food bank near you, call (312) 263-2303 or log on to <www.secondharvest.org>. You may also write: America's Second Harvest, 116 S. Michigan Ave. #4, Chicago, IL 60603.

*Log on to help the hungry.* With just a click of your computer mouse, you can donate food at The Hunger Site — and it doesn't cost you anything. The donations are paid for by corporate sponsors who hope you'll follow the links to their Web sites. You can make a free donation as often as once a day. Log on at <www.thehungersite.com>.

# Brew a free beverage

You took the first sip of a new beverage and discovered it wasn't your "cup of tea." But you didn't waste your money if you were testing a free sample — like one of these.

**Sip some cider.** One tea bag of Crow's mulled cider mix is enough to spice up 16 ounces of your favorite juice, apple cider, or wine. Or enjoy it simply as a tea. To get your free sample, send a long, self-addressed stamped envelope (LSASE) to:

J. Crow Co.
P.O. Box 172
New Ipswich, NH 03071

To find out more about their teas and other products, go to the Web site <www.jcrows.com>, call 800-878-1965, or e-mail your questions to jcrow@jcrow.mv.com.

**Relax with a free cup of tea.** For The Health Of It! offers samples of tea with exotic names like Hibiscus Medley. Or you might prefer a blend called Healthful Heart, Ultra Eye Bright, or Tranquillity. A description of these and other natural, caffeine-free teas can be found on the Web site <http://members.aol.com/JB2117/tea.html>.

Get your free sample by sending an LSASE to:

For the Health of It!
P.O. Box 142
Esko, MN 55733
218-878-1597

Be sure to tell them which sample you want. Include your e-mail address, and they'll send you their free health and fitness newsletter.

WebTea is another Web site offering free tea. Just be one of the first 1,000 people each week with the correct answer to a question about tea. You'll receive a free tea sample in the mail.

It's not hard because you can find the answer somewhere on the Web site. Check it out at <www.WebTea.com>. They also have a free Teazine, an e-mail newsletter that will tell you about their specials and discounts.

Stash Tea doesn't have a free sample. But if you order the Internet special of the week, you'll get a forest-green matte-finish canister for free. Go to <www.stashtea.com> to see this week's special. And check out their online Discount Factory Outlet Store for other specials. Recently they offered boxes of 16 paper-wrapped bags — with a dozen different choices of teas — for only 99 cents each.

Stash Tea has a free 36-page, full-color mail-order catalog, too. And if your first order is over $20 without shipping and handling, you'll get $5 off. Order the catalog online, phone 800-800-TEAS or 503-684-9725, or send your name and full postal address by e-mail to catalog@stashtea.com.

**Pour yourself a mug of hot coffee.** Is something a little stronger more to your liking? For a generous coffee sample, write:

100% Colombian Coffee Sample Offer
P.O. Box 8545
New York, NY 10150

And from time to time Taster's Choice gives away free samples. Check their Web site at <www.tasterschoice.com>.

## Save up to $1,000 on groceries

The online Grocery Card Network can save you money at all grocery stores that deal with coupons. You can pick out the coupons you want — $50 worth each month — from a list of hundreds.

You must pay a monthly membership fee of $6.95, but your yearly investment of $83.40 could bring you more than $500 in savings. Shop on double coupon days and increase the value to more than $1,000. If you shop where you get triple value, your coupons will net you even more. To get the details, go to the Web site at <www.grocerycoupons.com>.

## Dine out 'on the house'

It may be cheaper to eat at home than in a restaurant, but you don't have to break your budget when you go out for a nice meal. In fact, there are ways to get that meal for less or even for free.

**Taste and tell.** Shoney's and Captain D's want opinions about the food, hospitality, and cleanliness in their restaurants. In exchange, they will refund the cost of meals. If you'd like to be one of their mystery shoppers, get the details and fill out an application at their Web site <www.shoneysrestaurants.com/mystery.htm>. Check with other restaurants to see if they have similar programs.

The Restaurant Guide, a Web site that lists the menus of participating restaurants, also would like to pick up your dining tab. They want you to encourage restaurant managers to include their menus in the guide. They will feed you for free — up to $25 per meal — for each restaurant that joins at your recommendation. Find out how it works at <www.the-restaurant-guide.com>.

Whenever you eat out, especially if you're not happy with your dining experience, fill out those "tell us what you think" cards you find on your table. Or write a letter to the restaurant manager. Chances are you will be sent coupons for discounts or even a free meal.

**Be an early bird.** Food costs tend to rise as the day goes along so if you eat out for breakfast or lunch, you'll save a bundle over those hefty dinner prices.

If you prefer to eat out at dinnertime, look for restaurants that feature "early bird" specials. Plan to eat at those places before the main crowds arrive and prices go up. And dine out during the week rather than on the weekend. Many restaurants have lower prices on weeknights.

Here are some other ways to lower your dining-out costs:

★ Look for specials on the more expensive dishes. Lots of restaurants have certain nights when they lower prices on one feature of their menu — like a seafood night, for example.

★ Have an appetizer at home before going out. It will keep you from being hungry and ordering more than you can eat. And since alcoholic beverages and desserts have high markups, save those for when you get home afterward.

★ If you are a hearty eater, look for an all-you-can-eat buffet. If you have a modest appetite, just order a salad or appetizer, or share an entree with another light eater. If no one else cares for the dish you want, go ahead and enjoy it. Just ask for a food container and take the leftovers home for another meal.

## Save money and support a cause

Two good things happen when you buy Entertainment coupon books. You save a lot on dining costs with the two-for-one deals, and you help a good cause.

Many organizations use the Entertainment book as a fundraiser. It features two-for-one meals at area restaurants as well as discount coupons for fast-food, attractions, and services — all for one low price.

New coupon books usually become available in September in limited numbers. Call local schools, charities, and civic organizations to find out who might be selling them in your area. Or contact the publisher at:

Entertainment Publications
P.O. Box 1068
Trumbull, CT 06611
800-374-4464

## Log on for a free lunch

Yes, there is such a thing as a free lunch. In fact, there's little need to pay full price for any meal these days — not when so many restaurants offer free or discount coupons.

You can't miss the ones that come through the mail and in magazines and newspapers. But have you seen what's available on the Internet?

**Grab these coupons while they're hot.** Hot Coupons at <www.hot coupons.com> is one Web site that offers coupons for specials at restaurants all over the country. Dine4Less at <www.dine4less.com> is another. Put in your city or zip code to find the eateries in your area that will give deals like these:

★ From Dairy Queen, get $1 off on a chicken strip basket, or 50 cents off the price of any sandwich.

★ Purchase one meal from a variety of restaurants, and the second one is free.

★ At Subway, buy any two sandwiches for the price of one.

★ Get a free order of chicken wings with a pizza purchase.

★ Receive $5 to $10 off your bill at some first-rate restaurants.

Just print the coupons you want directly from your computer, and use them when you dine out.

**Save with regional restaurant offers.** Some Web sites offer coupons for use in limited areas of the country. For example, if you live in certain parts of Virginia or Texas, you might find free coupons at <www.billo fare.com>. Look for a Blimpie Buck, good for $1 off on a salad or sand-wich. Perhaps you'll find a deal on meals at Long John Silver's, or get a special price on an Arby's roast beef sandwich.

Some New Orleans restaurants offer free drinks, free appetizers, and cash discounts. You can take $3 off a dinner jazz cruise on the Steamboat Natchez. Eat at Dominique's in the French Quarter Sundays through Thursdays and get $15 off two entrees. Find out more at <www.new orleanscoupons.com>.

For coupons for restaurants in Alabama, Florida, and Georgia, go to <www.CouponTown.com>. In Massachusetts, check out <www.diningin mass.com>. If you are in Ohio, see <www.ohiocoupons.com>.

You can register to receive e-mail coupons for some of Connecticut's best restaurants at <http://ConnecticutRestaurants.com/coupons.html>. Find offers for fast food or gourmet meals in Arizona at <www.azeats.com>.

Diners in Colorado and California can look for restaurant specials at <www.restauranteur.com>. This Web site publishes recipes by various chefs of participating restaurants. So if you prefer to dine at home, you can save even more by cooking the same meals you might have ordered out.

**Play with your meal.** When you take your favorite youngsters to Chuck E. Cheese restaurant for pizza, they can enjoy games and rides as well. Just use the tokens you get with a coupon you can find at <www.chuckecheese.com>.

## Extra cash in the cookie jar

It's always great to find a sale on the foods you enjoy. But by using these tips you can make your own discounts every time you shop.

**Choose big chunks of cheese.** A bigger block or wedge of cheese is usually the best buy. You can cut it into smaller portions and freeze it if you aren't likely to eat it all before it grows mold.

As a rule, you'll pay more for shredded cheese. But if you need only a little bit for a recipe — and it's a kind you don't often use — check the price at the supermarket's do-it-yourself salad bar. It may be cheaper per ounce and you won't have any waste.

**Talk cheaper turkey.** Frozen turkeys usually cost a little less than fresh ones and generally taste just as good. Buy a bigger turkey and you'll save money as well. A 15-pound bird should feed 18 to 20 people. A 10-pounder will serve only six to eight. Watch for great prices on turkeys right before Thanksgiving and Christmas.

**Don't pay top dollar for produce.** Fresh fruits and vegetables are cheapest when they are in season. Stop at a farmer's market, buy through a food co-op, or pick your own to save even more. And don't forget gardening as another low-cost way to enjoy the freshest produce.

Get extra savings in the supermarket, too. For example, no bag of potatoes or onions will weigh exactly three or five pounds. So always select a bag that looks bigger than the others. You can weigh it to be sure. Since they all are priced the same, the additional amount is free. Weigh produce that is sold by the head or the bunch — like lettuce or carrots — as well.

Also look for reduced prices on vegetables and fruits that are past their prime. Spotted bananas make delicious smoothies, and overripe tomatoes are good in soups.

**Increase calcium at a lower price.** Do you drink milk mainly to get calcium for stronger teeth and bones? If so, the lower fat varieties are your best buy. They cost less and are higher in calcium than those with higher fat content.

Since milk is good for five days after the expiration date on the carton, why not buy it discounted and use it right away or freeze it? You'll save money as well by using dried milk in at least some of your recipes. It's cheaper and you waste less because it doesn't spoil quickly.

**Add flavor to beverages for less.** There's no need to buy those expensive flavored teas. Lemonade, orange juice, or fresh mint from your garden will add zest to a pitcher of plain iced tea.

Make coffee special by adding your own cocoa, cinnamon, or almond or vanilla flavoring. And to make coffee go further, grind the beans to a super-fine powder. You won't have to use as much, so you'll save money.

**Make a sweet substitute.** If you are tempted to satisfy your sweet tooth with expensive candies, try this nutritious treat instead. Combine one-fourth cup each honey and peanut butter with three-fourths to one and one-half cups powdered milk. Shape into balls, and if you'd like, roll them in sunflower seeds or shredded coconut.

**Spring for real chocolate.** Those artificial chocolate sprinkles from the supermarket may look pretty on your cookies or ice cream. But they can be expensive and not as tasty as the real chocolate ones. Go to an ice cream bar and ask if you can buy a few ounces of their richer sprinkles.

## Slice up to 50 percent off your grocery bill

Follow the advice of expert coupon clippers, and you may save up to 50 percent on your grocery bill. How? By combining special sales — like buy one, get one free — with double or triple coupon days. Senior citizens can often find stores that offer additional savings on certain days.

Now, with the Internet, you have even more ways to get coupons and save money on groceries.

**Locate online coupons.** You can print some coupons directly from your computer. Pathmark Stores, for example, recently offered a coupon worth 99 cents for a free one-pound box of Ronzoni pasta. If they have a store near you, check out their current coupons as well as their weekly specials at the Web site <http://pathmark.com>.

For free coupons for PAM cooking spray, go to the Web site at <www.pam4you.com>. You can also get a free recipe booklet. Give your name and address, and they will be mailed to you.

---

### Share your time and get low-cost food

How would you like to help improve your community and get low-cost food in return? Sounds like a win-win situation doesn't it? World SHARE is an organization that will provide you with affordable food just by sharing some of your time.

You simply donate two hours of volunteer work a month to a project of your choice, then save 50 percent on a monthly food package. (You pay $14 for $30 worth of meat, fresh fruit, vegetables, and staples such as pasta, rice, and beans).

You can volunteer at the SHARE warehouse or a host site, or you may choose to coach Little League, volunteer at Special Olympics or your local nursing home, or teach adults to read. SHARE lets you decide where you would like to donate your time and talents.

For more information and to find a SHARE office near you, call 888-742-7372 or visit the Web site at <www.worldshare.org>.

---

# Free samples from soup to nuts

It's fun to sample food that's free for the asking. And sometimes you're lucky enough to get more than just a taste.

**Slurp some free soup.** The soups that E.D. Foods have to offer aren't your ordinary samples. They are restaurant-size, weighing more than a pound — enough to feed 23 people. Or you can choose the free sample of chili that will feed seven people.

You'll have to send $2.75 for shipping and handling, but the soup regularly sells for $7.99 and the chili for $6 before this fee is added. To order your free sample, write them at:

E.D. Foods
6200 TransCanada Highway
Pte-Claire, QC H9R 1B9
Canada
Or call 800-267-3333, ext 235.

You can also order and view their specials online at <www.ed-foods.com>.

**Get lucky, get ice cream.** Check out the contests at the Dreyer's Web site at <www.dreyers.com>. You may win a gift certificate for a free quart — or even a year's supply — of ice cream. You'll find the same contests on the Edy's Ice Cream Web site at <www.edys.com>.

**Pick peanuts.** Bertie County Peanuts holds a weekly online drawing for free North Carolina-grown peanuts. You can sign up for the giveaway and order a free peanut catalog at <www.bertiecopeanuts.com>. Just click on "request form" to reach the giveaway site.

The Web site also includes recipes for peanut dishes like peanut-carrot salad and peanut muffins. And you can even sing along to the "Found a Peanut" song. Remember that one from your childhood?

You might want to order some peanuts — in bulk for the best prices — at their Web site. Or contact them at:

Powell & Stokes, Inc.
217 US 13 North
Windsor, NC 27983
800-457-0005

## Spices to tickle your taste buds — and your wallet

It's fun to experiment with spicy seasonings, but buying a lot of different herbs and spices gets expensive. Try these free samples of blended seasonings. If you like the way they perk up your dishes, you can buy more. That way you won't spend money on lots of individual spices that might go to waste.

A Better Seasoning
3104 Belmont Court
Jacksonville, NC 28546

Send a long, self-addressed envelope (LSASE) for your free sample. You might like to try this blend in the tuna salad or potato salad recipes you can find on their Web site at <www.abetterseasoning.com>.

Magic Seasoning Blends
P.O. Box 23342
New Orleans, LA 70183-0342

Go to the Web site <www.chefpaul.com>, print and fill out the form, then send it with either $1 or an LSASE with three first-class stamps. Along with this sample, you'll get a free copy of Chef Paul Prudhomme's most recent catalog. If you don't have access to a computer, send your name, address, and phone number with your sample request.

Cahaba Products, Inc.
P.O. Box 691
Selma, AL 36702-0691

Send an SASE for a free sample of their delicious Southern Flavor Seasoning.

KSP Spices
P.O. Box 892
St. Johns, AZ 85936

Send an LSASE for a sample of their natural seasoning. They don't use preservatives and other enhancers, so you might try your recipe first with half the usual amount. They will send a price list for bulk spices with the sample.

Everglades Foods, Inc.
P.O. Box 595
LaBelle, FL 33975

Send an SASE with your request for their free Everglades Seasoning sample. If you like the sample and want to order more, you can call them at 800-689-2221. For recipes using their herb and spice blends, go to their Web site at <http://hometown.aol.com/bjprophet/EGS/index.htm>.

## Help yourself to some hot stuff

If you really like the spices that bring tears to your eyes, consider these offers:

**Send for a sizzling-hot sample.** Heart of Texas promises to rush you a free sample of their habanero powder. All you have to do is send a long self-addressed stamped envelope (LSASE) to:

H.O.T.
9026 China Spring Hwy
Waco, TX 76708

If you don't want to mix your own hot sauce from the powder, you can order a ready-to-use 4-ounce bottle for $2.95. Get more information at their Web site <www.hotexas.com>.

**Read it and weep.** Subscribe to *Chile Pepper Magazine*, and the Mild to Wild Pepper & Herb Company will send you a free 8-ounce bottle of hot sauce from a choice of flavors.

To learn more, go to the Web site at <http://wildpepper.com>. While there, you might also check out their specials. If you'd like a chili sauce without the heat, look for Chile Caribi at $4 for a quarter of a pound. You can also contact them at:

Mild to Wild Pepper & Herb Company
81 Martin Place
Franklin, IN 46131-1745

**Enter monthly give-aways.** Are you looking for even hotter offers? You might want to enter a monthly online contest. The Bandera Chile Peppers company gives away a 2-pound box of their best gourmet dried chile peppers each month. Register online at <www.banderachilis.com>.

If your taste buds don't want you to leave it to chance, you can place an order. Request as little as 1 pound of chili peppers, or, if you are planning a really big barbecue, order 4 pounds and get an additional pound for free. Place orders online or at:

Bandera Chile Peppers
9010 S. Cage Blvd
Pharr, TX 78577-9769
956-781-7799 or 888-306-3336 (toll free)
Fax: 956-781-2323

**Triumph with trivia and red-hot recipes.** Coyote Moon also holds a sweepstakes. To enter, you must correctly answer a trivia question. But for the best prizes, check out their recipe contest. Recently they were asking for original chili-with-beans recipes. With several winners and a variety of good prizes, it's worth going online at <www.coyote-moon.com> to get the details.

While you are at the Web site, you might want to look at their recipes and order their free catalog. And check out their specials — like good prices on sample sizes.

You can also reach them at:

Coyote Moon
P.O. Box 17062
11632 Frankstown Road
Pittsburgh, PA 15235
412-370-4023
Fax: 412-371-6784

# Sweet temptations at a sweet price

Is your sweet tooth just aching for a treat? If so, bite into these free and discounted goodies.

**Jump for jelly beans.** If your timing is right, you can get free Jelly Belly gourmet jelly beans. They give away at least 600 free samples each day on their Web site at <www.jellybelly.com>. But they get so many requests, they can't provide them for everybody.

To be fair, they vary the time of day they make the jelly bean offer available. So if you don't hit the jackpot the first time you visit, try again later.

Really devoted jelly bean fans might want to join the Jelly Belly Taste Bud Club. It costs $14.95 for a two-year membership. But you get a genuine Taste Bud Club T-shirt, a Jelly Belly lapel pin, an autographed photo of Mr. Jelly Belly, and, of course, some jelly bean samples. In addition, you become eligible to win prizes, get special offers on Jelly Belly merchandise, and receive a quarterly newsletter.

Go to the Web site to print an order form that asks for your name, address, age, and T-shirt size. Send it with your check or money order to:

Jelly Belly Taste Bud Club
P.O. Box 803
Fairfield, CA 94533-0080

To use your credit card, contact the Taste Bud Club Hotline at 888-522-3267 (weekdays 7 a.m. to 7 p.m. CST).

**"Chews" chocolate.** If you like cooking with chocolate, you might want to share your recipe with Green River Chocolates. They'll send you a free chocolate sampler if they use your recipe on their Web site. Go to <www.grchocolates.com> to give them your recipe and to sign up for e-mail notices of their specials.

You can also contact them at:

Green River Chocolates
P.O. Box 421
Hinesburg, VT 05461
802-482-6727

J.S. Bach Classic Chocolates may also have a sample for you. Their online offers, which change frequently, have included a single sample, a four-box sampler (6.6-ounces) for a $4.95 shipping and handling fee, and a dozen chocolates free with the purchase of three dozen.

To see their current offerings, go to their Web site <www.bach-chocolate.com>. Or contact them at:

J. S. Bach Classic Chocolates
4952 Warner Ave., Suite 100
Huntington Beach, CA 92649
877-4-JS-Bach

You'll find chocolate and any other candy your heart desires on the Web site <www.candybarrel.com>. This company even carries low-fat sweets and "nostalgic" favorites you may remember from your younger days. You can choose from two discount specials each month.

# CLOTHING STEALS
# AND DEALS

A few years ago, a Georgia woman made a New Year's resolution not to buy any new clothes for one full year. She was concerned about the overuse of landfills and felt inspired to follow the practice of "using it up and making it last." Expecting to wear the clothes she had on hand until they were threadbare, she thought this would be a year of sacrifice. To her delight, she actually ended up with the best wardrobe she'd ever owned.

Respecting her commitment to the environment, friends examined their own closets, found beautiful clothes they never wore, and passed them on to her. Others shared tips for finding quality clothing at bargain prices at yard sales, thrift stores, and consignment shops. Some even had suggestions on how to find free clothes.

You don't have to give up buying new clothes, however, to find bargains and freebies. In this chapter, you'll learn secrets for dressing well for less cash no matter what your fashion philosophy. Discount catalogs, free clothing sites, Internet bargains — they're all here at your fingertips. And for more information on where and how to find the best deals, check out the ***How to find the best deals*** chapter.

# CLOTHING

## Finding free fashions can be fun

You may think that nobody really gives away free clothes. But think again. Sometimes it's a way for merchants to get you into a store in the hopes you'll see other items you can't resist buying. Or clothes may be taking up much-needed space, so someone will appreciate your taking them away. Here are some examples:

**Buy two, get one free.** When your favorite clothing store has this kind of deal on turtleneck pullovers, for example, it's a good time to stock up for the winter. Look for these sales in the store or advertised in the newspaper or on television. Sometimes the freebie is a different item — a free tie, perhaps, with the purchase of a dress shirt. Just be sure the item you buy is priced right, so the other is truly free.

**Ask about unclaimed clothes.** Do you know there are people who take good clothes to the cleaners and then forget about them? After a time, if they aren't picked up, they have to be cleared out. Ask your dry cleaner periodically about any unclaimed items. You can usually get them for free if you are willing to pay the cleaning bill.

Other free clothes may require a little more effort on your part. For example:

**Arrange a clothing swap.** Your friend has a blue linen dress you know would look great on you. So offer her a trade — maybe that skirt and blouse in her favorite shade of green, the one she always raves about. And if that trade turns out to be fun, broaden your choices with an organized clothes swap.

Get your club or church group involved. Have people bring in clean clothes in good condition. Everyone should go home with at least one "new" outfit. And when the trading is done, you'll feel even better if you donate what's left over to a charity thrift store.

**Case the curbside on moving day.** The end of the school term is an especially good time to check the curbs and dumpsters near a college campus for discarded clothes and other items. And also watch for boxes to appear along the street when spring cleaning is in full swing.

**Scout out treasures hiding in the trash.** Look behind apparel shops or clothing factories for discarded leftover or imperfect items. The idea of digging in dumpsters may seem distasteful, but it's worth a look for clean boxes that are easily within reach. (See the story on dumpster diving in the *How to find the best deals* chapter.)

**Fit yourself with free fabric.** If you sew, check out any clothing factories nearby for free or cheap remnants. You may still have to pay for a pattern and thread, but you save the main cost, which is the cloth.

**Hang out in hand-me-ups.** Did you like the grownup feeling you got from wearing an older sister's hand-me-downs when you were a kid? Now you might enjoy a taste of youthful rebellion when you kick up your heels in threads passed up from your children or grandchildren. Just let them know you'd like to borrow an item they no longer wear. They'll get the hint and offer you "first dibs" when they have others to give away.

**Make a withdrawal from a clothes bank.** Churches and other organizations collect donations of clean, usable clothes for those who have fallen on hard times. If someone you know doesn't have enough to wear, you might help them locate one of these clothes banks.

These ideas should put you on the lookout for other free clothing. With a little effort, you will quickly see a big difference in your clothes budget.

## Watch for free wearables on the Web

When you are searching for free clothes, the Internet is a source you shouldn't overlook. Some online merchants offer free items to encourage you to get into the habit of shopping with them.

Here are some examples that were available at the time of writing. If they interest you, go to the Web site given and see if the offers are still good. If not, perhaps they'll have others you'll like.

**Get free unmentionables.** Buy any bra, get a free pair of panties. Not only that, for every $50 purchase, receive $25 in "realwomen $s" that you can use in the future. A Christmas-time special included a gift certificate for $30 off your next purchase of $75 or more, or $75 off a $150 purchase. And you could also register to enter a sweepstakes for a new iMac computer. Go to <www.lanebryant.com> to see what's free today.

**Slip into some free stockings.** The Silkies company will send you a free pair of pantyhose along with two identical pairs for $1 each plus postage and handling. After trying the free pair, you can decide if you want to keep the others and pay for them. If not, just return them within 10 days. You keep the free pair, and the Silkies company will pay the return postage for the others. This is for new customers only, and you have to be age 18 or older. To order your stockings, go to <www.silkies.com>.

Or write to Hosiery Corp. of America, P.O. Box 8235, Philadelphia, PA 19101-9949.

**Select a free silk tie.** At a pre-Christmas sale, the Silk Tie Factory offered their wide selection of designer silk ties, regularly priced at $20-$36, for only $8.99 each. And with any order of $40 or more, shoppers could get one tie absolutely free. To find out what's available now, go to their Web site at <www.thesilktiefactory.com>. You can also call 718-601-4055, or write: The Silk Tie Factory, 5715 Mosholu Ave., Riverdale, NY 10471.

**Fancy a free shirt.** The Paul Fredrick Company believes if you try their men's clothing, you'll be back for more. So they'll give you free merchandise if you are a first-time customer. The offer may be for a dress shirt, a silk tie, or another quality item. Your only charge is the regular shipping and handling fee of $7.50. And to encourage you to order more, they offer to pay the shipping charges on any order totaling $50 or more. Claim your free gift at <www.paulfredrick.com>.

Keep an eye out for more freebies on the World Wide Web. But to be on the safe side, see the tips and warnings about online shopping in the *How to find the best deals* chapter.

## Free catalogs make shopping a snap

If you're like most people, you're probably tired of paying for clothing catalogs. Here are some companies that won't make you pay before you buy and will send you their catalogs for free.

The Ultimate Outlet, a Spiegel's catalog, has discount prices on clothing for men, women, and children as well as on household goods. Reach them at:

The Ultimate Outlet
P.O. Box 182557
Columbus, OH 43218-2557
800-332-6000
781-871-4100
Fax: 800-422-6697
TDD (telecommunications device for the deaf): 800-322-1231

You'll find hosiery, lingerie, and casual wear in the Hanes catalog. Get your free copy at the Web site <www.onehanesplace.com> or request it from:

One Hanes Place Catalog
P.O. Box 748
Rural Hall, NC 27098-0748
800-300-2600
Fax: 800-545-5613
TDD: 800-816-4833

The Bridgewater company sells clothing and accessories for men, women, and children. Write, call, or fax for your free catalog.

Bridgewater
Box 1600
Brockton, MA 02403-1600
800-525-4420
508-583-7200
Fax: 800-448-5767
TDD: 800-978-8798

To get a catalog that offers Legg's hosiery at a 50-percent discount, write or call:

Legg's Brand, Inc.
P.O. Box 748
Rural Hall, NC 27098
919-744-1790
800-522-1151

Find women's clothes in large sizes in this free catalog:

Just My Size
P.O. Box 748
Rural Hall, NC 27098
800-522-9567
<www.justmysize.com>

If you are a tall woman, this catalog has just the clothes for you:

Long Elegant Legs
5 Homestead Road, Suite 9
Belle Mead, NJ 08502
800-344-2235
Fax: 908-359-0691
<www.longelegantlegs.com>

Order a free Carabella catalog of swim, sports, and evening wear online at <www.carabella.com>.

For women's classic clothing, sizes 12 and larger, order a catalog from:

Ulla Popken
10610 Beaver Dam Rd.
Hunt Valley, MD 21030
800-245-8552
Fax: 410-329-1320
<www.ullapopken.com>

Wearguard offers a full line of durable work clothing, mostly for men, but some for women. Their free catalog is available at:

Wearguard Corp.
141 Longwater Drive
Norwell, MA 02061
800-272-0308
781-871-4100
Fax: 800-436-3132
<www.wearguard.com>

For women's casual and business attire in a wide range of sizes and at attractive prices, check out this catalog:

Willow Ridge
421 Landmark Drive
Wilmington, NC 28410
800-388-8555
Fax: 910-343-6859
TDD: 800-945-1118

Chadwick's of Boston claims to be the nation's first, and now largest, women's fashion catalog offering brand-name merchandise at discount prices. You can see for yourself by ordering it online at <www.chadwicks.com> or calling 800-525-6650.

If you like cowboy-style clothes, order this western wear catalog:

Sheplers
6501 W. Kellogg
P.O. Box 7702
Wichita, KS 67277-7702
888-835-4004
Fax: 800-900-7437
<www.westernwear.com>

The Eddie Bauer catalog of casual clothes and sportswear is available online at <www.eddiebauer.com> or by calling 800-789-1386. And if you place your order from a telephone in one of their stores — there are over 600 worldwide — they will deliver it for free.

"If it's not comfy, we don't have it!" claim the creators of this catalog of women's and men's casual clothing:

Northwest Express
P.O. Box 1548
Medford, OR 97501-0400
800-727-7243
Fax: 800-648-6640
<www.northwestexpress.com>

If you have access to a computer, you can find other clothing catalogs online at <www.freeshop.com>.

# Bargains abound on the Internet

Shopping for clothes on the Internet is a lot like shopping from a catalog. You'll likely feel right at home while browsing through the pages of familiar companies. And it's fun to check out the bargains offered on unfamiliar sites as well.

Just keep in mind that some Web sites are easier to navigate than others, and Web pages change faster than those in catalogs. Here are some sites where you can always find outstanding bargains.

**Log on to the ultimate outlet.** You may not live close to any of Speigel's 17 catalog outlet stores, but you can still get discounts of up to 70 percent by ordering online. For example, a mock-neck tunic for $18.99 is 60 percent lower than the regular price of $49. To see this or other bargains, go to <www.ultimateoutlet.com>.

**Bag outdoor gear at bargain prices.** You can save money with regular discounts from REI at <www.rei-outlet.com>. But watch for their closeouts to get the really good deals. Recently, men's Swedish wool pants were only $12.93.

**Get discounts on name brands for men.** Go to "clearance" at <www.savi shopper.com> and see if they still have four pairs of Geoffrey Beene cotton and nylon ribbed dress socks for $11.99. The regular price is $32.

**Find deals on "funky" clothes.** If your taste in clothes is a little off-beat, you'll appreciate the discounts at <www.droog.com>. And hunt for roaches — yes, the insects. You can save even more when you spot those critters hidden on their Web site.

**Make tracks for outdoor wear.** Get bargains on brands like Patagonia, Marmot, and Nike at <www.altrec.com>. If you are a first-time customer, take another 15 percent off your order.

**Save on what you wear to work.** The Wearguard Corporation sells work clothes and outerwear online. Look for their close outs for the best prices, like men's or women's Dura-Press 100% cotton pleated pants, regularly $34.99, on sale for $12.95. Find them at <www.wearguard.com>.

**Click on "clearance" to save.** Scoop up remaining close-out items at <www.bargainclothing.com> and <www.jcrew.com>. Look at the sale store at <www.llbean.com>. Or go to "Overstocks" at <www.landsend.com>.

These are just a few of the clothing sites where you'll find good deals. Maybe your favorite store has a Web site, too. Just type the name into your search engine to check it out. Before shopping online with companies that are unfamiliar to you, however, you might want to read the tips and warnings in the ***How to find the best deals*** chapter.

## Shirts that suit you to a T — for free!

Chances are, you have more than a few T-shirts in your wardrobe. Whether they're plain and simple or filled with clever designs, T-shirts are always handy to have around. They're also one of the easiest items to get for free.

Groups of all kinds use T-shirts to advertise their products or spread their messages, and they would love to have you sport their logos. Just look around, and you are sure to find one that appeals to you.

**Trade time and talent.** When you volunteer with just about any group, they are likely to give you a free T-shirt to wear. Run a foot race for charity, or participate in a bike marathon — you get a T-shirt. Volunteer to help at a sporting event or a community fundraiser, and you'll get another shirt. The options are limitless; you just need to keep your eyes open for opportunities you enjoy.

**Win with originality.** The Baby Net has a T-shirt featuring the Baby Net duck for your favorite infant. Get it for free if they use one of the following on their Web site:

★ Your special "while I was pregnant" recipe. They are looking for nutritious, low-fat dishes that are fairly easy to prepare.

★ An original "sing to your baby" rhyme. (All you grandmas should have a few of these!)

★ Your idea for a fun baby shower. If they post this idea, you'll also get a free "We have the Cutest Baby" bumper sticker.

For more information, go to <www.thebabynet.com>. While you are there, check their coupon page. A recent offering was $5 off on the purchase of a diaper bag.

**Get one free with three.** You can often get a free T-shirt, or at least a discount, when you buy others. Watch for these sales in stores, catalogs, and on the Internet.

If you order three or more from the TShirtGuy.com Web site, for example, they'll send you a free T-shirt with their name and slogan printed across the front. Just tell them when you order that you would like the free one. To see their choices, go to <www.tshirtguy.com>.

**Buy smart.** People often buy T-shirts for emotional reasons — team spirit, the excitement of travel, the thrill of seeing a favorite entertainer perform, to name a few. But the enthusiasm often fades quickly so a lot of these turn up at yard sales and in thrift shops. They aren't new or free, but you are sure to find some you really like at rock-bottom prices.

## Win a T-shirt sweepstakes

You have nothing to lose, not even the price of a postage stamp, when you enter these online T-shirt giveaways. Each of the following companies listed holds a monthly drawing. You can enter every month, but if you enter more than once within a given month from the same e-mail address, your entries may be deleted.

**Him's My Boy Golfwear** gives away a T-shirt with its clever logo — a dog breaking a golf club — that sells for $13.99. To register, go to the Web site <www.himsmyboy.com>.

They also have a photo contest for the funniest picture of a pet or the goofiest golf photo. They pick a winner in this contest every two months. If they choose yours, you'll get a free T-shirt, and they'll publish the photograph on their Web site. Send your pictures to:

Him's My Boy Photo Contest
P.O. Box 11883
Memphis, TN 38111

If you want your pictures sent back, include a self-addressed stamped envelope. If you want to e-mail your entry, go to the Web site for more information. They can also be reached by telephone at 800-663-8575.

**Geographics** is a T-shirt company that specializes in science-related designs — like biology, geology, and what they call "computer-geek-ology." To register for its monthly giveaway, go to <www.usabest.com/geographics>.

If you buy Geographics T-shirts, you'll get a discount if you order more than one. The more you buy, the bigger the discount. For details, see the Web site, or contact them at:

Geographics
7 Commerce Drive
Eureka Springs, AR 72632
E-mail: geograph@ipa.net
501-253-6830 (for information)
800-243-6830 (to place an order only)

**Space Shirts** holds a monthly drawing for a free T-shirt with a NASA space exploration or UFO design. Register at its Web site <www.space shirts.com>.

If you are interested in buying their T-shirts, you'll find child-size shirts ranging from $8 to $13, and adult sizes, $10 to $17.50. To get a free hard copy of their catalog, call 800-451-7453, fax 407-452-3302, or e-mail bmulberry@spaceshirts.com.

**Cool Clothing** sells T-shirts with pictures of pets. Enter its monthly drawing at <www.coolclothing.com>. You can buy a wide selection of T-shirts for $9.95 each. Or pick out a picture of your own pet, and they'll put it on a shirt for only $10.99. Send the photo and check to:

Cool Clothing
292 Fifth Avenue
New York, NY 10001-4513

Call first to find out the total with tax and shipping. You can reach them at 212-613-2237, or send an e-mail to Sales@coolclothing.com.

**California Rainbow Tiedye** lets its monthly winner choose from a selection of T-shirts that regularly sell for $19.95 to $23.95, depending on size.

If you don't win the first prize, perhaps you'll win the second — a certificate worth up to $15 toward the purchase of any of their tie-dye T-shirts. The third prize is a $2-off certificate.

To register, go to their Web site at <www.catalog.com/giftshop/tiedye/td.htm>. While you are there, give them your e-mail address, and they will notify you when they have special discounts on leftover shirts from sales at arts and craft shows.

# SHOES

## First-class deals on footwear

High-quality leather shoes and boots can be expensive. But it's possible to get good used ones for free and new ones at a discount.

**Shop at the shoe repair store.** Sometimes people take shoes or boots for repairs and never come back for them. That means the shop is stuck with merchandise it doesn't want. If you're willing to pay for the repairs, chances are you can get the shoes for free. So drop by your shoe repair shop from time to time, and see if there is any unclaimed footwear that fits you.

**Click on comfortable savings.** You can get discounts on sandals, clogs, and walking shoes at Birkenstock's "sale shelf" of discontinued and as-is items. Log on to your computer and go to <www.birkenstockexpress.com> for great bargains. They'll also repair your Birkenstock shoes, and they sometimes have specials on that service, too.

While you are at the Web site, you can order a free catalog. Or if you prefer, you can write, call, fax, or e-mail to request one at:

Birkenstock Express
301 SW Madison Avenue
Corvallis, OR 97333
800-451-1459
Fax: 541-752-6313
E-mail: mailorder@birkenstockexpress.com

**Get free in-store delivery.** If you have a Payless Shoes store near you, check out their Web site <www.payless.com> for a great deal. Buy your shoes online, and they'll ship them free if you have them sent to the store. And watch for their online sales. Recently they had up to 50 percent off on all their athletic shoes.

**Fit yourself from a wide selection.** If you are looking for men's shoes in hard-to-find widths, go to Hitchcock Shoes' Web site at <www.wideshoes.com>. You can save $20 or more on selections from their discontinued styles.

Request a free copy of their 56-page color catalog with sizes 5-13, EEE through EEEEEE while you are online, or contact them at:

Hitchcock Shoes, Inc.
225 Beal Street
Hingham, MA 02043
800-992-WIDE
Fax: 781-749-3576
E-mail: hitchcock@wideshoes.com

**Look for large deals.** If you are looking for large sizes in women's shoes, go to <www.shoexpress.com> and check out Shoe Express' online clearance sale. Recently they featured several styles for $19.99 a pair that were regularly priced for as much as $69. If you live close enough, you might visit their store in Lafayette, Louisiana, or you can call 318-235-5191 for more information.

**Focus on value.** The Knapp company has been selling work shoes and boots for nearly 80 years. They have walk-in stores and a traditional catalog, but you can also buy online. At their Web site <www.knappshoes.com>, you'll find the "Closeout Closet" with special deals on shoes for men and women. A recent feature was men's waterproof insulated boots for $64.90 — regular price, $124.99.

You can order a free catalog online, or call 800-869-9955 during business hours. Fax them at 800-276-1070, or write:

Knapp Boots and Shoes
One Keuka Business Park, Ste 300
Penn Yan, NY 14527

If you have a favorite shoe store, you are probably in the habit of watching for their sales. If you haven't checked to see if they have online specials as well, try typing their name into your Internet search engine and see what savings turn up. Before ordering from an unfamiliar Web site, you might want to check out the tips and warnings in the online shopping story in the ***How to find the best deals*** chapter.

## Free shoe advice from the experts

You've found great discounts on high-quality shoes, but they're only a bargain if you wear them. If they aren't comfortable, they'll just sit in your closet, gathering dust. So consider some helpful advice from the pros before you buy.

**Step into a pain-free fit.** You can avoid blisters, corns, calluses, and bunions with the information in the pamphlet, *10 Points of Proper Shoe Fit.* To get it, simply send a self-addressed stamped envelope (SASE) to:

American Orthopedic Foot and Ankle Society
1216 Pine Street, Suite 201
Seattle, WA 98101

You can order single copies of their other pamphlets as well. Send an SASE to the same address for each title you want from the list below.

- ★ *A Guide to Children's Shoes*
- ★ *10 Points of Children's Shoe Fit*
- ★ *The Adult Foot*
- ★ *Getting in Step With Arthritis*
- ★ *How to Select Sports Shoes*
- ★ *The Diabetic Foot*

**Locate hard-to-find footwear.** For a list of retail shoe sellers that carry less common sizes and widths, write:

National Shoe Retailers Association
9861 Broken Land Parkway, #255
Columbia, MD 21046-1151

**Find a professional for special needs.** Do you have a foot problem caused by a disease or injury? If so, you may need specially designed shoes or foot devices called orthoses. To get a list of board certified pedorthists, the specialists who can help you, contact:

Pedorthic Footwear Association
9150 Columbia Gateway Drive, Suite G
Columbia, MD 21046-1151
410-381-7278
800-673-8447
E-mail: info@pfa.org
<www.cpeds.org>

Follow the advice of the experts, and you'll walk comfortably through the largest mall or the longest flea market in your search for bargains.

### Fix it by mail

If you can't find a good local shoe repair service, try the Houston Shoe Hospital. They do mail-order repairs. Write 5215 Kirby Drive, Houston, TX, 77098; or call 713-528-6268

## Save money by swapping extra shoes

If you, like millions of other Americans, have different-sized feet, you probably buy two pairs of shoes to get one pair to fit. Is there a way to avoid paying double?

Or maybe you wear only one shoe and would like to know what to do with the other one. Two non-profit organizations can help you with these concerns.

**The One Shoe Crew (TOSC)** provides new shoes, single and "mismated," to adults and teenagers who are no longer growing. Currently they don't supply children's shoes.

There is a one-time registration fee of $3, and you must pay for postage — $2.50 for a single shoe, $5 for a pair. A $5 charitable donation is also requested each time you get shoes, but it's not required for those who can't afford it. If you're a U.S. veteran, you pay no fees at all.

TOSC can also match you with someone who wears the same sizes you do, but on the opposite feet. You can then make direct exchanges with that person. You'll pay a $10 partnership fee when a suitable partner is found.

Call 916-364-SHOE (7463) for more information or to request a registration form. Or write and send a self-addressed stamped envelope (SASE) to:

The One Shoe Crew
86 Clavela Ave.
Sacramento, CA 95828-4647

In most cases, you will want to exchange your unused shoes with your shoe partner. But they do accept donations of new shoes from individuals and businesses. Mail them to:

The One Shoe Crew
920 South River Road
West Sacramento, CA 95691

**The National Odd Shoe Exchange (NOSE)** provides shoes directly to those who register with them. There is an annual fee of $35, but as long as your registration is current, you can get shoes as often as you need them. Donations are requested to help cover the cost of shipping.

Children may also be registered with NOSE, and there is no fee for those age 5 and younger. For more information and registration materials, contact them at:

National Odd Shoe Exchange
3200 North Delaware Street
Chandler, AZ 85225-1100
480-892-3484
Fax: 480-892-3568

Since these are non-profit organizations, your donations of new shoes are tax-deductible. If you wish a receipt, put your name and address with that request inside the package. They do not accept used shoes. But cash contributions, also tax-deductible, are welcome.

# ACCESSORIES

## Brighten your outfit with freebies

Accessories — like belts, bags, ties, and scarves — can really perk up a basic wardrobe. Here are some you can get for free, although for most you must pay shipping and handling.

**Hold your hair with a free scrunchie.** Indicate your color preference, and the folks at Prairie Flower will try to match it from their assortment of bright-colored prints and solid scrunchies.

Or, if you prefer, you can order the materials to make your own scrunchie. (You must provide the needle and thread.) Be sure to indicate which you want — do-it-yourself or ready-made. Send $1 for shipping and handling to:

Prairie Flower
P.O. Box 8664
Riverside, CA 92515-8664

**Order a free bindi.** According to a legend from India, a person could steal a woman's beauty by staring at her eyes. So Indian women wore bindis — tiny stick-on face decorations — in the center of their foreheads to draw attention away from their eyes.

You can see examples and purchase bindis on the Profoundia Web site at <www.olywa.net/jpl/>. But to get a free sample, you must send a self-addressed stamped envelope (SASE) to:

Profoundia
P.O. Box 1323
Olympia, WA 98507

**Pack Power Rangers in your hip pocket.** A child will love to carry his money in a free Mighty Morphin Power Rangers black satin wallet. It has separate compartments for coins and bills. Send $1 for shipping and handling to:

Danors
9360 NW 39th Street
Sunrise, FL 33351

**Get a free silk or cotton bow tie.** These are valued at $5 to $25, but you can get one free if you pay a $2 shipping and handling fee.

Request a clip on, or ask for a traditional tie-your-own style. Also indicate the size you need — small, medium, or large. The address is:

Parker Flags
Dept. S
5746 Plunkett Street, Suite 4
Hollywood, FL 33023

**Decorate your shoes for the holidays.** Get two pairs of Christmas shoelaces, one with red Santa Clauses and the other with green trees. Send $1.25 for shipping and handling to:

McVehil's Mercantile
45 Bayne Ave, Dept. CL
Washington, PA 15301-8864

Prefer something you can wear all year long? Get a pair of bright colored neon shoestrings with black dinosaurs for $1 from the same address, Dept. DD.

**Baby his head in a warm hat.** Rainbow Kids sells children's clothing online. But they want to be sure all newborns keep their heads safely warm, so they will send you a free hat for a baby up to 6 months old. Go to <www.rainbowkids.net> and print an order form. Put 55 cents postage on a large (6x9 or bigger) self-addressed envelope, and send it and the filled-out form to:

Rainbow Kids, Inc.
Dept. Free Hats
P.O. Box 31817
Bellingham, WA 98228

**Pull back your ponytail.** Get a nice assortment of elastic ponytail holders —18 pieces, in fact — in a variety of colors with gold threading. Send 50 cents and an SASE to:

Savon
P.O. Box 1356
Gwinn, MI 49841

You can also send 25 cents and an SASE to the same address for a free eyeglass holder. This device keeps your glasses from falling or getting lost when you aren't wearing them.

Look for more free accessories in clothing and department stores, especially around holidays. That's when you are most likely to find a free scarf or tie, for example, with the purchase of a dress or suit.

## Accessorize your wardrobe for less

You can find amazing bargains on secondhand accessories at yard sales, thrift stores, and consignment shops. Once in a while, you may even turn up new items that haven't been worn or have been donated by merchants, usually at stores operated by charities.

For other good deals on new accessories, watch for end-of-the-season sales in stores and catalogs. The Internet is another helpful resource for good prices on new stuff. And you can bid on quality used items at online auctions.

**Try calling on Avon.** This company may be better known for beauty products, but it also sells jewelry — and not just door-to-door. If you haven't seen the catalog lately, ask your friends and family if they know an "Avon lady" who can give you one.

If you have a computer, you can check their online weekly specials at <http://shop.avon.com>. A recent example was a pair of blue topaz earrings with emerald-cut stones set in filigreed sterling silver for $39.99, $10 off the regular price.

**Reap end-of-the-season bonanzas.** The regular Tweeds catalog has a clearance section with good discounts on hats, gloves, scarves, and other accessories. For even more special deals, ask for their end-of-the-season catalogs. Call them at 800-999-7997. They also have a Web site at <www.tweeds.com>.

**Bag a good deal.** Orvis, established in 1856 as a sporting goods company, today sells a wide variety of products, including fashion accessories. Go to their Web site <www.orvis.com> to order a free catalog or to shop online. You'll find specials like a black beaded velvet evening bag and belt for $12 (regularly $24), a chenille handbag for $19 (regularly $29), or a beaded inlaid enamel on copper pendant for $19.99 (regularly $29.99).

**Tip your hat to low prices.** Check the "current specials" at the Sheplers Hat Wearhouse Web site at <www.hatwearhouse.com>. Look, for example, for hats by Stetson or Resistol, regularly $45, reduced to $24.99–$29.99.

**Bid for your bargain.** Auctions, both walk-in and online, are good places for good deals on accessories, both new and used, modern and antique.

Ebay, a popular online auction site, regularly offers a variety of accessories. And a recent check of <www.liveauctiononline.com> found several 14-karat gold jewelry pieces with bids starting under $20. For a list of online diamond auctions, go to <www.diamond.com>.

Most companies that sell clothing also sell accessories. Look for them at the same locations mentioned in the other clothing stories in this chapter.

# If it glitters, it could be free

Jewelry can really add sparkle to your appearance. And you may be surprised at how often you can find those glittering pieces for free. Sometimes you are asked to pay the price of shipping and handling. Other times you are required to first make another purchase. But there are free jewels out there. Consider these choices.

**Nab a free necklace by mail.** Just send a self-addressed stamped envelope (SASE) with a request for "Free Jewelry" to:

Laurie's Jewelry
2431 Buck Road
Harrison, MI 48625

(Limit one per household)

**Have fun with fairy earrings.** Get 14-karat gold-plated earrings, stamped in the form of fairies and dangling from fishhook earwires. Mail $2 shipping and handling to:

Prouty Enterprises
6325 Randon School Road
Rosenberg, TX 77471

**Let angels protect you.** Get a white enamel guardian angel pin for free when you pay $1 for shipping and handling. Or send 75 cents for an adjustable angel ring. Include an SASE with your request.

Phil Labush
9360 Northwest 39th Street
Sunrise, FL 33351

**Make your own earrings.** This free kit has enough materials — flower beads, pearl beads, and findings — to make six pairs of earrings in assorted colors. Send $2 shipping and handling to:

Mom and Me Originals
Box 54
Orrville, OH 44667

**Create a friendship bracelet.** Wear a friend's name — or another happy word — around your wrist. Get embroidery thread and instruction by sending $1 for shipping and handling to:

Friendship Bracelet
P.O. Box 11
Garnerville, NY 10923

**Claim a colorful pin.** You can choose between two lovely pins, each hand-painted in shining cloisonné colors. One is a mask design, the other a butterfly. Send $1.25 for shipping and handling. Be sure to specify which one you want. Mail your request to:

Florida, Inc.
2072 Edgewood Drive
Lakeland, FL 33803

**Sport a sparkling bracelet.** A diamond-cut metal bracelet will be selected for you from an assortment of colors. Just send 25 cents and an SASE to:

Savon
193 E. M-35
P.O. Box 1356
Gwinn, MI 49841

**Wear seashells from the seashore.** How would you like a ring made from a genuine seashell? Or how about a shell bracelet or necklace? For the ring, pay 75 cents in shipping and handling, or send $1 each for the necklace and bracelet. Send your request with an SASE to:

Danors
9360 NW 39th Street
Sunrise, FL 33351

And for those of you with access to a computer, check out these online offers:

**Dangle a free gold pendant.** A company called Fortunes in Gold wants to introduce you to their line of gold jewelry by offering you a free 14-karat gold pendant. You have to cover the insured shipping charge of $4.95. You can choose from more than 50 different pendants at their Web site <www.fortunesingold.com>.

**Grab a gift of garnet and gold.** JewelrySpotlight.com wants to show their appreciation to new customers. So those who place a $200 order or more online will receive a garnet necklace valued at $75. The 54-carat stone is set in 14-karat gold. Go to <www.jewelryspotlight.com>. Look for this item or other current specials.

**Make off with free jewelry every month.** Jewelry Impressions at Web site <www.jewelryimpressions.com> offers one free jewelry piece each month. For example, one month's offer was a free 7-inch, 4-mm gold bonded herringbone bracelet with a lobster claw clasp. Shipping and handling was $4.99.

In addition to the free piece, you could order a matching 18-inch, 4-mm herringbone necklace or a contemporary heart pendant and matching earring set for $4.99 each. And you could have it gift-wrapped for just $1.25 more.

**Put free pearls around your neck.** If you have never shopped online at Buyjewel.com, they want you to have an introductory gift. For a free 16-inch cultured freshwater pearl necklace with a 14-karat gold clasp, go to <www.buyjewel.com>. You'll pay $3.95 for shipping and handling.

And while you are at the Web site, look at the other specials. You can save 20 to 50 percent on a variety of other jewelry pieces.

# LOOKING YOUR BEST FOR LESS

To most people, looking good means feeling good about yourself. As a result, there are more personal care products on the market today than you could count in a lifetime. And advertisers want you to believe that only theirs will bring you true success and happiness. If you are not careful, you can spend a fortune before you know it.

But there are ways to look great and still balance your budget. Watch for big sales on cosmetics, for example, and shop at stores that give good prices every day. As a rule, department stores will be more expensive than discount stores. And grocery stores are generally higher, too. So don't yield to that temptation to toss a few beauty aids into the cart when shopping for food.

And be on the lookout for great freebies and discounts like the ones you'll find in this chapter. Check out the discount drugstores mentioned in the **Cures for High-Cost Health Care** chapter, too. Most of those also carry personal-care items.

## Sniff out free samples of perfume or cologne

Sometimes looking good just isn't enough — you want to smell good, too. You can find just the right scent for you with free samples of perfume or cologne. Several samples are available for only a small shipping and handling fee.

For a free sample of Jeanne of Beverly Hills, you can send a self-addressed envelope plus $3 for shipping and handling to:

Jeanne of Beverly Hills, Inc.
9304 Civic Center Drive, #3
Beverly Hills, CA 90210

Or visit the Jeanne of Beverly Hills Web page at <www.jobh.com> and charge the shipping fee to your credit card.

Feel like a princess for free with Isis, a blend of white roses and violets originally created for Princess Diana. Send $2 for shipping and handling to:

Isis International Inc.
47 Halstead Avenue
Harrison, NY 10528

You can also request your free sample online at <www.isisfragrance.com>.

If you're looking for Mr. Right, try Pure Instinct, the first pheromone fragrance formulated for romance. For a free sample, send a $2 check or money order to:

C'est Moi
P.O. Box 297
Neotsu, OR 97364

For additional free samples, place an order with either <www.perfume mart.com> or <www.1000perfumes.com>. Both feature original designer perfumes, with the latter boasting savings up to 70 percent off department store prices.

## Catch the scent of fragrance discounts

It can be fun to sample fragrances at the cosmetic counter of a posh department store. But that's probably not where you'll get your best buys. Try these mail-order and online companies instead.

**Save with "interpretation" fragrances.** The Essentials Products Company makes new versions of well-known perfumes and colognes for men and women. They sell them under the brand name Naudet at a fraction of the cost of the fragrances they mimic.

For a price list and free sample cards, send a long self-addressed stamped envelope (LSASE) to:

Essentials Products Co. Inc.
90 Water Street
New York, NY 10005–3587
212-344-4288

**Net good scents — online or off-line.** If you prefer the convenience of buying on the Internet, check out these sites for savings.

At <www.fragrancenet.com> look for deals like a variety of Bill Blass fragrances for women at 17 to 40-percent discounts. And for men, you may find Michael Jordan colognes at up to 17 percent off regular retail prices. You'll also get free shipping and handling — maybe even a free gift. And FragranceNet promises to beat any price you find on the Internet by 5 percent.

You can get a price list from FragranceNet by calling 800-987-3738 between 9 a.m. and 5 p.m. EST. Or write to:

FragranceNet
2070 Deer Park Ave.
Deer Park, NY 11729

The company has plans to move, so it may be best to call first before to check its current address.

Stock up on overstocks from Scentiments at <www.scentiments.com>. The clearance department offers items like Chloe's Narcisse 3.4-ounce spray tester for $21, regularly $55. Save more than $70 when you get Bulgari 3.4-ounce spray for $46.99. (The regular price is $120.) Or find an "ugly box special" like Casmir 3.4-ounce spray, regularly $75, on sale in damaged boxes for $33.99.

Parfums Raffy at <www.parfumsraffy.com> features specials like Demi-Jour by Houbigant, 3.3-ounce spray, for $39. They list the retail price at $79. And if there's a perfume you've wanted to try, but weren't sure you'd like wearing it, check out their long list of miniatures that sell for between $4 and $16. If you don't use the Internet, you can call or write to see if they have what you are looking for.

Shipping is free in the U.S. and Canada. You can order online, call 818-807-4459, or send a check or money order to:

Parfums Raffy
6327 Ethel Ave.
Van Nuys, CA 91401

With the super specials — like five scents for $25 — you may be tempted to go a little crazy at Perfumania. You can choose from a selection of brand-name perfumes, colognes, and scented shower gels and deodorants. You might find Only, for women, by Julio Iglesias. Or maybe you'll dance away with a scent for men by Baryshnikov. You have quite a good deal when you pay only $5 each for these scents that retail for $27.50 and $22. The Web address is <www.perfumania.com>.

## Skin-deep bargains on skin care

Sun and time can play cruel tricks on your skin. Dryness, wrinkles, and spots keep you from looking your best. Fight back with skin-care products that moisturize and protect your skin — and don't dry out your pocketbook.

Faciei Domani, which specializes in men's skin treatment, offers a free sample of All Day Moisturizer. Just call 408-395-2490. For a catalog and samples of DHC skin-care products, which are free from perfume, dyes, and allergens, call 800-342-2273.

Get a free sample of Epex Face and Hand Rejuvenation System by sending a self-addressed envelope plus $2 for postage to:

Advanced Skin Products
320 Superior, Suite 395
Newport Beach, CA 92663

If you can get online, check for more free samples from skin-care product Web sites. Some of the available deals include:

★ A three-to-four-week trial supply of Jus' Judy Facial Wash and Conditioning Gel at <www.jusjudy.com>. You can also call 800-867-7897.

★ A sample of Royal Gold Anti-Wrinkle Serum or other skin-care products and an HMS catalog of anti-aging products at <www.hmscrown.com>. Also, 800-867-7897.

★ A free sample from Zia Natural Skincare at <www.zianatural.com>

★ A one-week trial sample of Lametco's "New You" skin rejuvenating system at <www.appleaday.com/ny-sample.html>

★ A choice of free samples from Olay at <www.olay.com>

★ A free gift, including sunscreen, fresh lemon towelette, and adhesive bandage, from Lustra at <www.sunandskin.com>

Another neat way to get free skin-care products is to become a product tester. At InvigorateYou.com, you can rate new products using a star system. Just send an e-mail with your name, address, phone number, e-mail address, and reason for wanting to be a product tester to invigorate order@aol.com for this four-star deal. Make sure you specify any allergies you have so they don't send you products containing ingredients that might harm you.

---

## Free beauty tips

Get the latest how-to beauty tips for free in Cover Girl's personalized newsletter, *Connection Buzz*. You can keep up with the latest trends and get personal advice from beauty professionals. It all comes to you by e-mail each month when you sign up for Cover Girl's free members-only club at <www.covergirl.com>. Just fill out the questionnaire, and all the information will be tailored to fit your color preferences and lifestyle.

---

# Beauty comes at a (lower) price

Do you hesitate to try a new lipstick or a different brand of eye shadow — afraid you'll spend a lot of money then end up hating it? You can solve that problem by buying cosmetics from companies that let you try their products first. Don't hesitate to ask for lots of samples. It's hard to tell if you will really like something until you've worn it several times.

Also, ask about exchange policies. Some companies will let you make a swap if you find that a product just doesn't suit you when you put it on.

And watch for gift-with-purchase specials in the cosmetics departments of major stores, especially around holidays like Christmas and Mother's Day. Often a featured item will be reduced and have a free gift attached as well.

The companies below will help you stretch your beauty dollars even more.

**Free catalog, fantastic discounts.** The Beauty Boutique sells a wide range of brand-name cosmetics, perfumes, and skin-care products. Look for discounts up to 90 percent off the original price in their 80-page catalog. To get your free copy, call 440-826-3008, or write to:

Beauty Boutique
6836 Engle Road
Cleveland, OH 44101–4520

**How to recycle and save.** Sometimes it pays to think of the beauty of the environment as well as your personal good looks. At least it works that way where The Body Shop is concerned. This company — which uses all natural ingredients and does no animal testing — will give you a discount on a refill when you take back your empty container.

To get a free Body Shop by Mail catalog, with discounts about 30 percent lower than the retail prices, call 800-541-2535. To locate a store near you, call 800 BODYSHOP (263-9746). Or, for more information, go to the Web site at <www.usa.the-body-shop.com>.

**Good buys on lip balm.** Kettle Care offers specials like a moisturizing lip balm in a 1/4-ounce screw-top jar for $2.25 each — or get a pack of any six for $12.

Choose from tangerine, root beer, peppermint, lime, vanilla spice, and cherry-almond flavors. They are made with natural ingredients like beeswax, almond and jojoba oils, aloe, and cocoa butter.

The free Kettle Care catalog of beauty products contains a coupon for additional savings. And you can get a 25-cent credit for each container you return. Write or call:

Kettle Care
Pure Herbal Body Care
6590 Farm To Market Road
Whitefish, MT 59937
406–862–9851 (telephone or fax)
info@kettlecare.com

## Beautiful deals await you online

Many Internet sites have great deals on beauty products. The specials change regularly, so check them frequently to find the best deals on your favorite products. Here are a few you might want to know about:

★ My Beauty Center at <www.mybeautycenter.com> carries a full line of lipsticks, lip pencils, nail polishes, and other cosmetics. You'll probably find a free gift offer and free shipping with purchases over $5. Other good buys include things like a four-pack lip gloss or lipstick, regularly $18, for $8.95.

★ BeautyBuys at <www.beautybuys.com> sometimes rewards you with non-cosmetic freebies when you buy beauty aids. For example, they have offered a free $50 long-distance phone card with a $30 order for first-time customers. Check to see what specials they currently offer.

★ Ibeauty.com at <www.ibeauty.com> has free offers with a minimum purchase — a free travel case when you spend $80 or more, for example. You may also find buy-one-get-one-free specials on name-brand products like Elizabeth Arden and Liz Claiborne.

## Surf for fresh savings

Just like the discount stores you walk into, many online discount stores carry a wide range of products to keep you pretty, clean, and fresh. Here are some examples of the kinds of freebies and bargains you can expect to find.

★ If you are a first-time customer at <www.planetrx.com> you may get to choose three free products from a choice of 18 possibilities when you make a purchase of $10 or more. Or the newcomer special may be a "Sun Pack" — filled with suntan lotion and other products from Coppertone or Hawaiian Tropics. Look, also, for weekly specials that can save you up to 50 percent on selected items.

★ Specials at <www.mothernature.com> include deals like 4 ounces of Alba Botanica fragrance-free sunblock, SPF 15, for $5.15. It regularly sells for $7.93. Or look for a 2-ounce Burt's Bees poison ivy soap, regularly $5, for $3.25.

★ Get a 25-percent discount on your first non-prescription order at <www.drugemporium.com>. And look for the clearance items in each department for regular savings.

★ A recent search for sale items at <www.cvs.com> uncovered more than 200 products from companies like Aussie, Ban, Colgate, Fixodent, Gillette, and Oil of Olay. And shipping is free if you place a $30 order.

## Try a new — and free — shampoo

You want your hair to be clean and attractive, but daily shampooing and conditioning can make hair care expensive. So take advantage of those free samples you get in the mail or with your Sunday newspaper.

And if you have a problem with flaking and itching, Nizoral A-D dandruff shampoo is just a phone call away. Dial 888-NIZORAL (649-6725) for a free sample. Since you only need to use it twice a week to control your dandruff, you can enjoy trying those samples of regular shampoo between times.

The Internet is another source of free samples. Here are a couple that were available recently.

At <www.pertplus.com> Pert Plus offers a free sample of shampoo for you and another for a friend. Even without the samples, the humor on this Web site makes it worth the visit.

Check <www.helenecurtis.com> for a free coupon from the makers of Helene Curtis shampoo. You can also sign up for their free monthly e-mail newsletter, *Hairline*. It will keep you up to date on the latest hairstyles, tips and trends.

Most major brands now have a Web site, so go to your search engine and type in the name of one you'd like to try. They just may be giving away a free sample.

## Hair surveys net you free products

If you have the time to fill out surveys and forms, you could net your-self a bevy of free products. These particular questionnaires will help give you the beautiful hair you've always wanted.

**Make every day a good hair day.** How would you like to have a pro-fessional beauty consultant analyze your hair type and give you a customized hair-care prescription? Throw in a free kit of hair-care products to fit your profile — trial sizes of John Amico shampoo, conditioner, and styling aids — and you've got a great deal.

To take advantage of this offer, go to the Web site <www.johnamico.com> and fill out the questionnaire. You'll pay a $4.95 fee for processing, shipping, and handling.

**Take pride for free.** Women of color can take advantage of special hair colors, conditioners, braid sprays, and weave products for both natu-ral and synthetic styles. The people at African Pride will be happy to send you free samples of their products if you complete a brief questionnaire at the Web site <www.african-pride.com>.

**Pump up the volume on thinning hair.** If you are worried about hair loss, why not try some products designed especially to help you grow a fuller head of hair? You can get a free set of Apollo hair-care items — as well as an informational brochure and a free video — just by filling out a form at the Web site <www.apollohair.com>. For more information, call 800-806-9729 or send an e-mail to scw@apollohair.com.

## Get color to 'dye' for

Do you like to change your hair color from time to time? You can save a bundle by doing it yourself. And Clairol can help you get just the color you want — by phone or over the Internet.

If you have a computer, go to their Web site at <www.clairol.com>. All you have to do is answer a few questions, and they will make recommen-dations about the right color treatment for you.

While you are there, request a free subscription to Clairol's *Color Source Magazine* to keep up to date on the latest in hair care and hair coloring. With your first issue you'll get a $1 coupon.

For your specific questions, call 800-CLAIROL (252-4765), and talk to a hair color expert.

---

### Get a haircut — not a scalping

A new haircut can make a big difference in your appearance — and in your pocketbook. Use these tips to avoid getting skinned at the barbershop or beauty parlor.

- Get a bargain trim at a local barber college or beauty school. It's true that students do the work, but they are carefully supervised by professionals.

- Try a unisex style. Women's haircuts in a barbershop are likely to be cheaper than in a beauty salon.

- Learn to cut hair so you can trim your own or your family's, or swap cuts with a friend.

- Just get the cut. Don't pay for things you can do on your own — like shampoo, blow dry, or set your hair.

---

## Cute curls at pretty prices

You'll flip your old wig when you see the new styles in Beauty Trends free catalog. And you'll be even more excited by the good prices on wigs and accessories.

Start by ordering the catalog from:

Beauty Trends
P.O. Box 9323
Hialeah, FL 33014-9323
800-777-7772

When your catalog arrives with a wide range of stylish wigs by Cheryl Tiegs, Dolly Parton, and Adolfo among others, look for prices $10 to $15 lower than the regular cost. In addition, you may find a coupon inside for another $5 off a $40 to $69 purchase, or $10 off a total of more than $70.

You'll find discounts on other items as well — like a Dolly Parton wig-care kit, regularly $50.95 for only $24.95. Or a Revlon portable wig stand for $4.50, regular price $9.

When you order your first wig, you'll get a free kit with a video of tips for wearing and caring for your new purchase. It also contains a wig misting bottle and a wig styling comb.

A point system will net you even more savings and free products — even a free wig — if you continue to make purchases from Beauty Trends.

## Rub-a-dub-dub with free soap in the tub

A little pampering never hurt anyone. Washing with scented, hand-made soaps doesn't have to hurt your pocketbook, either. You can clean up with these deals on unique soaps.

Get a free sample from Anne-Marie's Soapworks by writing to:

301 W. Holly
Suite M6
Bellingham, WA 98225

Include $1 for shipping and handling. You can also order online at <http://amsoapworks.hypermart.net>. Other deals include $2.50 per bar for "not-so-pretty" bars or discontinued scents.

Sample the wares of Sierra Soap (trial-size bar of soap, shampoo, conditioner, lotion and massage oil) by writing to:

PARODON
P.O. Box 1863
Pollock Pines, CA 95726

Include $5 for shipping and handling, and indicate scented or un-scented soap.

Sierra Soap also features the Frugal Norwegian offer. Buy a soap, lotion, and a small shampoo for $19 (including shipping), and get a free bar of soap valued at $20. You can also call 800-223-0650 or visit the Web site at <www.sierrasoap.com> to order.

Whether you prefer lavender, peach, gardenia, cucumber, or just plain unscented, you can get more mileage out of any soap by opening it as soon as you get it. Dried-out soap lasts longer.

## Trim the cost of shaving

Shaving every day can cut away at your pocketbook as well as your whiskers. Watch for specials at discount drugstores, and check for deals like these on the Internet.

**Get a cheap shave.** Pay only 10 cents each for twin-blade disposable razors by Dorco. To place your order for 40 razors for just $4, go to the Web site <www.bluegoldusa.com>.

And while you are there, check to see if they still have the retractable razor — with a twist of the handle the shaving head disappears into a tube. A great travel razor, it's a steal at $7.95. The manufacturer's suggested price is $19.95.

**Sample a solution to keep razors sharp.** Do you find you have to throw away your razor blade after one use or you'll get painful nicks, cuts, or razor burn? That happens because the blades corrode more rapidly when you rinse them, then store them in open air.

You can keep both regular and disposable razor blades sharp, however, by soaking them between shaves in RazorGuard solution. Get a free sample of this product when you complete a survey on the Web site at <ww.razorguard.com>.

And if you are pleased with RazorGuard, describe your experience in seven words or less on the Web site, and you may be the winner of a whole year's supply.

## Exceed expectations with free denture cleaners

Removing stubborn tobacco, coffee, or tea stains from your dentures can be as easy as dialing your telephone. Just call 204-888-5031 for a free sample of Exceed Denture Cleaner. You can also order a free sample on the Web at <www.exceeddenturecleaner.com>.

If you'd like to try a different brand, send for a free sample of Sparkle Denture Cleaner. Just mail a long self-addressed stamped envelope with your name and address to:

Western Denture Center Inc.
1055 Court Street, Suite B
Medford, OR 97501

## Exercise your right to discounted equipment

You want to stay in shape, but walking can get pretty boring after a while. And the weather doesn't always cooperate. You might consider a treadmill or exercise cycle for a strenuous workout from the comfort of your own home.

If you're in the market for exercise equipment, check online at <www.workoutwarehouse.com> for brand names at bargain prices. You can save up to $600 on brands like NordicTrack, ProForm, HealthRider and Reebok. It even has an auction site where you can bid for new, brand-name equipment. You can also register to win a free treadmill or exercise bike every month.

To register for the drawing by mail, send a postcard to:

Win It from the Warehouse
P.O. Box 313
Logan, UT 84321

# CUT YOUR CAR COSTS

If you're like most Americans, transportation is one of your biggest expenses. As a car owner, you know how expensive it is to buy, use, and maintain an automobile. Most people, unfortunately, spend much more on them than they need to.

In this chapter, you'll learn how to find the best deals when buying your car, how to get the most for your money at the repair shop, and what to do about high auto insurance premiums. The more you know, and the more you're willing to work the system, the more money you'll save.

## Save 1,000s of $$ on a new car

Buying a new car can be overwhelming, especially if you're worried about spending too much. But unlike other types of retail stores, you don't ever have to pay the sticker price. You can save thousands of dollars by following these simple strategies.

**Investigate your options.** Do your homework before you ever talk to a dealer, and learn everything you can about the car you want. Most libraries carry periodicals on new cars, such as the *Consumer Reports* annual car guide, which gives you information about options, gas mileage, and typical maintenance costs. For some up-close research without the sales pitch, stop by and look at cars when a dealership is closed.

**Know the numbers.** Learn the dealer cost of the vehicle you want, then begin negotiating from that figure. A discount off the sticker price is not necessarily a good deal, since the sticker price usually represents a big markup from what the dealer paid for the car.

**Choose wisely**. The trendiest and flashiest cars basically sell themselves, so the dealer feels no pressure to move them quickly. Salesmen are more likely to offer discounts if you're shopping for a less popular model. If you find the car of your dreams, don't let the salesman know, or he won't have any incentive to lower its price.

**Use the phone.** Once you know the car you want, all the options, and the dealer cost, call several dealerships in your area and ask them to name their best price. You won't have to drive all over town, and you'll avoid the sales-pitch routine. If all the prices are pretty close, call around again and find out who's willing to give you the best discount.

**Watch the calendar.** Most car salesmen work on monthly quotas, so toward the end of the month, they're much more willing to make deals. Your position to negotiate a bigger discount gets stronger as the end of the month approaches and the salesmen scramble to fill their quotas.

**Take your time.** Don't let yourself be pressured. Take all the time you need with a dealer, and ask as many questions as you want. If a salesman is pressuring you, ignore his tactics. The cooler you are, the more likely you'll get what you want.

**Just walk away.** Your greatest weapon in dealing for discounts is a willingness to walk out the door. If the price is not right, walk away. Once a salesman realizes you're willing to leave, he's more likely to offer you a better deal.

## Let the pros dig up the discounts for you

Shopping for a new car can be costly in both time and money. Could a professional car-buying service be the answer? If haggling for deals and discounts is not your strong suit, they might be worth a look.

Your credit union or auto club may provide its own car-buying service, either at no charge or for a small fee. For more comprehensive service, however, you might have to lay out a few bucks. These outfits charge anywhere from $12 for a breakdown of model costs and fees to $400 for a complete search, purchase, and low-price guarantee.

Several hundred dollars might seem like a hefty additional expense, but consider this: Because they deal in volume and know the tricks of the business, these services often secure prices low enough to offset the fee they charge, which can end up netting you a nice discount.

Call one or more of the following companies to start your search. Describe exactly what you're looking for, and they will contact dealerships in your area and around the country to find the car you want.

★ AutoAdvisor — 800-326-1976

★ Car-Bargains — 800-475-7283

★ CarPuter — 800-221-4001

★ Nationwide Auto Brokers — 800-521-7257

Most of these services provide some sort of guarantee to protect you. Typically, if you can arrange to purchase the same car for a lower price on your own, the service will refund your money.

---

## Homework pays off in new-car negotiations

Alan Kelly followed the advice of experts and wound up with a new-car deal worth bragging about. "I just did my homework and it paid off," he said.

Kelly began his car search by deciding how much he wanted to spend. Then he read *Consumer Reports* and *Consumer Digest* and used information from the Internet to see which cars fit his price range and preferences.

He discovered the top-rated car was sold under two different brand names. "I decided I wanted the one that had the best resale value, but I kept that under my hat while negotiating a price. I let them think that I might buy the other make if I got a better deal."

Kelly's research revealed the invoice price the dealer paid for the car, so he used that figure to help set his price limit. Then he called his credit union for pre-approval of the loan.

He was fortunate to live near a large city, which gave him a good choice of dealerships. "It helped that the salesman knew he had competition nearby that wanted me as a customer," he said.

Since Kelly wasn't trading in another car and had his own financing, the negotiations were fairly simple.

"They tried to do their song and dance, but I stuck to my guns. When they saw I wouldn't go any higher, they agreed to my price. They tried to say they had lost money on the deal, but I knew better. They made a profit — but not a killing!"

---

## Warning: A trade-in is not a discount!

Many new car buyers are lulled into the feeling that by trading in their old car, they are getting a discount — and therefore a better deal — on their new car.

Don't be fooled. If the trade-in allowance offered by your dealer is not at least equal to the Blue Book value of the old car, you're getting ripped off. And new car dealers are notorious for offering less than the car's worth, simply because they know people are anxious to get rid of their old car.

You're better off selling the car yourself. But if you're in a hurry and want to trade it in, be sure to take some precautions.

**Know your car's worth.** Don't count on a dealer to tell you what your old car is worth; ask the experts. Go to the Web site <www.edmunds.com> on your computer, and enter your car's information into their evaluation program. This will help you distinguish between a fair offer and a questionable one. The annual Blue Book can also give you this information. Along with various Edmunds publications, it is available at bookstores, libraries, and some news stands.

**Know your price.** Before discussing your trade-in with the dealer, settle on a price for the new vehicle, then find out what he's willing to give for the old one. By keeping the two figures separate, it is easier to see and remember what kind of deal you're getting on each transaction.

**Know the competition.** If you've done your homework during your car search, you may have found more than one dealership with the car you want at the price you have set. Now that the price has been settled, ask each dealer what they're willing to do for you in terms of a trade-in. A little bit of healthy competition can help drive your trade-in allowance much higher.

## Get paid for a test drive

Yes, you read it right. The Saturn car company will actually give you a free $25 gift certificate to test drive one of its new cars. Just call 888-889-2392, and ask them to send you a test-drive certificate.

Take this form to your local Saturn dealership, and after taking any model for a quick ride around the block, ask the salesman who's helping you to validate the form. Then, simply mail or fax your validated certificate to Saturn headquarters. Within four weeks, you'll receive a $25 certificate for Land's End, Border's Books & Music, or your local movie theater.

Mail validated certificates to:

Program Headquarters
P.O. Box 5037
Troy, MI 48007
Fax: 800-704-7161

## Don't pay big bucks for little service

You're a cautious person who believes in the phrase "Better safe than sorry." So when you buy a new car, you spend some extra money for an extended warranty, or service contract. Safe, right? Alas, when you take your car in for repairs, you might be sorry.

The extended warranty sounds like a great idea. It's a chance for you to get extra protection after the standard three-year, 36,000-mile warranty runs out. It's also a chance for your car dealer to make a bundle.

Most of the time, an extended warranty is simply unnecessary — and overpriced. For example, if you trade in your car for a new one every three years, you'll never use the extended warranty because it doesn't kick in until the standard warranty has expired.

Often, you spend more on the extended warranty itself than you would on the repairs. And that's assuming the dealer will pay for the repairs you think are covered in the warranty. Many of the parts most likely to break down aren't covered. And almost any car problem can be attributed to "wear and tear" rather than "mechanical breakdown," giving dealers an easy way out of holding up their end of the bargain.

Complicated? You bet. That's why, before you decide to spring for an extended warranty, you should follow these steps.

**Study your standard warranty.** Make sure you understand the warranty that comes with your new car. Ask specific questions about what is covered and what is not. If you don't like the answers, or if the salesman won't provide them in writing, don't buy the car. Most major problems that could arise with a new car should be covered by the standard warranty. If they're not, it's not a very safe purchase.

**Read the fine print.** If an extended warranty looks like a good deal, look a little closer. The fine print on these contracts tells you what is not covered, and the coverage can be tricky, even deceiving. For example, the warranty may cover a part but not the labor needed to fix it. Or it may not cover extra repairs you need done because of damage caused by a covered part's failure.

**Take your time.** If you plan on keeping your car for a long time, an extended warranty might be the right choice for you. But don't let yourself be pressured by a high-intensity sales pitch. Take some time to think it over. Look at automobile and consumer magazines that rate cars. See which parts or systems are likely to break down in your car and if those parts are covered in the service contract.

**Shop around for a better deal.** You don't have to get your extended warranty through your dealer. Some third-party companies offer more comprehensive and less expensive warranties. (See *Go direct for the best deals* on page 130) Remember, there's no rush. If you think it over and decide an extended warranty is the answer, you can always purchase the plan later.

If you do buy an extended warranty, make sure you keep records of all the maintenance done on your car. This includes oil changes, tune-ups, and minor repairs. If you can't prove you took proper care of your car, the dealer might say the problem was your fault and you must pay for the repairs yourself.

It might be a bit of inconvenience, but like you always say, "Better safe than sorry."

## Used car smarts: How to drive away with big savings

A good deal on a used car is not hard to find if you know where to look and what you're looking for. Knowing how to minimize risk will let you buy a used car with confidence — and often at tremendous savings. Keep these tips and tactics in mind when you begin your search.

**Buy from a private seller.** The newspaper is the first place to look for a used car. People who sell their own cars usually charge less than dealers. Often, they just want to get rid of the car as quickly as possible, so there's a lot more room for you to negotiate a good price.

Besides the classifieds, you can find listings in trade publications and weekly auto sales magazines, available at many convenience stores and news stands. Ask your friends and neighbors, too. Buying from someone you know can take much of the hassle and guesswork out of the process.

---

## Go direct for the best deals

Thinking of buying an extended warranty for your car? Before you shell out big bucks to your car dealer, check out Warranty Direct.

This company, owned by Interstate National Dealer Services, Inc., can save you up to 60 percent off what dealers charge for extended warranties. The terms of the coverage are often better, too.

You can choose from four different levels of coverage with a wide range of terms. And you can learn all about them online at <www.warrantydirect.com>.

Even if you don't buy your warranty from Warranty Direct, you can get a free quote so you have something to compare the dealership's offer to. So give it a try. You have nothing to lose.

To contact Warranty Direct, write to:

Warranty Direct
333 Earle Ovington Blvd.
Uniondale, NY 11553

You can also call 800-632-4222 or e-mail them at info@warrantydirect.com.

---

**Choose a reputable dealer.** According to consumer expert Clark Howard, the best type of dealership is a used-car superstore such as AutoNation USA. They sell cars quickly so their markups are usually lower than independent or new car dealers. Many of their cars still carry manufacturer's warranties, and almost all come with limited 90-day warranties. Make sure to ask about a seven-day trial period. Most superstores will let you return a car within seven days with no questions asked. That gives you plenty of time to have it inspected by a mechanic.

**Check out the rentals.** Solid, reliable cars are often sold at big discounts by rental car companies. Companies like Alamo, Enterprise, and Hertz often use cars for one or two years, then clean them up and sell them to make room for newer models. Since this isn't their main source of income, these companies often offer great prices on their low-mileage, well-maintained vehicles.

**Educate yourself.** The more you know about fair pricing, the greater your bargaining strength. Check the Blue Book at your local library to find out the fair market value of any car you look at, or log on to <www. edmunds.com> on your computer. This Web site features a program that considers all the information about a vehicle, from year and model right down to extras and mileage, and calculates the fair market price.

Edmunds and magazines such as *Consumer Reports* also keep records on which makes and models perform well, last the longest, and give the best value for the money.

**Ask questions.** Don't be afraid to ask questions about any car you're thinking of buying. Here are a few to get you started:

★ Why are you selling the car?

★ Has it ever been in an accident, and if so, what kind?

★ How was the car driven? Was it used mostly for highway driving? Was it driven by one person or everyone in the family?

★ Did you keep it outdoors or in the garage?

★ Can I see the maintenance records? (This is a good indicator of how well the car has been treated during its life.)

All these questions can reveal a lot about the quality of the car and whether or not it will be a smart buy for you.

**Get a checkup.** Perhaps the most important step you can take to avoid a used-car rip-off is to take the car to a qualified mechanic before you buy. Ask a mechanic you trust how much he would charge to check out the car, then arrange with the seller to let you bring it in. Offer to leave a deposit if need be.

A seller who seems reluctant to let you take the car may know something he doesn't want you to find out. A mechanic can spot many existing or potential problems that are invisible to the untrained eye.

## Free form to help 'formalize' your sale

Don't take chances when you buy or sell a used car. Use the free standard form below as a bill of sale to protect you in case the sale is disputed later on. Of course, the title of the vehicle will need to be signed over to the buyer, but having an extra signed document on hand doesn't hurt. And remember, laws regarding the private sale of property vary from state to state, so be sure to check up on any special considerations where you live, and make the necessary adjustments to the standard form.

---

### SALE OF MOTOR VEHICLE

For value received, the undersigned seller, _____, sells and transfers to _____, buyer, the vehicle described therein.

Seller warrants that:
(1) seller is the sole owner of the vehicle;
(2) such vehicle is free of all encumbrances, security interests, and other defenses against seller;
(3) the cash price does not exceed a reasonable retail price at the time of sale;
(4) the vehicle has been delivered to and accepted by buyer;
(5) buyer was of legal age and legally competent to execute the contract on the date thereof;
(6) all disclosures to buyer and other matters in connection with such transaction, are in all respects as required by, and in accordance with, all applicable laws and regulations governing them.

Date: _____     _____Seller

_____ Buyer

---

## Discount financing: Use your credit union connection

Getting a good price on the car you want is only half the battle. How you finance it can make the difference between a good deal, a bad deal, and a steal.

One of the best sources for affordable financing is a credit union. If you belong to one, try to arrange a loan there first. If you don't, do your best to find one. You may be able to join through your company, fraternal organization, professional group, or a host of others.

Here's how to make the most of your credit union connection.

**Limit the repayment period.** You probably could get a loan for that Mercedes you love if you finance it over five years, but it'll cost you in the long run. When you finance for 60 months or more, you end up owing more than the car is actually worth. Also, if your car is stolen or wrecked, an insurance settlement might not be enough to pay off your outstanding loan. Stick to repayment plans of 48 months or less.

**Check out other perks.** In addition to sensible financing, credit unions offer other advantages as well, such as the CU Car Club, which helps locate good deals in your area on the car you want. You can access this free service by calling (888) CAR-CLUB.

**Avoid dealer temptation.** Even if the car dealer knows you've taken care of financing, he'll probably try to beat the deal. Dealers have been known to offer extremely low interest rates that they offset with markups in the price of the car. Once you've secured your credit-union loan, don't let the dealer talk you out of it. Rest assured that you've gotten the best deal possible.

## Secrets to a winning car lease

Financial experts will tell you that buying a new car is usually wiser than leasing. To convince you otherwise, car makers are making leasing more affordable, but finding a sound lease can still be a challenge. Dealers are notorious for hiding fees and other costs behind ultra-low monthly payments. So any discount you get, you'll have to dig up for yourself.

Follow these simple "do's and don'ts," and you'll come out with a winning car lease.

**Do read the fine print.** It's harder to compare prices on a lease than it is when buying because the costs are spread out over the down payment, the monthly payments, and the fees due at the end. Financing costs built into leases are also typically very high, so be suspicious if the numbers appear too good to be true.

**Don't be wowed by low payments.** Manufacturers and dealers like to use up-front fees to create ultra-low monthly payments that mask the actual cost of a lease. Buyers often accept this because it feels like they're making a down payment. They tend to forget that it won't benefit them because they're not buying the car.

**Do negotiate carefully.** Haggle with the dealer over price and payments just the way you would if you were going to buy the car, and don't let him know that you're really interested in leasing. When you've agreed on a price, then talk about the leasing option, and don't let the dealer deviate from the terms you've agreed on.

**Don't accept large end payments.** Watch out for large lump payments that are due at the end of your lease, which can easily be overlooked when signing up. Also, be sure you are aware of early termination penalties that will apply if you want to get out of your lease before it ends.

**Do consider your driving needs.** It's fun to trade in your car every couple of years, but it also limits the way you can use your car. Most leases limit your mileage to 12,000 or 15,000 miles per year. If you go over, expect to pay a penalty of 8 to 15 cents per mile.

**Don't shortchange your insurance.** Another hidden money-maker for dealers is something called an excess-wear-and-tear fee. This fee is assessed at the end of your lease if the dealer decides you've used the car too roughly. About one out of every three leasers ends up paying this fee, which averages about $1,650.

One way to get around this is by purchasing special insurance. Chase Manhattan and Bank of America offer lease provisions that cost from $100 to $400 but cover you anywhere from $1,500 to $2,500 on wear-and-tear costs. This coverage is tacked on at the start of your lease. Consider this option if you know you're hard on cars, drive a lot of miles, are messy, or have pets or kids.

**Do your homework.** Dealers have lots of tricks up their sleeves to make leases look like bargains. To protect yourself, send away for a checklist of hidden fees and costs that are common in car leases. Send $1 and a self-addressed envelope to P.O. Box 7648, Atlanta, GA 30357.

---

## How to lease for less

Once you've decided leasing is the right option for you, finding the right lease can be tricky. The best way to get a discounted lease is to be flexible in the car you plan to lease.

Manufacturers regularly offer special promotions of specific vehicles for many reasons; perhaps a particular model isn't selling well, or the new car market is unusually competitive. Whatever their reason, it's a good idea to take advantage of the specials they're offering. Look for leases that inflate the residual value of the car, cut the initial capitalized cost, or charge a low interest rate.

Investigate these three factors on any lease you consider. To learn whether a particular lease is a good deal, check out the Automotive Lease Guide at <www.carwizard.com>.

---

# Unbeatable discounts for auto insurance

When you're looking for auto insurance, be sure to tell the company everything about you and your car so you'll be eligible for any special discounts. Make sure you ask what's available because they may not always tell you. Some typical discounts are:

★ **Good driver.** Drivers with no accidents or violations on their records can get a discount from most insurers.

★ **Good grades.** If you're a student, you can qualify for a discount if you send proof of a good academic record.

★ **Defensive driving course.** Take a refresher course, and you'll benefit from lower insurance rates as well as better driving skills.

★ **Mature driver.** Drivers at least 50 or 55 years old can get discounts depending on how much they drive every year. And if you take the AARP-sponsored drivers' refresher course "55 Alive," you may be eligible for a state-mandated multi-year discount.

★ **Carpooler.** Drive to work with a friend, and you may get a 10- to 20-percent premium discount.

★ **Antitheft device.** Install an alarm, an ignition-shutoff system or a wheel-locking device, and you may receive a 5- to 15-percent discount.

★ **Safety measures.** Some insurers give discounts up to 30 percent for cars with automatic seat belts and air bags.

★ **Non-smoker.** If you don't light up, you may receive better rates on liability, no-fault, and collision insurance.

Remember to inform your insurer if your driving habits change. If you switch jobs or start working out of your home, the reduced use of your car could gain you a nice cut in your premiums.

This can be true even for short-term situations. Going out of town for a few weeks and not driving? Ask your insurer if he'll suspend your coverage for that period — and discount your premium for the uncovered time.

## A simple step to cheaper insurance

Looking for another discount on your insurance rates? Try etching your way to savings. A company in Kentucky offers an inexpensive kit that allows you to etch your car's VIN number into each of its windows, a step that makes your car much less likely to be stolen. In one study, nearly

7,000 vehicles were etched, and over the next year and a half, only 15 were stolen. Normally, about nine times that number would have been taken.

Automark Corporation charges $24.95 for its kit, but some insurance companies and police departments offer similar etching services for free. Call your insurer or local department to find out before investing in the kit. For more information, or to place an order, contact:

Automark
4323 Poplar Level Road
Louisville, KY 40213
800-274-6275

If your insurance company doesn't offer a discount for etched windows, ask Automark to send you detailed information on the above study as well as statistics from other studies showing that etching helps deter car theft. By sharing this data with a reluctant insurance company, you may well get them to change their tune.

## When a practical car is not a bargain

Many people believe that the flashier the car, the higher your insurance rates. While it's true that certain models, colors, and even accessories raise the "red flag," you may be surprised at the high premiums of more ordinary vehicles.

According to the Highway Loss Data Institute, such practical cars as the Honda Accord and Civic, and the Toyota Camry and Corolla are among those most frequently stolen. These statistics are factored in by insurance companies when setting your premiums.

Before you buy, get an estimate from your insurer on the car you want. If the quote is too high, you may want to consider buying another car or asking your agent how you can bring the insurance cost down.

For a free, full report on injury, collision, and theft losses for various models, write to:

Car List
P.O. Box 1420
Arlington, VA 22210

# How to ditch a lemon without losing money

Even the best and most reliable cars sometimes break down, but if you think you have a bona fide lemon, you don't have to take it lying down.

Almost every state in the Union has a lemon law, which states that a manufacturer has to buy back any seriously flawed vehicle. While the specifics vary, most of these laws cover problems that happen during the first 12 months or 12,000 miles after your purchase.

If you think you've bought a lemon, first try to resolve the problem with your dealer. If the dealer is uncooperative, contact your state government to find out the procedure for filing a complaint under your state's lemon law.

You can write for the free booklet *Lemon Law: A Manual for Consumers* to learn about your legal options and how to file for arbitration. This booklet will tell you everything you need to know to document your claim and get the results you need. Call 800-955-5100 for more information, or write to:

The Council of Better Business Bureaus
Autoline
4200 Wilson Blvd., Suite 800
Arlington, VA 22203

# Come out on top at the repair shop

Getting your car serviced can be almost as expensive as buying a new one if you're not careful. Too many people drop off their cars at the closest repair shop and then just pay the bill when it comes, whatever it turns out to be. Don't.

Take a little extra time to understand the work being done on your car and to shop around for the most reasonable price. Follow these tips for ways to cut high repair costs and get more bang for your auto buck.

**Put it in writing.** The safest way to know exactly what you're getting and how much it will cost is to have everything on paper. Before any work is done, tell the mechanic what the problem is and how much you're willing to spend, and have the deal written up. Make sure you state that all work must be pre-approved by you, just in case the mechanic happens to find little "extras" he thinks he should take care of.

**Watch out for bullies.** Since most people don't know much about auto repair, some mechanics will try to take advantage of their position of "power" by charging whatever you're willing to pay. By showing them that you're not afraid to take your business elsewhere, you level the playing field. If a quoted price seems too high, get a second opinion from another shop even if it means having your car towed. Although not always convenient, it's a good idea to get more than one quote for any repair.

**Go back to school.** Check your area high schools to see if they accept cars for use in their vocational classes. Students studying for automotive careers can turn out good work on small body repairs and simple engine problems at a fraction of the cost of a commercial body shop. Sometimes, it's even free.

**Get a full report.** You may get discounted or even free repairs if your vehicle is part of a recall or listed in a manufacturer's service bulletin. But don't rely on the government or car maker to disclose these defects. The Center for Auto Safety, a nonprofit consumer group, can let you know of any documented defect in your vehicle that could cause damage. For more information, visit its Web site at <www.autosafety.org> or call 202-328-7700. You can also write to:

Center for Auto Safety
2001 S Street NW, Suite 410
Washington, DC 20009

## Free services and discounts right under your nose

Keep your eyes open for free offers on routine car service. Many garages and oil-change companies will rotate your tires for free if they're doing other work on your car (and sometimes even when they're not). When it's time to decide where to get your oil changed, call around to find a place that does this, and save $10 every time.

To drum up business, new service stations such as tire stores, oil-change franchises, and general repair shops often advertise greatly reduced prices for routine maintenance such as oil changes, fluid checks, and tire rotation. Check for such deals in your local paper the next time your car needs servicing.

### Free help for do-it-yourself repairs

What better way to save on repairs than to do them yourself? Even if you don't know a fan belt from a spark plug, a little expert help can point you in the right direction.

Tune into any car repair call-in show on your radio, then dial up with your question. National Public Radio puts on a show called "Car Talk" featuring mechanics with all the answers. Even if you learn that you can't fix it yourself, they can often help you identify the problem based on your description. A bit of sound advice can save you a bundle in diagnostic fees from a local mechanic.

NPR broadcasts in most areas on the AM dial, but many local stations produce their own auto programs as well. Call a few talk radio stations in your area to find out when such shows air, then dial your way to substantial savings.

## A year's worth of oil changes ... free

Here's a great offer from an auto club that wants your business. Try AutoVantage for a free, three-month trial period, and get a certificate good for four free oil changes. Assuming you treat your car right and change your oil every three months or 3,000 miles, that means a whole year's worth of oil service free!

Cancel your membership after three months if you don't want to pay monthly dues, but check out their benefits first. They provide discounts on car and truck rentals, roadside assistance, car servicing, even reduced rates at certain hotels. Whatever you decide, be sure to take advantage of some of their great deals during your free trial membership.

Visit <AutoVantage.com> on the Web today to learn more about this outstanding offer.

## Pay pennies for parts

If you like to repair your own car, or just need a few items to spruce it up, don't settle for retail prices. Discounts are waiting out there, even in the high-priced auto-parts game. You just have to know where to find them.

**Look around the yard.** No, not your own yard — a junk yard. Your local auto salvage yard can be a gold mine if you know what you're looking for. When your mechanic quotes you a price on repairs, ask him what parts will be needed, then call around to several area salvage yards to see what you can find. One woman tried this after learning that a used transmission would cost her $600. She managed to find one for only $200 at a salvage yard, saving a huge amount on her repair bill.

**Get a cross-country quote.** Often, the cheapest parts aren't in your own backyard. They may be all the way across the country. Fortunately, mail-order, catalog, and online auto wholesalers make these good buys accessible nationwide. Next time you find yourself faced with a steep repair bill, check out these valuable parts sources before agreeing to the service.

Cherry Auto Parts
5650 N. Detroit Avenue
Toledo, OH 43612
419-476-7222

This Midwestern company features quality used and rebuilt parts for Jeep and Chrysler vehicles, plus parts for Asian and European imports at discounts of up to 70 percent. Call for a quote on your specific needs, or visit its Web site at <http://www.cherry-auto.com> for an e-mail quote.

Discount Tire Direct
7333 E. Helm Drive
Scottsdale, AZ 85024
800-589-6789

Specializing in tires, wheels, and suspension parts for all cars and light trucks, Discount Tire Direct features all the major brands you'll find at your corner tire store, usually for much less. Go online at <http://www.tires.com> and request a quote by e-mail.

Worldwide Auto Parts
Route 38
Maple Shade, NJ 08052
800-500-PART

Worldwide has stayed in business since 1962 by offering more than two million parts for foreign and domestic cars. The company sells genuine factory parts that can be costly when dealing with local mechanics. Search its online database at <http://www.wwparts.com> to find the exact part you're looking for. While you're there, browse the Tech Tips section for hints on getting better performance out of your vehicle, or follow the car-related links to other interesting car sites.

## Super savings on parts and accessories

You might think that auto superstores have cornered the market on low-cost parts and accessories for your car, but don't be misled. Catalog companies may offer you even better prices because they also buy in bulk, but they don't have the extra costs of paying a sales staff and keeping up a showroom.

Here are two catalog dealers that will help you cut the high cost of auto parts and accessories. J.C. Whitney & Co. in Chicago features more than 55,000 products in their 200-page general catalog. Their specialty parts and accessories are discounted up to 50 percent off retail. They also have separate catalogs for Jeeps, Volkswagens, sport utility vehicles, recreational vehicles, pickups, motorcycles, and automotive tools. You can order up to three free catalogs by writing:

J.C. Whitney & Co.
P.O. Box 8410
Chicago, IL 60680
312-431-6102

Specializing in recreational vehicles such as motor homes, trailers, and hitches, RV Direct promises the best price on anything for your RV, as well as parts for other vehicles. Their guarantee states that if you find an ad that lists any of their products for a lower price, send it in, and they'll beat it. Contact them at:

RV Direct
P.O. Box 1499
Burnsville, MN 55337
800-438-5480

## Free membership deals from Carclub

Get a free $10 pre-paid gas card when you sign up for a three-month trial with Carclub.com. Or register for 30 days and get a free Rand McNally road atlas. Those are some of the free offers you may find at Carclub.com, an online automobile club. Carclub claims it can save you more than $550 a year in auto expenses. And though their membership offers may change, their valuable discounts and services remain the same.

Learn all about Carclub's benefits on its Web site <www.carclub.com>. Or call 1-800-CARCLUB (1-800-227-2582) to talk to a customer service representative. You can also write them at:

Carclub.com
221 Main Street, Suite 250
San Francisco, CA 94105

# MAKE THE MOST OF YOUR MONEY

Money may be the root of all evil, but we'd all like to have a little more anyway. Or know how to keep more of the money we've earned — and make the money we invest work harder for us.

In this chapter, you'll get answers to all your money questions. You'll learn how to save on taxes and receive free help filing them. Get free expert investment advice. Learn helpful tips for banking and using your credit card wisely. Think the government owes you money? We'll tell you who to contact to get back what's rightfully yours.

And it's all free, which never hurts your bottom line. Invest some time and read on — it's guaranteed to pay dividends.

## BANKING

### Avoid ATM nightmares — get your cash for free

One of the ways people throw money away is by paying ATM fees to withdraw their own cash from their own accounts. About 78 percent of banks charge non-customers a fee — usually around $1.50 — for using their ATMs. Of course, that leaves 22 percent of banks that don't charge such fees, and finding them isn't as difficult as it may seem.

**Use your own bank's card.** Obviously, this is the easiest way to avoid ATM fees, as most banks don't charge customers to use their own machines.

**Look for an alliance.** If you prefer a small bank or credit union, which might not have as many ATM facilities, look for one that belongs to a selective surcharge alliance. Member institutions of these groups (around 2,200 nationwide) agree not to charge ATM fees for customers at member banks or credit unions.

**Get credit at the union.** To attract customers, many credit unions and small banks provide fee-free ATMs, even to non-members. These machines are often posted with signs advertising this service, so keep your eyes open. A few quick phone calls around town can also help you discover which free ATMs are most convenient to your daily schedule.

**Ask for cash back.** You can avoid ATM fees — and ATMs altogether — if you plan ahead. Most grocery stores offer free cash back when you use your debit card while shopping.

**Find free ATMs online.** Perhaps the quickest way to find a free ATM near you is by logging on to your computer. Visit Compubank's Web site at <www.freeatms.com> to find a non-charging ATM anywhere in the country.

People are getting so tired of paying ATM fees that the topic is a hot one in Congress these days. Some places, like San Francisco, have even outlawed surcharges. Maybe someday this will be true all over, but until it is, a little bit of planning can save you a whole lot of money.

## Bank on freebies

Credit unions are known for free and low-cost services, but loyal customers can get many free benefits from regular banks as well. By keeping a regular balance of $2,500 in any type of account, you may qualify to have your banking fees reduced or even eliminated. These freebies include such perks as:

★ Free checking
★ No-fee credit cards
★ Free cashiers checks
★ Free use of ATMs
★ Special loan rates

Often, a bank won't advertise these free perks but will give them to you if you ask. When faced with the threat of losing a loyal customer who keeps a consistent balance, banks have a way of finding free stuff.

And if your own bank doesn't want to play ball, keep your eyes open for another option. Banks frequently offer promotional savings and checking plans to attract new customers that offer virtually free banking to people who maintain a balance, sometimes as little as $500 or $1,000.

## Free stuff for banking online

Save yourself trips to the bank and the hassle of balancing your checkbook by using one of these online banks.

**Net yourself a free T-shirt.** Try online banking with NetCity.com. This Internet banking service allows you to shop, pay your bills, transfer funds, and keep track of your accounts — all from the convenience of your home computer. NetCity members are also entitled to free e-mail and Web pages to further simplify your life.

When you sign up, you will be issued a free "Smart Card," complete with a personalized PIN number, which takes the place of your current ATM card. By downloading funds from your account to your Smart Card, you can use the card to make purchases either online or at stores, and your online account even keeps a detailed record of your spending. Each time you use the card, you earn points that can be redeemed for free products and services.

Visit the NetCity Web site at <www.NetCity.com> to get more information or to sign up today.

In addition to simplifying your financial life, NetCity will also send you a free T-shirt featuring the NetCity logo if you take an extra minute to answer a few general survey questions.

**Sign up for free money.** Simplify your financial life by taking advantage of free online banking from Paypal.com. This Internet payment service will give you $5 — absolutely free — just for setting up an account. Simply visit their Web site and use a credit card, bank account number, or personal check to transfer money into your new Paypal account. You can then use the account to shop on the net, participate in online auctions, pay bills, or transfer funds to family or friends anywhere in the world.

Each transaction takes only a few seconds, and the service is free. Paypal will simply charge your credit card or bank account for the funds you wish to move. If you use the service to pay your bills, they'll even keep a detailed record of when your bills are due and when they've been paid. In addition, for every person you refer to the service, Paypal will credit your account an additional $5.

Log onto your computer and visit <www.paypal.com> to make your banking chores simpler than ever before and to start collecting your free cash.

# CREDIT

## Plastic power: Using your credit cards wisely

You almost need a credit card to get by in today's world. But just because you need one doesn't mean you need 10 or 12. Or that you have to spend the rest of your life in debt.

Following are a few tips for saving money and making the most of your credit cards, from the number of cards to carry, to paying off your balance, to making sure you get what you pay for.

**Remember that more is not merrier.** You don't need more than one or two credit cards. A good rule of thumb is to have one for emergencies and one for a credit line. More cards just mean more trouble.

Not only are extra cards unnecessary, they could be harmful. If you have access to too much credit, it could hurt your chances for a mortgage or loan. For example, the bank giving you the loan for your home might be suspicious that you'll use all that credit to furnish it and not have any money left to pay off the loan.

When you come across a new credit card deal too sweet to pass up, make sure you cancel one of your old cards before adding a new one to your wallet.

**Stop the balancing act.** If you already have several cards and are finding it tough to climb out of debt, try these suggestions.

★ Stop using your credit cards. This is probably the most obvious tip, but people in debt often keep charging. Use your money to climb out of the hole you're in, not to dig a deeper hole.

★ Pay more than the minimum. If you only make the minimum payment month after month, you'll never make a dent in your balance. You'll just be paying the interest.

★ Pay off the higher-interest-rate card first. Interest adds up faster on cards with higher rates. The sooner you pay it off, the more you'll save.

**Fight back with chargeback.** Say you used your credit card to prepay for a new dining room table, and the table was never delivered. In other words, you didn't get what you paid for.

You can use your card's chargeback option. As long as you file your claim for a chargeback within 60 days, you'll get a refund from your credit card company. If the table eventually does arrive, you can drop the chargeback claim.

The chargeback is one advantage of using a credit card and a good way to protect yourself from losing money for nothing.

To contact one of the major credit card companies, write or call one of the following:

VISA International Customer Service
P.O. Box 8999
San Francisco, CA 94128
800-227-6811 (traveler's checks)
800-847-2911 (lost or stolen credit cards)

MasterCard International
Public Affairs Department
888 7th Avenue
New York, NY 10106
212-649-5476

# 4 ways to fight credit card fees

If you're like most Americans, you probably spend more than enough money on your credit card payments. Why give the credit card companies even more money by paying unnecessary fees?

Whether you're shopping for a new credit card or want to stay with your old one, you can cut down or even eliminate extra fees by following these guidelines.

**Be picky.** Don't settle for a credit card with an annual fee, a low grace period or monthly service fees. With all the credit card companies competing for your business, you should be able to find a card without these burdens.

★ Ask your credit card company to waive its annual fee. Many companies will agree just to keep your business.

★ Try to avoid cards with low — or no — grace periods (the time between the billing date and when finance charges kick in). You'll end up paying more. Also watch out for monthly service fees, which are often piled on top of annual fees.

★ Beware of cards with fees that hurt you if you don't carry a balance. If you're what they call a "convenience user," someone who pays his bills in full by the due date to avoid paying interest, you're not profitable enough to the company. They might charge you an annual fee for low usage. They might also eliminate your grace period or even cancel your card.

★ Look for cards with low fees for paying late, going over your credit limit, or taking out a cash advance. In case you do any of those things, you won't be hit as hard.

**Be prompt.** Late fees can put you on the road to early bankruptcy. Being as little as one day late with your payment could mean a $30 fee.

Sometimes a late fee can snowball into even more fees. You might be near your credit limit, and your late fee pushes you over. Guess what? You probably get penalized with another fee for going over your credit limit. Or, if you're late a few times, your interest rate might be bumped up to as much as 22 percent.

Keep careful track of when your bills are due, and make sure you get them in on time to avoid any late fees. Remember, also, that the payment must arrive — not just be postmarked — by the due date.

**Be persuasive.** If you're not satisfied with the terms of your current credit card or if the terms change unexpectedly, call the credit card company and ask for better terms.

Point out that you've been a loyal customer for many years, even if you haven't been perfect with your payments. Often, they'll agree to your request to keep from losing you to a competitor.

**Be prudent.** Switch cards if you aren't happy with the terms, and your credit card company won't budge. There's no sense staying with a card that isn't working for you.

Just make sure that there is no fee for closing your account while you continue to pay off the balance or for transferring the balance to another card. These are common ways credit card companies harm you while you try to cut down your debt.

The bottom line — read the fine print. With all its hidden or unpublicized fees, your credit card offer might not be so fine.

## Check your credit for free

It's always a good idea to make sure your credit report is accurate and up to date. But unless you've recently been denied credit, you'll find that reporting bureaus tend to charge a nice stiff fee for the privilege. Don't pay it.

Instead, send your full name, date of birth, Social Security number, spouse's name, and a list of your addresses for the past five years to:

TRW Consumer Assistance
Box 2350
Chatsworth, CA 91313

Include a copy of a document, such as a bill, that has your name and address on it.

Protecting your good credit is essential to your financial stability, so send for your free report today.

# Guard your card from fraud

You get an offer for a pre-approved credit card in the mail. Figuring you don't need another card, you toss the envelope in the trash. For you, that's the end of it. But for a thief, it's just the beginning.

He responds to the offer, pretending to be you, and gets a card in your name. In other words, he's got a license to steal. And that's exactly what he does, charging expensive item after expensive item to an account with your name on it. He might even switch the billing address so you don't realize what's happening until you apply for a loan and find your credit report is terrible.

That's just one of many ways a scoundrel can commit credit card fraud without actually stealing your card. Being aware of these types of schemes will save you a lot of time and worry — not to mention money — in trying to clear your credit report. After all, the money you protect from thieves is money you save.

Criminals don't need to snatch purses or pick pockets to rip you off. All they need is your credit card number, and they have many ways to get it. Here are a few of them and some tips to protect yourself.

**Clerks and jerks.** When you're buying something by credit card, keep your eye on your card during the entire transaction. A shady clerk might copy your credit card number and use it later to steal from you. Never sign a blank receipt or one with a blank line that the clerk can fill in later.

Also, like a good poker player, keep your cards close to the vest. Someone behind you in line might be peeking over your shoulder and memorizing your card number.

**Phony phone offers.** If you get a telephone call from a friendly salesman who asks for your credit card number, be careful. The voice on the other end of the line might belong to a con artist.

Never give out your credit card number — or any other personal information, such as your social security number or bank account number — unless you called them or you know you're dealing with a respectable company.

**Greedy garbage pickers.** A thief rummaging through your trash won't just take advantage of pre-approved credit card offers. He might also get your credit card number from the carbons that come with your credit receipt or your monthly bill.

The best thing to do is to shred any paper that contains your credit card number before putting it in the trash. You won't only be tearing the paper, you'll be tearing down fraud.

If you have been the victim of credit-card fraud, make sure you report it at once. If you notice any suspicious charges on your bill or if you don't receive a bill when you should, contact your credit card company. It could be just a mistake, but it could also mean fraud.

And if you've been the victim of an old-fashioned credit-card thief, report your card as stolen as soon as possible. That way, you'll only be responsible for up to $50 of whatever he's charged to your account.

By being alert, cautious and quick to report fraud, you can keep your money where it belongs — with you.

# TAXES

## Save at tax time all year long

You keep a close eye on your major deductibles, but little ones can add up, too. If you want to save big money on your taxes, you have to learn to keep track of those small, deductible expenses that you rack up every day. Some deductions seem so common you might not even know you can take them. For instance, driving:

★ **For business.** If your job puts you on the road, you can deduct 32.5 cents per mile.

★ **For charity.** Take 14 cents per mile when you use your car for charitable purposes.

★ **For health.** Trips to the hospital or to see your doctor can be deducted at 10 cents per mile.

It's not just the little things that people often overlook. Sometimes, bigger deductions slip through the cracks, and with them, your money.

★ **Job hunters.** As long as you're searching for a job in the same field that you already work in, most expenses are fully deductible. These include resume preparation, car mileage, career counselors and placement firms, and travel expenses if you interview out of state. You don't even have to get the job to claim the deductions.

★ **Self-starters.** If you're self-employed, you can deduct 45 percent of your health insurance premiums, plus those of your spouse and dependent children.

★ **Caregivers.** If your contributions make up more than half of a parent's or grandparent's support, you can usually claim them as a dependent, at a deduction of nearly $3000.

There are tons of deductions available that the IRS doesn't advertise. But then, saving you money isn't their job, it's yours. Fortunately, they are willing to lend a hand. If you're not sure about a deduction, or need a tax question answered, go straight to the horse's mouth and call the free IRS help line at 800-829-1040.

## Free help with your taxes

Doing taxes is a complicated chore that no one enjoys, but getting a tax pro to help you out can be expensive. Except when it's free. While they won't do all the work for you, the experts with AARP's Tax-Aide program stand ready to help.

Since 1968, the Tax-Aide program has helped more than 27 million Americans prepare their taxes by filling out returns, organizing paperwork, and providing answers. The staff is made up of retired and volunteer tax and accounting professionals, including many former IRS employees. The service is available to low- and middle-income individuals, with an emphasis on the special tax needs of seniors.

Temporary centers are set up each year at more than 10,000 convenient locations, such as libraries, malls, and senior centers. If travel is difficult for you, volunteers can even provide service in your own home.

The centers operate each tax season from Feb. 1 to April 15, but if you have Internet access, you can visit their free Web site year-round at <www.aarp.org/taxaide/home.html>. Ask your tax question online, or read up on helpful advice and frequently asked tax questions. Use their links to connect to the IRS Web site, or browse their help center finder to learn where they'll be setting up camp near you come February.

## Your direct line to the IRS

Who better to answer all your tax questions than the tax man himself? Visit the IRS Web site at <www.irs.ustreas.gov> and learn what you need to know before you file. Free tips and advice on how and when to file your return are just a few clicks away. You'll also find any tax form you might need, which you can print right from your computer.

But don't log off yet. After your federal return is squared away, visit <www.taxsites.com> for another great list of online tax resources. This convenient site also features links to state government tax sites, which offer printable forms, free guidance, and in some cases, programs that let you file your return right from your computer.

---

### Make the most of your donation

If you have the choice of donating a big-ticket item to your favorite charity, or selling the item and donating the proceeds, don't sell. Your donation will get you the same deduction either way, but if you sell first, you may end up being responsible for capital gains taxes.

Charities generally have the advantage of being taxed at a much friendlier rate, if at all. And if it turns out they'd rather have the money, they'll be happy to sell it themselves and might even get a better price from a soft-hearted buyer.

---

## Let the taxman take you on vacation

No the IRS isn't going to send you to Bermuda for two weeks, but if you travel for business, it does offer an easy way for you to cut the cost of a family vacation. When your business trip keeps you out of town over the weekend, both Saturday and Sunday are considered business days, so your expenses are tax deductible.

It doesn't matter whether you spend those days working, sight-seeing, or lounging around the hotel pool. This is true even if the only reason for your weekend stayover is to get the cheaper airfare that comes with a Saturday-night stay.

The nice thing is that you can use that time as a discounted vacation. You can even bring your family along to take advantage of the savings. True, you can't deduct their plane tickets or their meals, but you can deduct those things your family shares with you, such as your hotel room and car rental. By knocking these expenses off through careful planning, you could end up with a nice, cheap (if somewhat brief) family vacation.

Remember, for your trip to qualify as a business trip, most of your time has to be spent working. On days when you work, you can deduct:

★ 100 percent of your hotel bill.
★ 100 percent of transportation costs.
★ 50 percent of meals and general expenses.

It's better to be safe than sorry when dealing with tax issues, so if you're not sure about some deductions, check first. The IRS offers many publications that explain what's allowed, and their tax experts will be happy to help you figure it out. Call one of their local offices, or log onto your computer and visit <www.irs.gov>.

## Veterans — don't miss big tax exemptions

If you're a veteran, or the spouse of a veteran, you may be paying some taxes unnecessarily. You probably get some benefits for serving your country, but your state may offer special tax exemptions that you don't know about.

For example, in the state of Florida, veterans who have a 100-percent service-related disability are exempt from paying property taxes. That benefit is extended to their spouses when they die. Depending on property values where you live, that could be a couple of thousand dollars you're paying unnecessarily every year.

Different states have other types of tax benefits for veterans and disabled veterans, so check with your local county or state veterans representative. If you can't find a veterans office near you, try contacting the national headquarters.

Department of Veterans Affairs Headquarters
810 Vermont Ave. NW
Washington, D.C. 20420
202-273-5400
<www.va.gov>

# MONEY MANAGEMENT

## Free help to get out of debt

If you find yourself in a financial hole, the most important thing you can do to improve your situation is to get out of debt. Whether your debt is due to outstanding credit card balances, loan problems, or just an inability to pay your bills, free help is out there if you know where to look.

Many nonprofit organizations offer free counseling, advice, and debt restructuring programs that help people who've fallen behind get back on their financial feet. One such group is Myvesta.org (formerly Debt Counselors of America), which can be reached by calling 800-680-3328 or by logging on to the Internet at <www.myvesta.org>. If you live in the Washington, D.C. area, you can visit their office at 6 Taft Court, Suite 200, Rockville, MD 20850.

This agency offers free information on how to change your spending habits, stick to a budget, and reduce your debt. For a voluntary donation, they will also consolidate your debts, giving you one monthly bill to pay, usually at a reduced interest rate.

Debtors Anonymous is another agency that offers free counseling on how to get out of debt and stay ahead of your bills. Look in your local phone book to find the branch nearest you, or call 212-642-8220.

## Know what you're worth — fast and free

Knowing your personal net worth is important when planning your financial future. Having this information will help you decide if you are investing enough, if your money's in the right place, or if you should be doing things differently.

The fastest way to figure your net worth is by using the free Net Worth Calculator at the American Express Web site. Log onto your computer and visit <www.americanexpress.com>. Click on Planning Tools under the Financial Planning section you'll see listed in the box. Then click on Net Worth, and enter your figures into the appropriate spaces. The calculator will automatically compute your net worth for you.

If you don't have a computer, follow these simple steps to get a better picture of your current financial standing.

★ **Add up your assets.** Make a record of everything you own and how much each item is worth. List your house first, then your cars, investments, other real-estate holdings, home furnishings, jewelry, clothes, and anything else of significant value. When your list is complete, add up the total.

★ **List your liabilities.** Make a second record listing everything you owe. This should include your mortgage; auto, personal, and student loans; and any outstanding credit card debt.

★ **Crunch the numbers.** Now simply subtract the total of your liabilities list from the total of your assets list. This figure is a pretty good estimate of your net worth.

## Uncle Sam may be holding your cash

About one out of every 10 people is owed something from the government — usually a few hundred dollars, but sometimes much more. Right now, there's more than $10 billion in unclaimed money out there just waiting to be picked up. If you think some of it might be yours, it's time to take action.

This missing money is usually in the form of:

★ Forgotten bank accounts
★ Valuables left in safe deposit boxes
★ Unclaimed life insurance
★ Lost stocks, bonds, and dividends
★ Unknown oil and gas royalties
★ Social Security and Veterans Affairs benefits
★ Tax refunds
★ Neglected pensions
★ Apartment, utility, and rental deposits

How do you find out if any of this money belongs to you? It's easy. Every state government has a department responsible for returning unclaimed money to its rightful owners. It's usually called the Unclaimed Property Division and is most often run by the state's Treasury Office, or sometimes by the Banking Division or Controller's Office. Simply get out the phone book and contact the appropriate government office of each state where you have lived.

An even faster way to find your money is by using the Internet. Forty states have their own unclaimed property Web sites, which you can reach by logging on to the site of the National Association of Unclaimed Property Administrators at <www.unclaimed.org>. This easy-to-use tool can also provide you with the mailing address of the right department in any state you wish to search.

## Does the government owe you money?

Goodness knows, the government isn't perfect, but thank goodness, its workers do keep pretty good records. Unfortunately, the size of the government and its many departments make it easy for things to slip through the cracks. If you think you've been shortchanged, here's how to get in touch with four of the most common Washington culprits.

**Taxes.** Think you've overpaid on a return or missed a refund? Call the IRS toll free at 800-829-1040, or get the number for their local office from your phone book.

**Social Security.** Checks coming late or not at all? Maybe you're eligible for benefits and don't even know it. Most areas have a regional office you can call, or check the Social Security Web site on the Internet at <www.ssa.gov>.

**Pensions.** Most people assume that if their company goes bankrupt, they lose their pension. This isn't always true. The Pension Benefit Guaranty Corporation insures 42 million individual pensions, and yours could very well be covered. Contact this government agency by writing to:

Pension Benefit Guaranty Corporation
Pension Search Program
1200 K Street NW
Washington, DC 20005

**Military benefits.** Veterans and their families are entitled to many benefits long after leaving the service. To find out what you're entitled to, call the Department of Veterans Affairs at 800-827-1000 or write:

Department of Veterans Affairs
810 Vermont Avenue NW
Washington, DC 20420

# Let Uncle Sam find your lost savings bonds

Did you know that the government will pay you full cash value for lost savings bonds? Even if you haven't seen them in years, or if they've been stolen or destroyed, the Bureau of Public Debt will search down the records of your bonds and pay up, absolutely free. All you have to do is ask.

Simply call the Bureau at 304-480-6112 and request Form PDF-1048. Fill out the form, providing information about the issue dates, serial numbers, and denominations of the lost bonds. When you're done, have the form certified by a notary public or bank officer, then send it in.

As you fill out your request, keep these tips from the Bureau in mind:

★ The most helpful facts are the social security numbers and registered names of the owners as well as the serial numbers of the bonds.

★ The more previous home addresses you can provide, the better.

★ Listing a few possible spelling variations of your name can help, too, in case the name was spelled wrong on the bond.

★ If you know the bonds were stolen, be sure to include a copy of the police report.

Don't worry if you can't answer all the questions, but the more information you give them, the better the chance your search will succeed.

You can also get the necessary forms at Federal Reserve banks and most commercial banks. If you have the Internet, you can download the forms from the Bureau's Web site at <www.savingsbonds.gov>.

Because the government processes about 800,000 of these inquiries every year, results may take a few weeks or even months. But then, free money is always worth waiting for.

# INVESTMENTS

## The secret to stock market success

So you want to make a killing in the stock market? Then do your homework. The one secret shared by all successful investors is that they get their information before they buy. Knowing a company inside and out — how it runs, its history, and its potential — will help you predict how valuable its stock will become. Follow these hints from one highly successful investing club to root up sources of free information on smart stock buying.

**Check out the library.** Respected magazines such as *Fortune*, *Forbes*, *Kiplinger's Personal Finance Magazine*, and *Business Week* offer insight into hot industries, new companies, and even legal changes that affect your company's success.

Look for stories about both your company and the industry in which your company is involved. Value Line's *List of Timely Industries* offers suggestions about the types of companies that are likely to be big winners in the near future. And for daily coverage and up-to-the-minute details, check out *The Wall Street Journal*, the daily bible of the financial world.

**Glance over the expert's shoulder.** The National Association of Investors Corporation (NAIC) is a nonprofit group that helps educate and advise private investors. Their *Better Investing* newsletter is a good source for stock tips, market information, and profiles of companies. Look for their Web site at <http://www.better-investing.org> for some sound investing tips.

**Spend a day at the fair.** Different organizations sometimes host regional investment fairs, which bring together representatives from many companies and investment firms. The NAIC also puts on its own informative convention. Stop by one of these events, and hit up the experts for some free answers.

**Go to the source.** Annual and quarterly reports, stockholder's documents, and even certain advertising materials can give you a good feel for a company's standing, all for free. Call the investor relations department of the company you wish to research to find out what materials are available.

Take advantage of all these free resources to get the scoop on any company in which you plan to invest.

## Free expert advice for the self-investor

It's tough to go it alone in the tricky game of self-investing, especially if you're just starting out, but it can be done. You've heard the old expression, "knowledge is power," but in the world of investing, knowledge is money.

The best way to prepare yourself to make sound investing decisions is to learn all you can about how the market works, what types of companies and stocks are likely to perform well, and what exactly you want your investment strategy to do for you. You can learn more about free sources for developing your financial savvy in other stories in this chapter, but two of the best can be accessed directly.

National Association of Investors Corporation (NAIC)
711 W. Thirteen-Mile Road
Madison Heights, MI 48071
810-583-6242

International Association for Financial Planning
Two Concourse Parkway — Suite 800
Atlanta, GA 30328
404-395-1605

These associations are aimed at helping the individual investor. Give
them a call for more information, and for free answers to some common
investing questions.

## Score a touchdown with the SEC

Sports fans who see the term "SEC" probably think of Georgia,
Alabama, Tennessee and the other college teams in the Southeastern
Conference. But if you're thinking about investing, "SEC" stands for the
Securities & Exchange Commission, and unlike the college athletic con-
ference, this SEC can save you lots of money.

Just dial the SEC Toll-free Investor Information Service at 800-732-
0330. You can get a full background check on a company before you decide
to invest with it or find out if your broker or brokerage firm has been in any
kind of trouble. It's also a prime source for general information about federal securities laws, investor alerts, and instructions on how to file a complaint.

The SEC offers several free publications packed with information
about investing. A few examples include *Invest Wisely: An Introduction to
Mutual Funds, What Every Investor Should Know* and *Invest Wisely: Advice
from Your Securities Industry Regulators.* You can get them by calling the
same toll-free number. Or you can write to:

Securities & Exchange Commission
Office of Consumer Affairs
450 Fifth St. NW
Washington, DC 20549

The SEC also has a Web site at <www.sec.gov>.

Before you make an important investment decision, check out what
the SEC has to say — their free advice could save you a bundle.

Just think of it as scoring a financial touchdown.

# Investing secrets revealed for free

Get the most out of your money by learning the secrets of smart investing. The LA Times Business Academy has a free online service that guides you through the ins and outs of successful personal investments. Check out the topics covered in "Investing 101" to learn how you can benefit from these valuable secrets.

★ **Risk management.** Learn to weigh risk against profit and how to decide the right amount of risk for your age, financial situation, and personality.

★ **Diversification.** Look at different ways to spread out your investments and reduce the chance of big losses.

★ **Stock selection.** Review the basics for knowing what qualities make a stock successful, such as steady growth and smart company management, and where to find this key information.

★ **When to sell.** Learn how to keep your cool and ride out scary moments in the market, and how to bail out wisely if you need to.

★ **Bond investing.** Forget the old wives' tale that bonds are practically risk-free, and get the inside scoop on how to invest in them safely.

★ **Mutual funds.** Although safe and convenient, mutual funds can be tricky. Making the right choices at the right time can mean a lot more money in your pocket.

★ **International stocks.** Discover ways to make these risky investment options a bit safer, and use them to make your investment portfolio more secure.

★ **Tax breaks.** Putting investment money into IRAs, 401(k) plans, and other tax-deferred accounts will save you money and can double your profits.

★ **Record keeping.** Staying organized helps you avoid paying too much in taxes, keeping bad stocks too long, and other costly mistakes.

★ **Expense management.** Find out how to save money by cutting unnecessary expenses, like broker fees and commissions.

Once you've mastered "Investing 101," you can move on to the more advanced series on investing and other topics at the Business Academy Web site. To begin your free lessons, log onto your computer and visit <http://www.latimes.com/business/invest101/overview.htm>.

## Take the trouble out of T-bills

If the roller-coaster ride that is the stock market makes you a little weak in the knees, you might want to consider a safer way to invest your money. Treasury bills, notes, and bonds that are backed by the U.S. government might be your answer.

Here's how they work. You buy these securities at less than face value. Then after a designated period of time — one year or less for T-bills, one to 10 years for notes, and 10 years or more for bonds — the government pays you the face value. Your interest is the difference between what you paid and the face value when it matures. For example, a $10,000 T-Bill purchased for $9,750 will earn $250 in interest.

The lowest denomination for any of these securities is $1,000. They will cost you even more if you buy through a broker. But you can avoid extra fees by dealing directly with the U.S. government in a program called Treasury Direct. With Treasury Direct, you cut out the middleman and a lot of paperwork because you can use the telephone or even the Internet to buy Treasuries.

Just contact your local branch of the Federal Reserve Board to find out how to participate in Treasury Direct. You should find a listing for it in your phone book. You can also call the Treasury Direct hotline at 800-943-6864, or write for information to:

Bureau of Public Debt
U.S. Department of the Treasury
13th and C Streets SW
Washington, DC 20239

If you have access to the Internet, you can get lots of information about T-bills, notes, and bonds and the Treasury Direct program at <www.publicdebt.treas.gov>.

# Want to make money? Join the club

The stock market can be scary. With all the choices to make, the discipline it takes to keep investing, plus the risk of losing money, the stock market could frighten anybody. Like a dark alley, it's the kind of place you might not want to go alone.

Well, you don't have to. One way to get your feet wet in the stock market is through an investment club.

Investment clubs can be made up of friends, family, co-workers or even strangers. Members pool their money, share the responsibility of researching companies, and also share the risks and rewards of investing. It's an inexpensive way to learn about the stock market and have fun, too.

Just ask Bill Kilgour, a 25-year-old account executive from Pittsburgh.

He recently joined the Big Unit Investment Club, which consists of 36 friends, family, and co-workers. For $100 up front and an additional $25 a month, he has learned about the world of personal investing while enjoying himself and making a profit.

"I think it's fun. We grab dinner and have a few drinks sometimes after our meetings," Kilgour said. "We alternate locations all over town to accommodate the different areas where people live. We set aside a group of tables and meet. It is as much a social outing as a business meeting."

During meetings, the club discusses potential buys, then members dig up information on the company before the next meeting. That way, every member has a chance to give an informed opinion before the group makes a decision.

"Personally, I have learned the essential importance and value of research," said Kilgour, who looks into a company's earnings, growth potential, and history before making a recommendation to buy, hold, or sell.

Once the club decides to buy, it purchases $1,200 worth of stock at a time, much more than the young account executive could afford to invest by himself. In fact, increased buying power was one of the reasons Kilgour joined the Big Unit Investment Club.

"I got in because if I can afford to buy one share of a stock, as a club we might be able to buy 10 or 20 shares," he said.

Like most investment clubs, the Big Unit Investment Club isn't trying to get rich quick. Its strategy is to buy a mix of blue-chip and strong technology stocks and hold them, reinvesting the dividends for stable long-term growth. Currently, their portfolio includes big-name stocks like Microsoft, Coca-Cola, Wal-Mart, AT&T, Cisco Systems, Pfizer and FedEx.

"Our strategy is very conservative," said Kilgour. "The club is usually up around an average of 4 to 8 percent."

If you're interested in starting your own investment club, you can get information and advice from the Investment Club Central online at <www.iclubcentral.com>. Or contact the following organizations:

National Association of Investors Corporation (NAIC)
P.O. Box 220
Royal Oak, MI 48068
877-ASK-NAIC (877-275-6242)
<www.better-investing.org>

Securities and Exchange Commission
Office of Investor Education and Assistance
450 Fifth Street NW
Washington, DC 20549
<www.sec.gov>

For more free advice, take a few tips from Kilgour.

"Establish very clear goals. Encourage group input. Be flexible, and have a good time," he said, adding, "Remember that there is always a risk of losing money, so be smart and do your research."

You just might emerge from the dark alley of the stock market with a brighter financial future.

# MAXIMIZE YOUR HOME INVESTMENT

For most people, a home is more than just a roof over their heads. It's a safe and secure haven from daily stresses, a family gathering place, a means of self expression, and a melting pot of memories. A house is also a big investment — for most people, the largest purchase of their lives.

This chapter will show you how to make the most of your home investment and how to turn it into a money maker, not a money trap. You'll find advice on smart strategies for buying and selling, ways to save on financing and moving, and more. You'll also find some realty-related freebies to help make the buying/selling/moving process a little less difficult.

## Get a free appraisal from the pros

Don't sell your home short. Before putting your house on the market, visit the HomeGain Web site for a free home appraisal and expert advice on the best way to sell it.

Simply log onto the Internet and go to <www.homegain.com> then follow the links to their Home Valuation tool. Answer a few simple questions about your property and your area, and HomeGain will give you a ballpark figure on how much your home is worth.

The detailed report also will include recent selling prices for homes in your neighborhood. This can help you price your home more realistically, improving your chance of a quick sale.

The HomeGain site also features other free tools to help you prepare your home for sale, drive a good bargain, and find a successful real-estate agent.

★ **Checklists.** These handy resources include a glossary of real-estate terms, a home seller's list of frequently asked questions, and a checklist to help you decide if an agent is right for you.

★ **Calculators.** Specially designed for home sellers, these tools let you figure out your profit as well as your capital gains tax. They'll also help you compare the expense of moving versus improving your present home.

★ **Library.** This feature lets you browse a great selection of consumer guides, articles by real-estate professionals, and other sources of free advice.

## Free form for sale of home

If you decide to cut out the middle man and sell your home without a real estate agent, you can save a lot of money. You can also save yourself some time, and perhaps some headaches, if you use free legal forms available on the Internet.

The forms are general, and you can alter them to fit your particular circumstances, but they at least give you a starting point. Go to <www.FreeLegalForms.com>, click on the list of downloadable forms, and choose "Contract for Sale and Purchase of Property."

## Drop PMI 'ASAP' to save big bucks

If you don't have at least 20 percent to put down on a new home, you'll probably have to cough up extra for private mortgage insurance (PMI). PMI is designed to protect your lender in case you default on your loan. It can be fairly costly, so if you can wait until you have a larger down-payment, you'll save a lot of money. If you just can't wait, however, ask your lender about the best deal on PMI or alternative finance options, such as "80-10-10" loans.

Once you've paid your mortgage down to 80 percent of your home's value, the PMI should be dropped. This may not happen automatically, though, so don't forget you have it. It's usually included in your monthly payment, so it's easy to write the check and not think about PMI. Big mistake. It's not just pocket change — PMI can add as much as $100 a month to your mortgage.

# Get cash from your home

Medical bills piling up? Property taxes getting to be too much? If you're at least 62 years old and own your home, you might be sitting on the answer to all your prayers. Older homeowners can apply for a reverse mortgage, which lets you borrow money against the equity you've built up in your home.

Instead of making payments to the bank like in a traditional mortgage, the bank gives you a loan based on your home's value, then actually makes payments to you. This money can come to you in a lump sum, monthly payments, or a line of credit. You only have to pay it back when you sell your home or die.

If you sell your home, you can just use the money from the sale to pay off the loan and keep the rest. If you die, your heirs can repay the debt with other money if they don't want to sell.

You can use the cash from a reverse mortgage for anything you want. Most seniors use it to pay real-estate taxes so they can afford to keep their homes, but others earmark it for:

★ home repairs
★ medical bills
★ travel
★ refinancing an existing loan
★ general income

And because the money comes to you in the form of a loan, it's tax-free and will not affect your Social Security or Medicare benefits.

So if you're ready to turn years of loyal home-investing into some free money, learn how to get started by logging on to your computer and visiting <www.reversemortgages.net>. If you're not online, get in touch with one of the following institutions, which all have reverse mortgage programs in place:

★ The Bank of New York — 800-677-9000
★ First Union (Florida only) — 800-922-6267
★ Wells Fargo Bank (calls from California, Colorado, Idaho, Oregon, Texas or Washington) — 800-999-3850
★ Wells Fargo Bank (calls from all other states) — 888-667-1772

You can also contact the Housing and Urban Development (HUD) field office nearest you or write to:

U.S. Department of Housing and Urban Development
451 7th St., SW, Room 9100
Washington, DC 20410
888-466-3487
<www.hud.gov/rvrsmort.html>

---

### Find a loan fast ... and free

Finding the right mortgage can be a chore, but if you can handle a "mouse," a great loan may be yours for the asking.

Simply pull up the Internet on your computer, and log on to <www. getsmartinc.com>. Answer a few questions about the property you are buying, your loan preferences, and your financial history. This convenient Web site will then set up a sample loan to suit you. After you look it over, GetSmart will connect you to banks that can offer you such a loan and will compete for your business.

The best part is, the whole process is free. Just fire up the old computer, and you'll be on your way to financing your next real-estate purchase.

---

# Get a dirt-cheap loan for rural housing

Meat isn't the only thing certified prime by the U.S. Department of Agriculture. If you're a low-income family, you can also get some prime deals on housing through the USDA's Rural Housing Service.

**Buy your home.** The Rural Housing Service's Direct Loan Program gives loans to families with low incomes who want to buy new or existing houses in rural areas. The interest rate can be as low as 1 percent and the term of the loan can be as long as 38 years depending on your income.

Eligibility varies from place to place. Your income is considered "very low" if you make less than half of the median salary of the area where you live. For example, a very low income in Albany, Georgia is $14,550, while in Atlanta an income of $22,100 is called very low.

**Build your home.** Handy? You might consider the Mutual Self-Help Housing Program, which lets you help build your home. You're obligated to do at least 65 percent of the work to get a lower-cost home. You also must help other future homeowners work on their homes.

**Rent your home.** If you're having trouble coming up with the rent, you might be able to get help from the Rental Assistance Program. To qualify, you must live in Rural Rental Housing or Farm Labor Hous-ing projects financed by the Rural Housing and Community Devel-opment Services.

**Repair your home.** When your house and your financial situation are both in pretty bad shape, you can apply for aid through the Home Repair Loan and Grant Program. It might be just what you need to fix your leaking roof or build a ramp for a disabled relative.

If you're 62 or older, you can get a grant for up to $7,500. Otherwise, loans with 1-percent interest are available for up to $20,000.

For more information and to see if you're eligible for any of these programs, contact your Rural Development State Office. Or get in touch with the national office at:

Rural Housing Service National Office
U.S. Department of Agriculture
Room 5037, South Building
14th Street and Independence Avenue SW
Washington, DC 20250
202-720-4323
<www.rurdev.usda.gov>

# 4 steps to smart refinancing

Interest rates are plummeting, and you're stuck with a high-interest mortgage. Should you refinance? Follow these few simple steps, and you'll know when and how to cash in on big savings through refinancing.

**Follow the 2-percent rule.** Whenever the current mortgage rate falls more than 2 percent below the rate you're paying on your own mortgage, it's time to seriously consider refinancing.

**Shop around.** Don't automatically choose to renew with your present lender. Check with other financial institutions to find the best rates and benefits. But let your own creditor know that you're shopping around. He may be more willing to offer you a competitive deal and may even waive extra costs such as refinancing fees.

**Cut your payments.** Whenever possible, shorten the term of your mortgage when you refinance. Even if you only shave a year or two off the length of your mortgage, the money you save on interest will really add up.

**Time your move wisely.** What's the best time of the month to refinance? Simple — the end. Never close on a refinancing loan near the beginning of a new month, or you run the risk of paying double interest. Avoid this needless trap by timing the close on your new loan carefully.

## Sure-fire tips for a cheap and easy move

If you thought buying a new house was expensive, wait until you see how much it costs to move in. Moving companies charge pretty steep fees, but if you play it smart, you'll find lots of free stuff out there to help keep the bill "under wraps."

**Look for free packaging.** When you use a professional mover, you pay for everything including the packaging material. Obviously, you can save money (and probably minimize breakage) by packing yourself, and you can save even more by getting your materials for free.

★ Pick up boxes at your local grocery or liquor store. Beer and liquor cartons are a good size and very sturdy. Also check paint stores, copy shops, schools, and furniture stores.

★ Hospitals, offices, and office supply stores are great sources for old Styrofoam, bubble wrap, and shredded paper for packing your breakables.

★ Kill two birds with one stone by using towels, old rags, sheets, and even your clothes as packing material. You've got to pack them somewhere anyway — why not wrapped around your dinnerware?

**Take advantage of free advice.** Mayflower Movers offers a free moving kit to help make your move easier. Write to:

Mayflower Movers
Box 107B
Indianapolis, IN 46206

**Rent at the right time.** When moving yourself, try to borrow a truck instead of renting. If you do rent, rates are usually lower during the middle of the week, the middle of the month, and during non-summer months. Be sure to shop around as rates between rental companies can vary considerably.

**Get rid of dead weight.** Moving companies charge by the pound, but you'll pay even if you move yourself — in gas mileage and effort. Cut down on your total weight by getting rid of anything you no longer need.

★ Weed through your wardrobe and give old, rarely used clothes to charity.

★ Try to eat all the food in your pantry before you move, especially heavy canned goods.

★ Ditch old magazines, newspapers, and other typical home "collectibles." A good house cleaning can save you big bucks on moving day.

## Cut costs by sharing your home

What should you do if you can't afford to live in the nice house you want or can't make full use of the large house you already have? How about sharing?

More than 400 shared-housing programs across the country bring people together to share living quarters — and expenses. Sponsored by various agencies, these programs can help you explore money-saving living options you've probably never considered.

Shared-housing programs work in two ways:

★ If you own a home, the program can match you with a boarder that will help with expenses by paying rent, doing yard work, splitting the bills, or helping around the home.

★ If you're looking for a place to live, the program will screen potential housemates to find compatible people who would be interested in sharing a house with you.

For more information on locating a shared-housing program in your area, write or call:

National Shared Housing Resource Center
431 Pine Street
Burlington, VT 05401
802-862-2727

Whatever your situation might be, shared housing is a great way to cut down on living costs by sharing rent and other expenses. Not only are the savings good for the wallet, but the companionship and security of living with others can be good for your spirit, your heart, and your overall health.

## Free guide to living in the Sunshine State

If you're planning on retiring to Florida, or just thinking about buying property there, send for a helpful book called *How To Buy A Home In Florida*. Pringle Development offers this resource free to anyone interested in moving to the Sunshine State.

Pringle has been named by *Where To Retire* magazine as one of the best 100 master-planned communities in America. Whether you choose to live in a Pringle development or not, the information will help you get a feel for your real-estate options in Florida. Topics include:

★ Overview of community living and housing types
★ Cost of living and other expenses
★ Financing and reselling in Florida
★ Homebuyer's checklist

To get your free book, write to: Pringle Development, Inc., 26600 Ace Avenue, Leesburg, FL 34748. Or visit Pringle's Web site at <www.pringle.com> where you can either sign up to have the book mailed to you or download the book to your computer. In a rush? Request your book over the phone by calling 800-325-4471.

## Smart advice for apartment savings

Owning your own home may be the great American dream, but most people have to spend at least some time in an apartment. And some people even prefer apartment living — you don't have to mow the lawn, fix the plumbing, or call the exterminator, and most apartment complexes have community perks like a clubhouse, pool, and laundry room.

Before renting an apartment, however, make sure you don't fall for common financial mistakes.

**Know what you're getting into.** Ask questions. It's the only way to decide whether a place is right for you. How much is the rent? How long is the lease? What deposits are required, and how much are they?

**Think before you ink.** Never sign a lease on the spot, no matter how beautiful the place looks, or how many people the rental agent says are lined up waiting to snatch it away from you. Take the lease home with you and read it thoroughly. Mark any items you have questions about so you can ask before you sign.

**Be sure of your decision.** Most apartment complexes require a deposit and/or application fee. If you change your mind after paying those items, you'll probably lose your money. Be fairly certain you want to lease a place before paying any fees.

**Secure your security deposit.** Getting a security deposit back when you move out can be the most frustrating part of renting an apartment. Some people even find they receive a cleaning bill in the mail after they've moved out.

To protect yourself, make sure you're present for the move-in and move-out inspections. Take videos or photos before you move in, and make notes of any pre-existing problems and have your landlord sign and date them. That could help protect you if a dispute arises later.

With a little forethought, you can make your apartment experience as inexpensive as possible.

# RETIRE WITH MORE

You work hard all your life, and you deserve a few years of retirement bliss. But many people sort of stumble into retirement without having prepared themselves for this new lifestyle. Retirement brings many changes — particularly financial — that you need to be aware of. This chapter is designed to help you hang on to your hard-earned money so you can enjoy your golden years in style and comfort.

Discover where to get legal advice and other services, how to build and protect your nest egg, and how to plan your estate so that your heirs reap the benefits — not the government. If you want to have a happy, secure retirement — and who doesn't — just follow the advice in this chapter.

## Building and protecting your nest egg

Retirement is something most of us look forward to — no more rat race, no more deadlines, just lots of time to travel and enjoy life. If you really want to enjoy your retirement, though, you need to make sure you build up a nest egg and then protect it.

**Set goals.** The first step to a secure retirement is to set your goals. Decide what you'd like to do in retirement. Do you long to travel to exotic places, or would you rather spend your retirement quietly puttering about in your garden? What you want can make a big difference in how much money you need to save.

**Make saving a priority.** Don't just save money whenever you have extra. Make saving a priority, not an option. Automatic drafts from your paycheck are an excellent savings strategy, because you never see the money so you don't miss it.

**Don't put all your nest eggs in one basket.** To maximize your savings, spread your retirement money out. Here are just some of the ways you can save your money.

★ **401(k).** This is the foundation of most retirement plans. Your contribution is automatically deducted from your paycheck before taxes. This makes it relatively painless, because your paycheck will only be reduced by 50 to 85 cents for every dollar you put into your 401(k). The extra 15 to 50 cents would have gone to Uncle Sam anyway. You will have to pay taxes on that money but not until you withdraw it, and until then, it's earning interest. Plus, most employers will also match a certain percentage of what you put in. Some employers even match 100 percent, contributing a dollar for every dollar you put in.

★ **SEP (Simplified Employee Pension).** These plans are usually provided by owners of small businesses, because they aren't as complex and expensive to administer as a 401(k) or other plan.

★ **IRA (Individual Retirement Account).** If you're self-employed, or if your employer doesn't offer a pension plan, you can start an IRA. Like a 401(k), the government doesn't tax the money you put into an IRA. It's only taxed when you withdraw it.

★ **Annuity.** When you buy an annuity, basically, you're buying an insurance policy that pays while you're still alive. Since annuities are underwritten by insurance companies, and insurance investments are protected from taxes, your money grows tax-free until you withdraw it. When you withdraw your money, it is taxed as ordinary income. Many annuities also provide a small death benefit for your beneficiaries. What's more, unlike other retirement plans, there's no limit to how much you can invest in an annuity.

For more detailed information on retirement planning, you can send for these booklets by contacting the Consumer Response Center (see address on next page).

★ *From Here To Security.* Reliable advice on steps you should take to ensure a secure retirement. (50 cents)

★ *Predictable, Secure Pension for Life.* Detailed information on pension plans and your rights. (Free)

★ *Annuities.* Are annuities right for you? Send for this guide and find out. (Free)

Consumer Response Center
Federal Trade Commission
Washington, DC 20580
202-326-2222
<www.pueblo.gsa.gov>

Another valuable source of retirement information is the Pension and Welfare Benefits Administration, which can be reached at:

Pension and Welfare Benefits Administration
U.S. Department of Labor
202-219-8776
800-998-7542 (publication hotline)
<www.dol.gov/dol/pwba>

## Save hundreds in legal fees

If you've always been a do-it-yourselfer, from installing your own car radio to fixing your own plumbing, you know it can save you a lot of money. Of course, sometimes if you don't know what you're doing, it can cost you more in the long run. The same applies to legal processes. If you do your homework, you can handle some of your own legal procedures.

**Hit the books.** Self-help legal books can guide you through some simple legal processes. Some contain standard forms that you can copy and use. One example is *101 Free Legal Forms for Personal Use* by Robin Leonard. While a book containing legal forms may cost $20 to $30, it could save you hundreds in lawyers' fees. Forms in these books usually include wills, bills of sale, rental agreements, powers of attorney, etc. Of course, you'll save even more money if you can find the book in your local library.

**Search the Internet.** If you have access to the Internet, you can find a wealth of legal information. You can also download free forms from the World Wide Web. Sites that provide free legal forms to download and print include:

★ Legalwiz.com at <www.legalwiz.com>

★ Internet Legal Resource Guide at <www.ilrg.com>

★ Legaldocs at <www.legaldocs.com>. This site offers some free forms and some that are available for a small fee. One of the advantages of this site is that it lets you customize your documents online.

When searching for a particular legal form, don't use the first one you find. You're better off checking three or four Web sites, then comparing the details of each form to find the one that best suits your needs.

**Know your risks.** Understand that there are risks in doing your own legal work. Some things are still best left to experts. Like plumbing repairs that seem simple until your house gets flooded, a mistake in a legal matter could be costly and stressful. If you use a fill-in-the-blank form for an important matter, it's a good idea to at least have a lawyer check it over. It won't be as costly as having him draw up the document, and it may save you a headache in the future.

## Getting top-notch low-cost legal advice

Everyone needs advice now and then, and when it comes to legal issues, it can be essential, especially as you get older.

If you're a member of the American Association of Retired Persons (AARP), you are entitled to a free 30-minute consultation with a lawyer who meets the association's standards. If you go through AARP, you can also get basic legal services at a discounted rate. Some sample rates as of July, 2000:

★ Simple Will: $50
★ Health Care Power of Attorney and Living Will: $35
★ Financial Power of Attorney: $35

For most other legal services, you receive a 20-percent reduction in regular attorney's fees if you go through AARP.

Another resource affiliated with AARP is the Legal Hotline Technical Assistance Project. It keeps an updated state-by-state list of hotline numbers and publishes a quarterly newsletter. For information, call 954-472-0997.

If you're not a member of AARP, or if you can't even afford discounted legal advice, the Administration on Aging may be able to find free legal aid for you. Seventeen states have special legal hotlines for people 60 and older. You can call for free advice on simple legal issues, and sometimes get referrals for more complicated matters.

- ★ California: 800-222-1753; 916-551-2140
- ★ District of Columbia: 202-434-2170
- ★ Florida: 305-576-5997
- ★ Georgia: 888-257-9519; 404-657-9915
- ★ Hawaii: 888-536-0011; 808-536-0011
- ★ Iowa: 800-992-8161; 515-282-8161
- ★ Kansas: 888-353-5337; 316-265-9681
- ★ Kentucky: 800-200-3633
- ★ Maine: 800-750-5353; 207-623-1797
- ★ Maryland: 800-999-8904; 410-539-5340
- ★ Michigan: 800-347-5297; 517-372-5959
- ★ Mississippi: 888-660-0008; 228-374-4168
- ★ New Hampshire: 888-353-9944; 603-624-6000
- ★ New Mexico: 800-876-6657; 505-797-6005
- ★ Ohio: 800-488-6070; 513-345-4160
- ★ Pennsylvania: 800-262-5297
- ★ Tennessee: 800-836-0128; 423-756-0128
- ★ Texas: 800-622-2520
- ★ Washington: 888-387-7111
- ★ West Virginia: 800-229-5068; 304-291-3900

## Where there's a will, there's a way to save money

Ask anyone about their long-term financial goals, and a comfortable retirement will probably head the list. Being able to leave something to their children will most likely be high on the list as well. Unfortunately, lengthy probate and lawyer's fees can eat up any inheritance they hope to pass on unless they take steps to prevent it.

The first step in protecting your property is to create a will. Everyone needs a will. If you die without one, the government will decide who gets your assets, and it may not be distributed the way you think. Once you've decided it's time to make a will, you have to decide the best and least expensive way for you to do that.

**Pay a lawyer.** As you know, attorney fees can be high, but simple wills usually aren't an expensive item. And if you're a member of the American Association of Retired Persons (AARP), you can get a discount from certain lawyers. If you decide to write your will yourself, it's probably a good idea to get a lawyer to review it. He won't charge as much to review a will as to create one, but it will protect you in case you've made an error.

**Refer to a book.** If you're the studious type, you can find books that will help you create your own will. Many contain forms that allow you to fill in the blanks. These may not work for you, however, if you have a lot of property or special situations to address in your will. One good book to look for is the *Complete Book of Wills, Estates, and Trusts* by Alexander A. Bove, a Boston attorney.

**Sit back with some software.** If you have access to a computer, a software program that helps you create a will can be an excellent choice. Most will walk you through the process by asking you a series of questions and will have multiple forms that you can print out and keep. It's cheaper than a lawyer, and you can do it in the privacy of your home. One of the most popular programs is WillMaker by Nolo Press. It currently costs $29.95 on its Web site <www.nolo.com>.

If you decide to save money by making out your own will, there are a few points you need to consider to ensure that your will is legal and binding.

★  In about half the states, a will must be typed or computer-generated. Some states accept handwritten or "fill-in-the-blank" wills. You should check to see what your state's requirements are or else assume that you need to use a typewriter or computer.

★  The document must state that it is your will.

★  You must sign and date it. The signing must be witnessed by at least two people. Some states require three witnesses. The witnesses cannot be anyone who is to inherit property from the will, and although they have to watch you sign, they don't have to read the will. Notarization isn't required.

For more information on estate planning, write for a free copy of *Wills & Living Trusts*. Send a postcard requesting publication D14535 to:

AARP Fulfillment
601 East Street NW
Washington, DC 20049

## Urgent warning on living trusts

Here's a warning, especially for elderly people — don't trust sales-people bearing living trusts.

A living trust is often used to bypass the probate process. Property held in a trust passes to your beneficiary immediately upon your death. A trust isn't a substitute for a will, but it can be a faster, less expensive way to pass high-priority items like a house or business on to your heirs.

Unfortunately, the sale of living-trust kits and estate-planning services has become a common way for the unscrupulous to make money. They tend to target elderly people, and they charge outrageous prices for services you may not even need.

Be suspicious of anyone who approaches you offering these services. They may even claim to be endorsed by the American Association of Retired Persons (AARP), but AARP is not associated with any company that markets living-trust kits.

Keep in mind that living trusts aren't for everyone. People in good health who are under 55 or people who don't own a lot of property probably don't need one. If you think you need a trust, AARP recommends that you hire a lawyer. Your state may require that a lawyer draw it up, but if you can do it yourself, you'll save money. A book on making out your own living trust costs about $30, and computer software costs about $50. A lawyer will generally charge $1,000 to $1,500 for writing a trust.

For more information, send for AARP publication #D14535, *Wills and Living Trusts*. Write to:

AARP Fulfillment
601 East Street NW
Washington, DC 20049

# Plan ahead to keep funeral expenses low

Nothing is certain except death and taxes, but neither topic is pleasant to think about or discuss. Nevertheless, you know that smart thinking about taxes can save lots of money. The same is true of death — funerals can be very expensive, and a little thought can save you and your family thousands of dollars.

When you have an unexpected death in the family, it's easier to let the nearest funeral home handle everything, but that's how funerals get so expensive so quickly. Take some of the difficulty out of a tough situation for your family by working out your own funeral arrangements ahead of time.

**Make your wishes known.** You don't want your family to pay for expensive perks you wouldn't have cared about. Make your own decisions, spell them out in writing, and make sure those closest to you know where to find that information.

**Save, don't prepay.** Some funeral homes offer prepayment options, but they usually aren't a good choice financially. You're better off setting aside money for your funeral in a savings account ear-marked for funeral expenses that your heirs will have access to in the event of your death.

**Buy separately.** You don't have to buy your casket, urn, or flowers from the funeral home. If you can get a better deal by doing it separately, do so. And be aware that FTC rules do not allow funeral homes to charge an extra handling fee for items purchased elsewhere.

**Consider an alternative.** Although many people are reluctant to do so, one of the best ways to save money is to arrange to donate your body to medical science. There's no body to deal with, and your family can arrange memorial services wherever and whenever is best for them. Plus you've made a contribution that may someday help save another person's life.

**Find free information.** Because you're a thoughtful and thrifty person, you may have planned in advance for your funeral, but not everyone has the foresight to do that. If you suddenly have to deal with making arrangements for a family member, one of your best bets may be to contact your local memorial society. These organizations work to keep funeral costs low and may be able to provide you with valuable information and assistance.

To receive a free pamphlet on the benefits of memorial societies as well as a list of local organizations, send a self-addressed stamped envelope to:

Continental Association of Funeral and Memorial Societies
33 University Square, Suite 333
Madison, WI 5715
800-458-5563

For more information, you can also send for *Funerals: A Consumer Guide* from:

Consumer Response Center
Federal Trade Commission
Washington, DC 20580
877-382-4357

## Free support services for the elderly

The years at the end of your life are often referred to as your "golden" years. Unfortunately, that term sometimes doesn't ring true. Often, older people become disabled physically or mentally, and unscrupulous people may take advantage of them. In 1965, the Older Americans Act established a network of agencies to protect elderly people and help them live a better life.

There are hundreds of local Area Agencies on Aging that provide services for older people. If the Agency can't provide the service you need, they may be able to direct you to an organization that can help. Call Eldercare Locator at 800-677-1116 Monday through Friday, 9 a.m. to 8 p.m. EST. Be ready to give them your county and city or zip code and a brief description of your problem.

You can also write:

National Association of Area Agencies on Aging
1112 16th St. NW
Washington, DC 20036

Services provided by these agencies may vary, but here are some of the more common services.

**Ombudsman Program.** The person with this odd-sounding title has a very important job — investigating nursing homes. An ombudsman is a public official who investigates citizen's complaints against organizations, government agencies, or officials.

Since its beginning, the ombudsman program has uncovered and resolved countless problems in nursing homes, ranging from cold food to physical abuse and wrongful death. Through their periodic visits, ombudsmen (many of them certified volunteers) also provide emotional support to nursing home residents. If you have a question or concern about a nursing home, this is the program that may help.

**The Elderly Nutrition Program.** This program provides nutritious meals for seniors, either delivered to their homes, or in community settings such as senior centers. Other services may include nutrition screening and health counseling.

**Transportation assistance.** As people age, their ability to drive a car often deteriorates. Sometimes public transportation is a good alternative, but not everyone has access to it. The national aging network provides rides to places such as the doctor's office, senior centers, and adult daycare centers. The National Transit Resource Center can also provide you with information on local transportation options for senior citizens and people with disabilities. Call 800-527-8279.

**Pensions and benefits counseling.** Financial difficulties can make your golden years seem a bit rusty. If you're having problems with your pension, or would like to avoid problems in the future, you can contact one of the Administration on Aging's Pension Counseling Demonstration projects.

These projects provide counseling and assistance in filing claims to obtain promised pensions. They may be able to answer questions about retirement benefits or help you find legal assistance for your pension problems.

# COST-CUTTING CAREER STRATEGIES

Most of us have to work at least part of our lives. And when we do reach the golden age of retirement, many of us find that we miss the challenges of the working world. Today, thousands of seniors are staying in the job market by postponing retirement or embarking on new "post-retirement" careers.

Whether you're returning to the job market, starting your own business, or simply looking for your first job, this chapter has something for you. Getting the best deal is usually a simple matter of knowing where to look, and the professional world is no exception. From free job-hunting services to discount office supplies to promotional items, you'll find everything you need to help you advance in the workplace.

## Aim 'hire' with free job-hunting services

Your company may have down-sized or pressured you into early retirement. Maybe you need some extra income. Or maybe you're just looking for something to do. Whatever the reason, you want a job.

Looking for employment can be a full-time job. Scouring the want-ads, making phone calls, and mailing out resumes is hard work. Sometimes you don't even know where to begin.

Here are some free services you can employ to help you find employment.

**Profit from experience.** It might seem like the job market is geared toward computer whizzes fresh out of college. But there are many companies who value the experience and dependability of a mature worker. Here are some services that help you find them.

★ Experience Works!, a free nationwide staffing service, provides older workers with temporary or permanent jobs as well as training. Call 800-598-9882 ext. 3500 to speak to someone about the program.

★ Green Thumb, the organization that sponsors Experience Works!, also offers the Senior Community Service Employment Program (SCSEP) and projects through the Job Training Partnerships Act. Both programs are for low-income older Americans. For more information about these programs, write to: Green Thumb National Headquarters, 2000 North 14 Street, Suite 800, Arlington, VA 22201. Or you can check out their Web site at <www.green thumb.org>.

★ Hire Potential, Inc. also helps older workers find temporary or permanent positions as part of a commitment to what they call the "Untapped Workforce," which also includes veterans, welfare recipients, and people with disabilities. You can contact them online at <www.hirepotential.com>. Or you can reach them by calling 415-986-3289 or writing to: Hire Potential, 414 Mason St., San Francisco, CA 94102.

**Untangle the Web.** If you use the Internet, you can find some great resources to help in your job search. Here are two of the best.

★ The Riley Guide at <www.rileyguide.com> features an extensive list of opportunities and resources you can access on the Internet. Everything from writing a good resume to researching a company can be found at this site.

★ The Jobhunters Bible at <www.jobhuntersbible.com> provides great advice about searching wisely for jobs online. It also lists recommended sites and explains the pros and cons of each.

All Internet job searches should start at one of these points. You'll spend a lot less time surfing and a lot more time finding what you need.

**Search these sites.** While you're online, you can get tips on writing a resume, interviewing, and negotiating your salary as well as view job openings and post your resume on a number of sites dedicated to the job search. Here is a small sampling of what's out there.

★ JobsOnline.com at <www.jobsonline.com> gives you 30 minutes of free long distance if you take a free career aptitude test. Once you register on this site, you have access to all sorts of job listings, and you can post your resume.

★ Monster.com at <www.monster.com> shouldn't scare you. This site offers a free job search, tips, and the opportunity to post your resume if you register. It also features a forum called "Aging in the Workforce" where older workers can post comments and ask or give advice on all aspects of employment.

★ CareerBuilder at <www.careerbuilder.com> provides many tips and resources. You can tailor your job search by city, job type, and pre-ferred salary.

★ Headhunter.net at <www.headhunter.net> is another popular site that boasts all the usual resources and search capabilities, but also features a "Boss Button" to help you if you're looking for another job while at work. Just hit the special button when your boss walks by, and your screen will change to something more innocent looking.

★ Career.com at <www.career.com> is geared toward workers looking for high-tech jobs. You can also reach them by calling 650-917-5510.

Regardless of which resource you use, you're bound to find something that will help you in your quest for a job. So, keep looking, apply your-self, and you'll see it pays to employ these free job-search services.

## Learn and earn with free resources

You've probably heard that knowledge is power, and time is money. If you run your own business or if you're thinking about starting one, you can get the information you need without spending hours hunting for it. Plus, this valuable business knowledge is absolutely free or extremely inex-pensive. That way, you save time and money. Just check out these amaz-ing resources. You'll feel pretty powerful.

**SCORE.** Score some points for your business with the Service Corps of Retired Executives, an organization "dedicated to the formation, growth, and success of small business nationwide." SCORE offers free face-to-face counseling, personal e-mail counseling, workshops, and "how to" tips from retired business experts. You can contact SCORE by writing to:

SCORE Association
409 3rd Street SW, 6th Floor
Washington, DC 20024

Or you can call 800-634-0245. You can also visit its Web site at
<www.score.org> which features a locator service to help you find a
SCORE chapter near you as well as links to other resources.

**U.S. Small Business Administration.** Another great resource is the
Small Business Administration. On this government agency's site, <www.
sba.gov>, you can find out about starting, financing, and expanding your
business and about government and other resources and services. It also
gives you the chance to post your business card online.

**Small Business Advisor.** This organization helps small businesses get
started and keep operating. On its Web site, <www.isquare.com>, you can
get tax advice, stock quotes, and tips. You can also read articles about all
aspects of business from marketing to customer service.

A free monthly e-mail newsletter, featuring tax and money saving ideas,
time saving hints and more, is available online. This company also provides
books, consulting services, and seminars. For more information, contact:

Small Business Advisor
Box 579
Great Falls, VA 22066
703-450-7049

**Professional City.com.** This all-in-one online service makes things
easier by breaking the big topic of "business" into smaller categories such
as accounting, human resources, law, or marketing. This impressive site
offers links to journals, news services, discussion groups and more — all
geared toward your specific field.

You can build a free Web site, access business newsletters, and get help
with just about everything, from speech writing to driving directions. It
even has a "cybrarian" who will do the research and write a report for you
for a fee. Check out the site at <www.professionalcity.com>. You can also
call 805-492-0738.

**Office Click.com.** Another all-in-one business resource, Office Click is
geared toward the administrative professional and features access to supplies,

travel, shipping and more. It provides articles with advice about the workplace as well as the opportunity to swap tips with other professionals.

You can also take advantage of the fun "Take a Break" feature that allows you to escape the world of business for the world of entertainment or politics for a while. To explore this valuable site, go to <www.officeclick.com>.

With all these great business resources at your fingertips, what are you waiting for? After all, time is money.

## Enjoy a bonanza of business information

If you prefer your information in hard copies, you can find dozens of free brochures filled with business and financial advice. Here are some prime sources of free information.

**The Federal Trade Commission (FTC)** publishes brochures on business and other consumer issues. Topics include advertising, investments, credit, and home. You can get anything from guides to buying a franchise to frequently asked questions about advertising your small business. For a complete list of available publications, write to:

Best Sellers
Consumer Response Center
Federal Trade Commission
600 Pennsylvania Ave. NW
Washington, DC 20580

You can also call 877-FTC-HELP (877-382-4357) or visit the FTC Web site at <www.ftc.gov> where you can read the brochures online.

**MetLife** is another great place for free information. MetLife offers more than 70 brochures about starting, running, or selling a business, reentering the workforce, doing taxes, investing for the first time, planning for your retirement, and more. Just call 800-638-5433, or check out its Web site at <www.lifeadvice.com> where you can view the publications.

**ArcaMax.** This last deal isn't free, but it's pretty close. ArcaMax offers a software package called the "Small Business Encyclopedia" for only $7.95, which features valuable information about running a business. As an added bonus, there are no shipping or handling charges. The "Small Business Encyclopedia" runs on Windows 95/98 and can be ordered online at <www.arcamax.com>. You can also write to:

ArcaMax, Inc.
860 Omni Boulevard
Newport News, VA 23606

Or you can call 888-ARCAMAX (888-272-2629), or fax your order to 757-369-6523. Include the promo code "ahpsbe-" when ordering any way other than online.

## Bargains for your office

It costs money to run a business. Whether you need a special kind of paper for your laser printer or an ordinary desk to work at, you're going to reach for your wallet. Even if you just have a home office, you probably need many of the same materials that businesses use.

But whatever your needs — office furnishings, office supplies, or packing and shipping products — you can find them at a discount.

**Furnish your office for less.** Shop for filing cabinets, bookcases, desks, chairs, and more for your business or home office with catalogs from these discount companies. Catalogs are free unless otherwise noted.

Alfax Wholesale Furniture
370 Seventh Ave., Suite 1101
New York, NY 10001
800-221-5710

Business & Institutional Furniture Company
Box 92039
Milwaukee, WI 53202
800-558-8662

Frank Eastern Co.
599 Broadway
New York, NY 10012
800-221-4914
Catalog: $1

K-Log
P.O. Box 5
Zion, IL 60099
800-872-6611
<www.k-log.com>

National Business Furniture Inc.
735 N. Water St.
P.O. Box 92952
Milwaukee, WI 53202
414-276-8511

**Save on supplies.** Get everything from paper clips to office machines at tremendous savings from these companies. Contact them for a free catalog of their products.

Business Technologies
3350 Center Grove Dr.
Dubuque, IA 52003
800-451-0399

Fidelity Products Co.
5601 International Pkwy.
P.O. Box 155
Minneapolis, MN 55428
800-328-3034

OfficeMax Inc.
3605 Warrensville Center Rd.
Shaker Heights, OH 44122
800-283-7674
<www.officemax.com>

Penny-Wise Office Products
6911 Laurel Bowie Rd., Suite 209
Bowie, MD 20715
800-942-3311
<www.penny-wise.com>

Reliable Corp.
P.O. Box 1502
Ottawa, IL 61350
800-359-5000

Sunrise Business Products
43 Royalston Lane
Centereach, NY 11720
800-222-PENS
<www.sun-rise.com>

Viking Office Products
950 W. 190th St.
Torrance, CA 90502
310-225-4500
<www.viking.com>

**Pinch pennies on packing.** These companies offer great deals on everything you need to pack and ship your products — boxes, bags, envelopes, labels, wrapping paper, bubble cushioning, and more. Contact them for a free catalog.

ULINE
2200 S. Lakeside Dr.
Waukegan, IL 60085
800-958-5463
<www.uline.com>

U.S. Box Corp.
1296 McCarter Hwy.
Newark, NJ 07104
800-221-0999
<www.usbox.com>

Whether you need furniture and supplies for a large company or just for your personal use, check out these great places for bargains. You and your business will profit from it.

## Promote your business for pennies

When you run a business, whether it's a law office or a landscaping service, you want more clients. Advertising, word of mouth, and a good reputation will help, but don't forget the little things.

You don't need a huge billboard along the side of a highway to get someone's attention. Pens, calendars, caps, or key rings will do the trick. Those are just a few of the promotional items you can find for a discount — or even for free.

**Ample samples.** Some companies that specialize in promotional products give you the chance to sample what they have to offer. For example, Effective Promotions provides free samples of their handy bags, postcards, pens, and pillboxes.

You can request your free samples online at <www.efpromo.com> or contact them by calling 518-274-0291 or writing to:

Effective Promotions
670 Pawling Ave.
Troy, NY 12180

Another source of promotional freebies is Excel Impressions, which offers you a free hat embossed with your company logo. The offer is only available online and limited to businesses who are seriously considering ordering more hats in the future. Check out their Web site at <www.nb.net/~freehat> or e-mail them at freehat@nb.net.

**Wise buys.** Even if a company doesn't offer free samples, it can give you great deals on promotional items.

Get an idea of just how many promotional options you have with Best Impressions. This company has rulers, mouse pads, mugs, sports bottles, flashlights, golf balls, pens, calendars, tote bags and more — all at up to 50 percent savings. For a free catalog, write to:

Best Impressions Promotional Products Catalog
P.O. Box 802
Lasalle, IL 61301

You can also call 800-635-2378 or reach them online at <http://best impressions.com>.

**Card sharks.** Despite all the unusual items available, the standard promotional item is still the old-fashioned business card. But just because it's old-fashioned doesn't mean it has to be boring.

Check out Lighthouse Colorprint, which specializes in full-color business cards. With this creative service, your picture or a picture of your business can be right there on your card. For $5, you can get an order kit, which includes price lists, order forms, samples, and a $25 certificate that you can use with your order. Just send it to:

Lighthouse Colorprint
P.O. Box 465
Saint Joseph, MI 49085

Or you can call 616-428-7062 ext. 2. You can also reach them on the Internet at <www.lighthousecolorprint.com> where you can view samples of their work.

Moore Business Solutions Direct provides two different catalogs, the "Moore Business Products" catalog and the "Image Street" catalog. Both are filled with useful business products as well as promotional materials. To get a catalog, log on to <www.moorebsd.com>, call 800-323-6230, or write to:

Moore Business Solutions Direct
111 Barclay Blvd.
Lincolnshire, IL 60069

You can save at least 50 percent on your printing needs from Mr. Z's Print Services. If you ask for information, you'll also get free samples of their business cards. Shipping is also free. Call 352-683-5683 or write to:

Mr. Z's Print Services
P.O. Box 3368
Spring Hill, FL 34611

Whether you're looking for a business card or a fanny pack with your company logo, you can spread the word about your business without spreading your money too thin.

# HOUSEHOLD DEALS AND DISCOUNTS

Your home is your castle, and you want it to be as attractive and comfortable as possible. However, you don't want to spend a king's ransom to achieve that.

Whether your goal is to decorate your home with style, furnish it for less, or just keep everything in working order, you'll find good advice in this chapter on how to improve your home without draining your bank account.

## Buying quality cookware for less

In many homes, the kitchen is the center of life. It's a warm place where friends and family gather to chat and, of course, eat. You want good cookware to help supply all that wonderful food, but you don't want to spend an arm and a leg to get it. Here are some tips for getting great cookware at cut-rate prices.

**Look for liquidations.** Many small restaurants go out of business within the first year, and their inventory is sold at auction. The cookware is usually top-quality and should sell for a fraction of the original cost. Keep an eye on the public notices in your local newspaper, and make sure you inspect all items carefully before placing your bid.

**Send for mail-order deals and discounts.** Catalog shopping can save you time and money. Here are some that offer free catalogs and discounts on merchandise.

Kitchen Etc. — This company will send you a free catalog offering china, cookware, and cutlery at prices from 20 to 40 percent below retail.

Kitchen Etc.
32 Industrial Dr.
Exeter, NH 03833-4557
603-773-0020
Fax: 603-778-9328

Zabar's — This famous New York City deli offers its wares — food, cookware, and housewares — by mail.

Zabar's
2245 Broadway
New York, NY 10024
212-496-1234
Fax: 212-580-4477

**Net some online savings.** If you're a "surfer," you can take advantage of Internet sites that offer discounts on cookware and other kitchen items. Of course, there are plenty of Web sites that sell at full price, but the good thing about the Internet is that it's quick and easy to do a little comparative pricing. Here are some sites that seem to always have good deals.

Chefstore.com — This site offers up to a 43-percent discount over retail. It also offers free ground shipping on orders over $50. To make the deal even sweeter, Chefstore lets you choose between several different free gifts. The gifts are based on the amount of your order — the more you order, the more valuable your gift. Log on to the Web site at <www.chef store.com> or call 888-334-CHEF (2433).

Variety.com — This site boasts prices that are 50 to 75 percent lower than manufacturer's suggested retail on cookware and lots of other products. You can visit the site at <www.varietydiscount.com> or send for a catalog. The catalog costs $5, but that will be deducted from the price of your first order.

VarietyDiscount.com
Catalog Orders
5018 Ashworth St., Suite G
Lakewood, CA 90712-1289

## Brew up a free coffee offer

If you're a coffee lover, these offers may be right up your alley.

**Free coffee maker.** Cafe Madelaine will send you a free West Bend Four Cup coffee maker when you sign up to receive regular shipments of their coffee. You'll receive four half-pound packages every six weeks. You can cancel your membership at any time and keep the coffee maker. Keep in mind that this offer, like any other, is subject to change, so if you're interested, call 800-248-3204 and ask for department D119CM.

**Free coffee grinder.** Coffee Direct will send you a free Grindmaster Minimill coffee grinder when you buy 5 pounds of their bulk beans. Recently, prices ranged from $27.86 for their "Breakfast Blend" to $118.42 for their "100 percent Pure Estate." Visit their Web site <www.coffee direct.com> or call 800-934-JAVA (5282).

## Major savings on major appliances

Your refrigerator is on the fritz, your washing machine has agitated its last, or your dryer won't dry a damp towel — time to go appliance shopping. Luckily, you don't have to replace large appliances very often. They can last 10 years, 20 years, or even more. But when you do need to replace a major appliance, it can be intimidating. The choices are almost limitless, and it seems as though the prices are, too. Here are some money-saving ideas for buying appliances.

**Save with "scratch and dents."** You can save as much as 50 percent or more by buying new appliances that have scratches or dents in them. Often the blemish is in a spot that goes against a wall, so you wouldn't notice it anyway.

Some department stores will have scratch and dent or repossessed appliances in the regular store, just separated from the unblemished ones. Others, like Sears, will sometimes have their scratch and dents in a separate outlet store. Always check the appliance thoroughly to make sure it contains all the parts you need, and ask about the store's return policy.

**Get lower prices with floor samples.** Even if your local department or furniture store doesn't offer "scratch and dent" discounts, they probably sell floor samples at a discount. There's usually nothing wrong with these appliances, but the model may have been discontinued, or they need to make room for newer samples.

**Consider returned rentals.** Rental stores often have great prices on previously rented appliances. They're not exactly new but usually haven't been used much. Because they've probably been moved several times, they're likely to have scratches or dents in them. Ask if you don't see these on the showroom floor.

**Buy used.** Check your newspaper for used appliances and moving sales. Large appliances can be difficult to move, or they just may not match the decor in the new house, so people will sell them cheap.

Before buying a used appliance, check *Consumer Reports* (back issues are available at most libraries) to see which models tend to last the longest. If you know which models are most reliable, you're more likely to find a used appliance that will last for years.

# Clean your house without cleaning out your bank account

Cleanliness is next to godliness, according to one old saying. Keeping your house clean, however, can be a lot of work and cost a lot of money besides. Cleaning supplies can take a bite out of your budget. Here are some ideas for keeping your home spotless for less.

**Think big.** Bigger is usually better when it comes to cleaning supplies. Large containers of soap, laundry detergent, etc. generally cost less per ounce than small containers. It's also a good idea to skip the fancy squirt or spray bottles. You pay for packaging. Invest in a plain spray bottle, then buy your cleaner in bulk containers with screw-on lids, and refill your spray bottle from the container.

**Make your own.** You don't have to buy commercial cleaners to keep your home sparkling. Some inexpensive household cleaners include ammonia, bleach, vinegar, and baking soda. Baking soda is particularly effective on greasy dirt, because it neutralizes and breaks up fatty acids, so you can then rinse them away. Be careful about mixing household cleaners. Bleach and ammonia, for example, form toxic fumes when mixed.

**Write for free housekeeping hints.** Stubborn spots and stains are the plague of housekeepers everywhere. Find out how to get rid of common stains by writing for a free folder.

Duraclean International
Customer Service Dept.
2151 Waukegan Rd.
Deerfield, IL 60015

**Get free samples.** Keep an eye out for free samples. Even if you decide not to buy the product, if you use the sample a couple of times, you've saved some of your own cleaning products.

★ Waljan Products, Inc. offers free samples of its cleaning supplies, which include products for carbon removal, degreasing, cleaning, and polishing. Call 800-835-7024.

★ Power Orange is a strong cleaning product that claims to remove grease, crayon, and ink from most washable surfaces. For a free sample, visit the Web site <www.yesclean.com/Power_orange.htm>.

**Save by mail.** Some companies offer bulk quantities of cleaning supplies by mail. Staples, an office supply chain, is one example. Call 800-333-3330 for a free catalog.

## Free know-how for home maintenance

If you're a homeowner, you know how expensive home maintenance and repair can be. And it seems to be a never-ending process. Once you get the plumbing fixed, it's time to paint the house, patch a hole in the wall, or replace a window.

The best way to keep more money in your pocket is to become a do-it-yourselfer. If you don't get good information, however, you may spend more time scratching your head in confusion than actually doing the work. You may also end up paying a professional to fix your mistakes.

So before you plunge into the do-it-yourself arena, make sure you're armed with the most important tool — knowledge. And you can get that knowledge for free if you know where to look.

**Ask your extension service.** Your county extension service probably has racks full of free pamphlets on various aspects of home maintenance, repair, and improvement. Look in the county government section in your phone book. Extension services are associated with universities and sometimes also offer seminars and workshops for free or a small fee. Some extension services have a Web site with free info. One good example is the Michigan State Extension Service at <www.msue.msu.edu>.

**Get help from home improvement stores.** As a way to lure you into their stores and encourage you to buy home improvement materials from them, many stores offer free seminars on home repair and improvement. For example, Home Depot and Lowe's both offer regular classes. Call the store nearest you to get a class schedule.

**Search for online aid.** If you have access to the Internet, it can provide a huge source of helpful information.

★ <www.household-helper.com>. On this site, you can sign up for a free e-mail tip to be mailed to you weekly. You can also e-mail specific questions.

★ <http://homeimprovement.netscape.com/homeimprovement>. This site provides how-to guides on a variety of home improvement topics, along with an interactive guide to finding a remodeler or architect in your area.

★ <www.remodeling.hw.net>. This online remodeling magazine has lots of informative articles that may give you ideas on how to improve your home.

**Take advantage of free government info.** Considering the high taxes you probably pay on your home, it's a little consolation that you can get free or almost free information on home maintenance from the government. The Federal Consumer Information Center offers informative pamphlets on a wide variety of topics. Examples include:

★ *Home Improvement.* Helpful advice on when home improvements pay off, how to select different home improvement specialists, and comparing financing options. (Free)

★ *Fixing Up Your Home and How to Finance It.* Information about hiring a contractor, doing the work yourself, and the HUD Title 1 home improvement loan program. (50 cents)

★ *Am I Covered?* Answers 15 common questions regarding homeowners insurance and explains what is covered in a standard policy. (50 cents)

★ *Home Sweet Home Improvement.* Handy tips for home improvement on everything from choosing a contractor to cleaning up the job site. (50 cents)

★ *Keeping Your Home Safe.* Use the crime-stoppers' checklist and other practical tips to protect your home from fire and theft. (Free)

★ *Rehab a Home With HUD's 203(k).* Learn how you can get a long-term mortgage that includes the costs of reconstructing, modernizing, and eliminating health and safety hazards in your home. Find out what properties are eligible, what improvements are covered, and how to apply. (50 cents)

★ *Repairing Your Flooded Home.* Step-by-step advice on cleaning up and repairing your home and its contents after a flood and how to protect your home in the future. (Free)

★ *Should You Have Your Air Ducts in Your Home Cleaned?* Tips on deciding if your ducts need cleaning, choosing a cleaning service, evaluating health claims, and keeping ducts clean. ($2)

To request any of these pamphlets, write or call:

Consumer Response Center
Federal Trade Commission
Washington, DC 20580
202-326-2222
<www.pueblo.gsa.gov>

# Home improvements that make you money

Your home may not need major repairs, but your bathroom still has the original olive-green color scheme, and you'd love to have a more modern kitchen. But is remodeling a practical investment? If you're smart about which improvements to make, you can raise the value of your home while making it more appealing.

**Choose projects carefully.** If you plan to stay in your house forever, cost and your personal preference may be the only considerations when choosing a remodeling project.

But if you ever plan to resell your house, it would be wise to consider what remodeling projects add the most value to your home. Some improvements will add so much value to your home, they will more than pay for their cost. Others may actually decrease the value or marketability of your home.

One improvement that commonly lowers the marketability of your home is a swimming pool. You may long for a pool to lounge beside in the summertime, but many potential buyers see only the expense of upkeep and the hazard to small children. That shouldn't stop you from putting in a pool if you want, but just be aware that your home may be more difficult to sell when the time comes.

According to the National Association of Home Builders, the following home improvements will return most of your investment through an increase in value to your home.

★ Minor kitchen remodeling — 104 percent
★ Bathroom addition — 95 percent
★ Major kitchen remodeling — 94 percent
★ Family room addition — 85 percent
★ Bathroom remodeling — 85 percent
★ Attic bedroom addition — 81 percent
★ Exterior remodeling — 75 percent
★ Deck addition — 78 percent
★ Sun-space addition — 70 percent
★ Home-office addition — 59 percent

**Don't over-improve.** Another thing to consider before remodeling is the average market value of homes in your neighborhood. If the average value of homes in your neighborhood is $120,000, and you make $50,000 worth of improvements to your home, you may not make that much money back when you sell.

If you use your head and do some research, adding those extra touches to your house can actually make you money in the long run.

## Nuts and bolts of hiring a contractor

You've decided to take the plunge and hire a contractor to remodel your bathroom or kitchen. How do you avoid throwing your hard-earned money away on a dishonest or incompetent contractor? Here are a few tips to help ensure that your remodeling project goes off without a hitch.

**Ask around.** Don't just pick up a phone book and call the first contractor listed. Ask friends to recommend contractors who have done work for them in the past, and ask if you can see the finished product. Most people are proud of the improvements they've made to their homes, and they'll be happy to give you the grand tour. Then you can judge the work for yourself.

If you ask around, you may not find the perfect contractor, but you may at least find out who you shouldn't use. One bad review should be enough to make you think twice about using a contractor.

**Check credentials.** Once you've found a contractor, don't let the fact that a friend recommended him prevent you from asking for references — and then check those references.

It's also a good idea to check with the Better Business Bureau to see if he's had any complaints lodged against him. Ask if he belongs to any trade organizations like the National Association of the Remodeling Industry. Often, members of associations are more likely to have a professional attitude and take pride in their work.

Some states require that contractors be licensed. If your state does, ask to see the contractor's license. Check to make sure he is insured as well.

**Get several quotes.** Even if a contractor has a sterling reputation, his prices should be competitive, so get several quotes. You can even get quotes from contractors you're not considering using. It will at least give you an idea of a reasonable price range for the job.

**Ask questions.** You should interview a contractor just as you would any employee. Learn as much as you can about the project so you can talk intelligently about it. Don't be afraid to say you want a second opinion.

**Work out a payment schedule.** Never pay the full price upfront. A shady contractor might never do the work, and an honest contractor won't expect you to pay right away. Arrangements depend on the length of the job and the people involved. Some people pay half when the job is half finished and the balance on completion. If it's a lengthy job, you may set up a weekly amount.

**Get it in writing.** A good contract will help you avoid many problems that can result from poor communication. Make sure you establish prices in advance, and specify a time frame for finishing the work.

---

### Get paid for your opinion

You can receive free products or cash awards if you're willing to spend some time answering a few questions. The American Consumer Opinion panel is a group of households that are regularly surveyed to gather information about certain products and services.

If you join the panel, they may send you a product sample to test before you give them your opinion, or you may receive a cash award up to $25 or more depending on the length of the survey. Members are also entered in a monthly drawing to win $250.

If you're interested in becoming a survey household, visit the Web site <http://acoi.cjb.net/> or call 800-262-5974 for more information.

---

# Cut-rate remodeling materials

One way to save when remodeling is to buy your own materials. Your local builder's supply store (Home Depot, Lowe's, etc.) will usually have the lowest prices because they deal in high volume. But sometimes you can get even better deals when you order supplies through the mail. Check out these manufacturers for some of your remodeling projects.

**Carpet:**

S&S Mills
200 Howell Dr.
Dalton, GA 30721
800-363-6943

Buying your own carpet may save you up to 50 percent off the retail price, but keep in mind that you'll have to pay shipping costs. The Dalton,

Georgia area is home to several carpet mills — this is just one of many. They'll send you samples and price information. If you'd like to check prices at other mills in the area, try calling directory assistance for more phone numbers.

## Bathroom fixtures:

Baths From the Past, Inc.
83 E. Water St.
Rockland, MA 02370
800-697-3871
Fax: 781-871-8533

Redoing your bathroom can add a lot of value to your home. If you're planning an old-fashioned motif, this company may help you do it more cheaply. They offer prices up to 30 percent below comparable items from other sources, and the fixtures are guaranteed for life. Catalogs are free.

## Windows and glass:

Arctic Glass & Window Outlet
565 County Rd.
Hammond, WI 54015
800-657-9276

If you're installing new windows, doors, or skylights, call this company for a catalog. Prices average 10 to 50 percent below retail, and the company promotes the use of insulated glass for ventilation and energy efficiency.

## Wallpaper and blinds:

American Blind and Wallpaper Factory
909 N. Sheldon Rd.
Plymouth, MI, 48170
800-575-8016
Fax: 800-575-2758
<www.DecorateToday.com>

This company offers an 8-percent discount off retail and claims that they will never be undersold. They will also send you a free blind kit and wallpaper catalog.

**Sunrooms and glass enclosures:**

Four Seasons Sunrooms
5005 Veterans Hwy.
Holbrook, NY, 11741
800-368-7732

If you want to enclose a deck or patio, or add a sunroom or skylight onto your house, call Four Seasons and ask for their free catalog. They offer factory savings up to 35 percent.

# Free home info galore

Keeping your home safe and beautiful can be a lot of work. Luckily, if you need help with your "homework," there's a lot of free information available to help you get the job done right. Just look at this array of free booklets that you can send for.

*How to Panel a Room*
Masonite Corp.
P.O. Box 311
Towanda, PA 18848

Free booklets on insulation (ask for list of educational material):

Consumer Inquiry Dept.
Owens-Corning Fiberglass Corp.
P.O. Box 901
Toledo, OH 43601

*Learn How to Wallpaper* (send long SASE)
Red Devil Tools Co.
Box W
Union, NJ 07083

*How to Choose, Use and Care for Tools*
H.K. Porter Co.
Hardware Division
355 5th Ave., #1335
Pittsburgh, PA 15222-2407

*EKCO's Guide to Tools of the Trade*
EKCO Housewares
Consumer Service Dept.
Franklin Park, IL 60131

*Window Idea Book*
Pella Windows Co.
100 Main Street
Pella, IA 50219

*Understanding Carpet Quality*
Free Project Planning Pack
Armstrong Tile
Consumer Affairs Dept.
P.O. Box 3001
Lancaster, PA 17604

*Beautiful Walls* (25 cents)
Georgia-Pacific Corp.
900 SW Fifth Ave.
Portland, OR 97204

*Stripping Paint From Wood* (booklet #331A — 50 cents)
Consumer Information Dept. R.O.
Pueblo, CO 81009-0011

*See Your Home in a New Light* (booklet gives proper use of lighting)
General Electric Lamp Division
Nela Park
Cleveland, OH 44112

List of do-it-yourself plans for the home craftsman:

Home Craftsman Plan Dept.
Western Wood Products Association
1500 Yeon Building
Portland, OR 97204

*Homeowner's Guide to Insulation and Energy Savings*
M.S.U. Meeks
Owens-Corning Fiberglas Corp.
Fiberglas Tower
Toledo, OH 43659

*Your House Is On Fire* (booklet #AA-2982)
Aetna Insurance
Public Relations Dept.
151 Farmington Ave.
Hartford, CT 06156

Free booklet with 16 pages of decorating ideas using ceramic tile (25 cents):

American Olean Tile Co.
1604 Cannon Ave.
Lansdale, PA 19446

## Fabulous furniture deals from the Tarheel State

Every year thousands of furniture buyers flock to the furniture mecca of the universe — North Carolina. If you haven't already heard of this phenomenon, you might be surprised to learn that 60 percent of the nation's furniture is manufactured within a 200-mile area of central North Carolina, around the towns of High Point and Hickory.

The area boasts huge showrooms, offering discounts from 40 to 70 percent — sometimes even more — off regular furniture store prices. If you live in North Carolina you're in luck, but if you live elsewhere, how do you take advantage of these great discounts?

**Do your homework.** Visit furniture stores in your area and decide what kind of furniture you want. When you've narrowed your choices to two or three styles, write down the manufacturer and number. Then you can focus your search on specific styles.

**Call ahead.** Find out which company carries the furniture you want. If you plan to make a trip, it will save you lots of time wandering through huge showrooms.

**Figure expenses.** You can fly to North Carolina and have your furniture shipped to you, or you can rent a truck and drive. If you drive, you'll save shipping and be able to bring your furniture home with you. If you have it shipped, you'll have to add about 10 percent to your purchase price, but you won't have to pay sales tax on items shipped out of state.

**Fly and buy.** If you decide to fly to North Carolina, you should know about fly and buy deals. Several furniture manufacturers, along with US Airways, offer package deals from selected cities that include discounts on hotels and rental cars. To check on current deals, send an e-mail to fly andbuy@ncnet.com, or call US Airways. You can also ask specific stores if they have package deals.

**Gather pertinent information.** You don't want to fly all the way to North Carolina and then try to decide what size sofa will fit in your living room or what colors will go with your carpet. Before you leave, take measurements, and if you have carpet, paint, or wallpaper samples, take them. If not, take pictures. This is probably a good idea even if you've settled on a specific style. You never know when something else might catch your eye.

**Time it right.** Twice a year, the furniture stores in North Carolina have a furniture market — one week in April and one week in October. During these weeks, the stores are closed to the public. The best time for bargains are after Christmas and during the August end-of-season sales.

For more information, call the North Carolina Division of Tourism, Film and Sports Development, 800-VISIT-NC (847-4862); High Point Convention and Visitors Bureau, 800-720-5255; or the Hickory Convention and Visitors Bureau, 800-849-5093.

Here's a sampling of store phone numbers to get you started:

- ★  Hickory Furniture Mart, 800-462-MART (6278)
- ★  Catawba Furniture Mall, 800-789-0686
- ★  Shaw Furniture Galleries, 336-498-2628
- ★  Rose Furniture, 336-886-6050
- ★  The Atrium, 336-882-5599
- ★  Carolina Discount Furniture, 828-396-2347
- ★  Medallion Furniture, 336-889-3432

## Cost-saving furniture finds

If you don't have time to make a trip to North Carolina but still want to save money on furniture, here are some ideas for finding great deals.

**Look at rental stores.** Most rental stores will sell furniture after a certain period of time. Check the yellow pages for stores near you. Inspect carefully before buying. If you find blemishes, you may be able to get a better price.

**Find out about floor samples.** Ask about floor samples at furniture or department stores in your area. Many will sell them at a discount when they need room for new merchandise.

**Tour a model home.** Many new subdivisions have beautifully furnished model homes to entice buyers. Stop in and ask what they plan to do with the furniture when the home sells. Sometimes the builder simply moves it into another model, and sometimes the new homeowner wants to keep it, but often they sell the furniture to the public at a discount. There may even be a model home furniture reseller in your area. Check the yellow pages.

**Consider buying used.** Check your local newspaper for moving sales and estate sales. You can often get great deals on nearly new furniture or sturdy antiques.

**Talk to a designer.** Interior designers sometimes have odd pieces of furniture that a customer ordered but decided not to use for some reason. If the piece works for you, however, you may get a great discount on it.

**Finish it yourself.** If you're willing to do a little work, you can save a bundle by purchasing furniture that's unassembled or unfinished and putting the finishing touches on yourself.

## Buying fine art on a poor man's budget

If you have a taste for fine art, but not the budget for it, don't despair. Decorating your home with art doesn't have to be expensive.

**Find hidden talent at art schools.** Wouldn't you love to have been one of the first people to buy a Warhol or an O'Keefe? If you check with your local university or art school, you may be able to get the early work of a future famous artist for next to nothing. Even if your budding artist doesn't bloom in your lifetime, if you like what you buy, you've made a good purchase.

**Check out charity auctions.** Unless you really know a lot about art, auctions may not be a good idea for getting deals. You might get caught up in the bidding process and actually pay more than a piece is worth. However, charity auctions conducted by art museums can be a smart move, because whatever you pay is usually tax-deductible. Besides, they're a lot of fun.

**Investigate artsy Web sites.** Buying art on the Internet may not be as much fun as attending a black-tie art auction, but it can save you time and money. Plus you have the convenience of searching through thousands of prints and more to find just what you need.

Interested in collecting prints from a specific artist? Just type in the name and browse through the selections. Or search by a particular style — it's simple. Here are a few good Web sites for buying discounted art.

★ <art.com>. This Web site offers discounts of 20 to 50 percent off retail on prints, limited edition prints, and original artwork. You can purchase most works framed or unframed, and standard shipping is free on orders of $30 or more.

★ <artselect.com>. This Web site offers 40 to 50 percent off custom framing. It also has a satisfaction guarantee policy. If you're not satisfied with your order, you can return it within 30 days for a full refund. You have to pay the return postage.

★ <momastore.org>. If you're a fan of modern art, but can't make it to New York to browse through the Museum of Modern Art (MoMA), you can surf its store's Web site for some great deals. There's a section for sale items with an extra discount for MoMA members. For example, the Web site recently featured a Pierre Bonnard poster for $19.95 that originally sold for $45. Check back often to get the best deals.

# A hodgepodge of free household items

You're a thrifty person, so you're sure to appreciate these freebies for all around the house.

**Bundle up in a wool blanket.** The Pendleton company, which makes wool products, holds a free drawing every month. If you'd like to win one of their warm wool blankets, just visit their Web site at <www.pendleton-usa.com>, fill out a form, and you'll be entered in their monthly drawing.

**Safeguard your children from window treatments.** Since 1981, more than 140 children have died by strangling on window treatment cords. One company would like to help prevent any more of those deaths. No Brainer Blinds will send you two breakaway tassels or two cleats (to anchor cords out of children's reach). Send a self-addressed stamped envelope (with two stamps) to:

No Brainer Blinds and Shades
One Brainer Tower
6135 Kirby Drive
Houston, TX 77005

Write "tassel" or "cleat" on your return envelope. You can also visit their Web site <www.nobrainerblinds.com> or call 888-466-2724 for more information.

**Learn to fancy-fold napkins.** Folding napkins in unusual designs adds an elegant touch to your dinner table. Find out how to master that skill for free. Send a business-size self-addressed stamped envelope to:

Homespun Fabrics Co.
P.O. Box 3223
Ventura, CA 93003

**Feel the warmth.** There's nothing cozier or more romantic than curling up in front of a fire. You can get a case of Duraflame firelogs for free if you win one of their online contests. One recent contest involved telling them how you spend your time in front of your fire. Another required you send your favorite Halloween photo taken in front of the fireplace. To participate, go to <www.duraflame.com>.

**Try an amazing wall primer.** Draw-Tite is a product that is used for preparing dry wall for paint or wallpaper. It also works to repair torn drywall. The manufacturer will send you a free sample so you can see for yourself how well it works. Write or call:

Scotch Paints
555 West 89th Street
Gardena, CA 90248
310-329-1259

**Light a candle in your home.** Candles decorate your home and provide soft, romantic light and sweet fragrances. Burning Desires, a candle manufacturer, offers a free dozen candles when you buy a dozen of the same type. Visit their Web site <www.freecandles4u.com> or call or write for more information.

Burning Desires — Free Candles 4 U
143 S. Main
Osceola, IA 50213
515-342-7058

**Child-proof your electrical outlets.** If you ever have young children in your home, it's important to take certain safety measures. Curious children can easily get hurt. To eliminate one hazard, you can get 20 free safety outlet plugs. Just send $2 for shipping and handling to:

F&H Baby Products
PO Box 566
Chagrin Falls, OH 44022

# Posters for pennies — or less

If you're decorating on a shoestring, posters can be an inexpensive way to dress up bare walls. You can sometimes even get them for free since posters are a popular promotional item.

**Just do it.** Keep an eye out at sporting goods stores for posters featuring athletes. They may have an advertising logo (Nike, Spalding, Reebok, etc.) on them, but they can be especially appropriate for decorating a young person's bedroom.

**View a video poster.** If you're into movies, your local video rental stores may be a source of decor additions. Some video stores give away the movie posters when the movie is no longer popular.

**Plant a tree.** Each year the National Arbor Day Foundation conducts a contest in which fifth-graders draw posters based on a theme. The winning drawing is then offered as a free poster to help educate people about the value of trees. Contact:

National Arbor Day Foundation
100 Arbor Ave.
Nebraska City, NE 68418
<www.arborday.org>

**Admire scenes from Minnesota.** The University of Minnesota will send you a colorful poster featuring scenes from their state. Send $3 for postage and handling to:

Free Poster Offer
University of Minnesota Press
111 Third Ave. South, Suite 290
Minneapolis, MN 55401

**Just say no to drugs.** The National Clearinghouse for Alcohol and Drug Information will send you a free anti-drug poster featuring Martin Luther King, Jr. Call 800-729-6686 and mention inventory number AV165.

**Show your love for music.** If you're a musician or music buff, D'Addario will send you up to five free gifts, including posters. Visit their Web site at <www.daddario.com>. And don't forget to check specialty music stores for freebies, too. Sometimes they give away posters featuring musicians with their favorite brand of instrument.

**Remember the 60s.** To get a colorful fractal poster featuring wild 60s-type button designs, send a self-addressed, stamped envelope to the following address. If you want the poster mailed flat, send an 8.5x11 envelope.

Web Page Fractal Poster Offer
P.O. Box 511411
Salt Lake City, UT 84151-1411

**Support the environment.** The Environmental Protection Agency offers a series of educational posters featuring water resources. The posters are available in color or black and white and are designed to join together to form a wall mural. Poster titles include:

★ *Water, The Resource That Gets Used and Used and Used for Everything!*
★ *How Do We Treat Our Wastewater?*
★ *Wetlands: Water, Wildlife, Plants, and People!*

★  *Ground Water: The Hidden Resource!*

★  *Water Quality: Potential Sources of Pollution*

★  *Navigation: Traveling the Water Highway*

★  *Hazardous Waste Cleanup and Prevention*

★  *Watersheds: Where We Live*

★  *Oceans — Coastal Hazards: Hurricanes, Tsunamis, Coastal Erosion*

If you're a teacher, or have children who would benefit from these posters, write to the following address and specify the poster title and grade level of the children it is intended for —K-2, 3-5, or 6-8.

U.S. Geological Survey
Branch of Information Services
Box 25286
Denver, CO 80225
800-ASK-USGS (275-8747)

**Promote girl power.** If you have a young girl in your life, or just feel like one yourself, you can order Girl Power merchandise, including posters, from the National Clearinghouse for Alcohol and Drug Information.

Visit their Web site <www.health.org > or call 800-729-6686. Offers change from time to time, but one poster offered is a Girl Power sports poster featuring girls playing different sports. The inventory number for that poster is GPSPTF. Another poster features the young gymnast Dominique Dawes. The inventory number for that poster is GPDDP.

# Decorate your fridge with free magnets

If you scratched your new refrigerator getting it in the door, or if you just like hanging your favorite child's artwork on your refrigerator, a refrigerator magnet can cover your boo-boo or secure your future Picasso's handiwork. Many companies offer free refrigerator magnets as promotional items. Here are some to choose from.

**Personalized magnet.** This company will make a personalized magnet from your photograph or drawing. Send your photograph (up to an 8x10 size) to:

Fridge Magnet Offer
P.O. Box 322
Montreal, Quebec
Canada H4A 3P6

Don't forget to include your name and address, or visit its Web site <http://freefridgemagnets.freehosting.net/page1.htm> for a form to print out and send. There's no charge for the magnet, but the company would appreciate $2 to cover postage and handling.

**Comic magnet.** If you'd like a comic book character on your refrigerator, send a self-addressed stamped envelope to:

Free Megaton Magnet Offer
c/o Fiasco Comics Inc.
P.O. Box 64
Wexford, PA 15090-0064
<http://www.megatonman.com/misc/sase.html>

**Programmer magnet.** Drop this guy a note saying you'd like a free magnet, and he'll send you one — providing he has any left. Send your business card and a self-addressed stamped envelope (55 cents postage) to:

Kwan Software Engineering, Inc.
1030 E. El Camino Real, PMB 243
Sunnyvale, CA 94087-3759
408-745-1538
<http://www.windowsprogrammer.com/freestuff.htm>

**Writer's magnet.** Send this author a business-sized, self-addressed stamped envelope with "Attn: Magnet Offer" on the outside, and she'll send you a free "Rebecca Sinclair" mood magnet.

Rebecca Sinclair
P.O. Box 15385
Riverside, RI 02915
<www.eclectics.com/rebecca>

# SUPER SAVINGS ON UTILITIES

They come to your mailbox every month without fail — those dreaded utility bills. And every month, you probably look at them in shock and wonder why you have to pay so much for water and electricity. They were once considered conveniences — luxuries even, but now they're just the necessities of modern life. Since you have no desire to live like the pioneers, you pay ... and pay and pay.

This chapter offers you valuable advice on how to cut your utility bills, how to wade through all the confusing telephone information, and how to avoid hidden costs. You'll even find out how to make long-distance calls for free. So turn down the lights, fire up the candles, and read on.

## Free your phone bill from hidden charges

Phone companies have lots of ways to make back the money they lose by offering those amazingly low long-distance rates. Regular charges are often hidden in the fine print of your calling plan, and you might not know about them until they show up on your monthly phone bill. Here are some common hidden charges to watch out for:

★ **The switch off.** Most companies charge a $5 fee to switch your plan from one long-distance provider to another. Ask to have this fee waived before agreeing to switch companies.

★ **Expensive help.** A few extra minutes to look up a number in the phone book can save you 35 to 50 cents in directory assistance fees every time you place a call. Long-distance directory assistance is even more costly, sometimes as much as $1 or more. For free long-distance help, look up your number on the Internet at <www.four11.com>.

★ **Busy signal blues.** If you need to verify a busy signal, you will be charged. Some companies even assess the fee for this service when it's used during an emergency.

★ **Callback payback.** Convenience features like Star-69 or auto-matic redial for busy signals usually charge around 75 cents per use. Like other optional features, you can put a block on these services to help yourself fight temptation.

★ **Anonymity fee.** If you don't want your number listed, it could cost you up to $2 per month. Same goes if you want to be listed under more than one name. To avoid the unlisted charge, some people list their phone numbers under a false name.

Always check your bill each month, and don't be afraid to dispute charges you don't understand. If your phone company sticks you with a lot of extra fees, don't stay with them. Sometimes, just threatening to switch can convince them to drop some of their extra charges.

## Long distance on the cheap

For someone with lots of friends and relatives who live out of state, or even just across the state, the long-distance phone bill at the end of the month can come as an ugly surprise. Lots of discount long-distance plans are in the marketplace today, but many have hidden costs that make them less than bargains. What you need is a simple, straightforward calling plan with no surprises.

Here are four long-distance plans that seem to live up to their billing as simple and money-saving. Their rates apply any time of day or night and any day of the week.

**GTC Telecom** is available in 47 states right now, with the other three (Alaska, Hawaii, and New Mexico) to be added in the future. Its long-distance state-to-state rate is 5 cents a minute if you pay by credit card. If you want your long-distance calls billed with your local phone company, you'll be charged an additional $1.95 per month.

Prices on long distance within each state vary from 8 cents to 15 cents per minute or more. You need to check on the cost for your own state. To contact GTC Telecom, call 800-486-4030, or visit the Web site at <www. gtctelecom.com>.

**Uni-Tel** sells you long distance calling for just 4.9 cents a minute if you use more than 307 minutes (5.12 hours) a month. This works out to about 30 minutes a day of talking time for just over $15 a month. If you use less time, you still get the 4.9-cent rate, but there is an extra charge of $2 per month.

You can also get a personal toll-free number for $2.50 a month. This allows people to leave voice messages for you, which you can retrieve at the regular rate from any remote location. It's a helpful feature for frequent travelers. Intrastate prices vary. You can reach Uni-Tel on the World Wide Web at <www.star69.net>.

**Five Cent LD.com** has long distance interstate rates of 5 cents a minute. You pay by credit card, but they will e-mail you a Web address every month where you can view your charges in detail. There are no added fees and no minimum number of minutes required. Their intrastate charges vary widely, but if they are high in your state you can choose Five Cent LD for your state-to-state calls only. You can write, call, or reach the company at their Web site.

National Accounts, Inc.
28 Hill Road
Parsipanny, NJ 07054
800-304-5267
<www.5centld.com>

**BigZoo.com** has some of the lowest long-distance rates around, with no hidden charges. Both interstate and intrastate long-distance calls cost just 3.9 cents a minute. The prices on international calls vary, but seem competitive. To use this system, you purchase a prepaid phone account in amounts of $5, $10, $20, or even $50 and pay over the Internet with a MasterCard or Visa. For $20, you can talk long distance for more than eight-and-a-half hours. Once you sign up, you access the system with an 888 (toll-free) number and your own PIN (Personal Identification Number).

You can use your Big Zoo calling card account from anywhere in the United States except Alaska and Hawaii. You can even use it on most cell phone accounts to save money on long distance. If you use Big Zoo from a pay phone, you must pay a 55-cent surcharge mandated by the FCC (Federal Communications Commission). Otherwise, that's it. You can reach Big Zoo on the Internet at <www.bigzoo.com>.

# Dial up a cheap phone bill

How would you like to know quickly and easily which phone carrier will give you the cheapest rates? If you have access to the Internet, you can use a Web site called Star69.net to compare the bottom-line costs and services of various calling plans.

This free service takes into account the type of calls you make most (within state or out-of-state), the average length of your calls, and the costs of service in your particular state. Using their formula, you can get a good idea of which plan would be the most economical for you to use.

To reach Star69.net on the World Wide Web, go to <www.internet offer.com/star69.net/longdistance101.html>.

Here are a few things to keep in mind when figuring out your phone costs:

★ Calling long distance within your state (intrastate) is usually more expensive than state-to-state (interstate) calls, and rates vary depending on where you live. You need to check the price in your state with each phone company.

★ The true price of your monthly long distance also includes two federal taxes. The PICC taxes the use of local phone lines, and the carriers pass the cost on to you. It is usually a small fee, less than $3 per residential line. The USF (Universal Service Fund) tax charges 4 to 8 percent on all interstate and international calls. This pays for phone lines in low-income or inaccessible areas, libraries, and schools.

★ With some plans, you must talk for a minimum number of minutes per month to get the advertised price. Decide whether or not your calling habits make this a good buy.

★ Some companies charge a connection fee, a flat monthly fee, or a fee per call in addition to the per-minute charge. Be sure to find out if such charges apply.

★ Calls may be billed by the full minute or by increments of six seconds. In the long run, it doesn't usually make a lot of difference in the price of the service unless you have a huge volume of long-distance minutes. The six-second plans often add a fee per call.

# Save big on overseas calls

Calling from the road can be expensive if you're not careful, but calling home from overseas can break the bank. Using these phone-company tips can save you a lot of time, money, and hassle when dialing from distant lands.

**Check your code.** The long-distance company you use at home can provide you with rates and access codes that you'll need to place international calls. Write these down before your trip. Without them, you may find yourself at the mercy of unknown foreign companies charging whatever they want.

It's possible that not every phone you find on your trip will accept your codes, but be patient. Taking the time to find one that does will ensure that you don't pay more than you should.

**Beware of check-in temptation.** Hotel room phones are pay phones just like any other and don't necessarily have the best rates for long distance or local calls. Be sure you know the rates before you opt for the expensive convenience of in-room dialing.

**Check with the help.** Desk clerks and hotel personnel can be helpful in finding phones and local companies with affordable long-distance rates.

**Keep the help in check.** Sometimes, hotel operators are told to connect callers to a specific long-distance provider, an arrangement that isn't always to the guest's advantage. Ask about direct-dial rates, which may be cheaper, before agreeing to connect to the hotel's regular provider.

**Double check posted rates.** Try to use phones that list competitive rates for long-distance calls, but don't take their word for it. Be sure to confirm with the operator before placing your call that the posted rates are what you'll be charged.

# Call on your computer for free long distance

Some of the best things in life are free, and now you can add to that list a phone call to a far-away friend. If you have a personal computer and Internet access, you can actually make long-distance calls for free. The call goes through your computer to the other person's phone, so they don't even need a computer to enjoy a free call from you.

How can Internet companies afford to give you free long-distance service? It works like radio — advertisers pay the companies to get their products in front of you. The banners and other ads on the Web sites pay for the service.

Here are three free long-distance providers you might want to check out:

**Dialpad.com** allows you to call anyone in the United States for free by downloading a small "applet" to your computer. You don't have to interact with any ads or advertisers; the banners simply run across your computer screen as you talk. You can talk for as long as you like. An online company linked to their Web site can sell you a headset for around $5 to make talking easier. You can reach them at <www.dialpad.com>.

**Callrewards.com** allows you to make free phone calls to anyone in the United States, and international calls are also available. All you have to do is download software from their Web site and you're in business. If you have an "Internet PhoneJACK," you can plug your telephone into it and dial as usual. If not, you can use a headset plugged into your computer to listen to the phone call, or simply use your microphone and speakers to talk and listen to your friend at the other end of the line.

You earn points toward the free phone calls by reading and listening to ads, visiting Web sites, and buying products from the advertisers. You also get points by referring friends to the service. The Web site is at <www. callrewards.com>.

**Hotcaller** allows you two minutes of long-distance calling in exchange for watching one of their Internet ads. For international calls, you need to view two ads for every two minutes of phone time. You simply decide in advance how many minutes you plan to talk, and watch the appropriate number of ads. A tone notifies you when you have 30 seconds of talking time left. You will find Hotcaller on the Internet at <www.hotcaller.com>.

The only catch to this free long-distance calling is that the sound quality is not as good as regular long distance. It varies depending on the speed of your modem and the traffic on the Web when you call. Also, because your voices are traveling over the Internet, there may be a slight delay as you speak.

If you can adjust to these minor problems, you may decide this is a great deal. After all, the price can't get any better than free.

# 9 ways to discount your energy costs

If your home is powered by electricity, you're spending almost half your monthly energy costs on heating and cooling. Lighting, cooking, appliances, and hot water guzzle the rest. With electricity averaging more than 8 cents a kilowatt hour, you're probably spending a lot more each month than you can afford.

Here are some easy and practical ways to give your budget an energy discount.

**Turn down the thermostat.** Keeping it at 55 degrees at night is one of the simplest ways to cut your energy costs. Throw on an extra blanket, and you won't miss the extra heat. Turn the thermostat to 65 degrees during the day when no one is home.

By setting back the thermostat 15 degrees, you can lower heating expenses by 30 percent. If your fuel costs average $1,000 a year, that's a $300 savings.

**Insulate intensively.** Install insulation with a value of R30 in your attic and underneath floors, especially those over crawl spaces and basement areas. If you live in an old house without insulation, you can have shredded or foam insulation blown into the outer walls.

**Protect those pipes.** When you insulate, think about your ductwork also. The pipes that carry warm or cool air through your house could be leaking and keeping your attic more comfortable than your bedroom. Have the ductwork checked, and seal any leaks, then insulate around it wherever you can for a really efficient air-handling system.

**Weatherize well.** Hunt for cracks, holes, and small leaks around the outside of your house. Then caulk, seal, and weather-strip anything you find. Don't forget the areas around electrical outlets and plumbing. You can save as much as 10 percent on your energy bill simply by plugging holes.

**Heat water wisely.** Save money by lowering the temperature of your water heater to about 115 degrees. You won't miss the extra heat, and it's actually safer for young children and seniors. You can also buy an insulating kit for your water heater that will keep your water hot at all times.

**Turn off the lights.** Use natural light whenever possible by opening drapes in the daytime and enjoying the sun. Turn off lights when you're not using them.

Buy compact fluorescent light bulbs instead of incandescent bulbs. Although expensive, they will last longer and use 90 percent less electricity, saving you $25 to $40 over their lifetime.

**Check your windows.** Even if your windows are tightly closed, some air will still get in and out. You can help insulate with some simple additions.

★ Tinted window film, applied directly to the glass, can help keep heat out in the summer and reflect it back inside in the winter.

★ Storm windows are a good investment and should pay for themselves quickly through the energy discount they provide.

★ If storm windows are too expensive, you can staple heavy plastic around the outside of your windows. Or tape thinner plastic on the inside to keep the air from sneaking through.

**Landscape luxuriously.** Plant trees to shade your home from heat in the summer. Use trees and shrubs on the north and west sides of your house to shield it from winter winds. Two fast-growing trees are the Leland Cypress and the Austree, an Australian import that grows eight to 15 feet in one year and flourishes in most climates.

**Use your fireplace properly.** Close the damper when you're not using your fireplace, or your warm air will go right up the chimney. When you do light a fire, open the damper, close the doors leading to the room, open a nearby window about one inch, and turn your thermostat down to 55 degrees. This will help reduce heat loss.

To make your fireplace even more efficient, you can install glass doors and a blower to direct the heat back into your house.

## Experts hand out free $-saving info

Everybody loves free advice on saving money. And who better to help you cut energy and utility costs than these experts.

**Think pink.** You know them by their pink Fiberglas insulation and their company spokesman, The Pink Panther. But more than that, the Owens Corning company can answer any question you may have about insulating your house properly.

They'll help you find insulating products in your area and can even locate a local installer or builder to help you put in the insulation. Call their Product Information Line, visit their Web site, or write for *The Homeowner's Guide to Insulation and Energy Savings.*

Owens Corning Corporation
P.O. Box 901
Toledo, OH 43601
800-438-7465
<www.owenscorning.com>

## A radiant idea for saving on heating bills

If you live in an older house with accordion-style radiators, here's a helpful tip for keeping in more of that cherished heat.

- Go to your local hardware store or home center and buy some sheets of foam-board insulation that are lined with foil on one side. These are used as insulation in new construction.

- Measure the size of each radiator and use a sharp knife or utility knife to cut a piece of foam board to fit just behind it, next to the wall.

- Slip the foam between the radiator and the wall with the foil side facing into the room.

The heat from the radiator will now be directed back into your house instead of out through the walls into your yard. The result? A home that is both beautiful and cozy.

**Call up Uncle Sam.** Replacing old or worn out-appliances is an expensive, long-term decision. To help you make the smartest investment, the government's Energy Star program identifies dishwashers, refrigerators, washers, televisions, VCRs, and lots of other items that are especially energy efficient. Get in touch with the people at Energy Star by mail, phone, or the Internet, and start saving money today.

U.S. Environmental Protection Agency
Energy Star Programs (6202J)
401 M Street SW
Washington, DC 20460
888-STAR-YES (782-7937)
<www.energystar.gov>

**Consume less energy.** Wouldn't it be great if there were organizations designed to give shoppers valuable, free advice? There are — consumer agencies like the Consumer Research Council. For their take on buying appliances and products that will save the most energy and money, request the booklet *Save Money & Save the Environment: A Consumer Guide To Buying Energy-Efficient Products for the Home.* Remember to include a long, self-addressed, stamped envelope.

Consumer Research Council
1424 16th St. NW, Suite 604
Washington, DC 20036
202-387-6121

**Hang some weather defense.** Don't throw money out the window. Apply "low-E" film to your windows, and keep heat in during the winter and out during the summer. You'll raise your comfort level and reduce energy costs at the same time. Gila Window Film comes in kits or in bulk rolls and is easy to apply without professional help. It's available in many hardware stores and home centers, or you can buy it through the mail from the manufacturer.

Just ask, and the folks at Gila will send you a free sample kit of their window films in 4-inch by 6-inch sheets. You can try the different styles and colors at home to see what might work for your windows. Contact them by mail, phone, or Web site.

Gila Window Film
P.O. Box 5068
Martinsville, VA 24115
800-528-4481

**Fix it yourself.** It's July and your air conditioner just died. Before you call an expensive repairman, try this free, money-saving alternative.

Visit the Warmair Web site at <www.warmair.com> for useful information and a troubleshooting guide for almost any kind of heating or cooling system. You'll learn how the systems work and how to maintain them. And your pocketbook will love Warmair's quick emergency repair tips for fixing simple problems.

---

### Guaranteed money-savers

Wondering where to find all those energy-saving devices that will cut 30 percent or more off your utility bill? Try the mail-order company, NRG Savers. This company is so confident its products will save you money that it has a full-refund guarantee.

If you don't think their products have performed as promised — even after using them a year — just send them back, and NRG Savers will refund 100 percent of your money.

Take a look at the Web site to get an idea of the amazing array of new energy-saving products. They even have a work sheet to help you figure out how much you'll save with any given product.

You can reach the company at:

NRG Savers
9805 320th Street
St. Joseph, MN 56374
877-363-4614
Fax: 775-406-7130
<www.nrgsavers.com>

---

# 8 easy ways to save water and $$

Water may be everywhere, but it's not free and you won't find any discount coupons for it. So, how can you get it for less? You have to make your own savings, and one way is to cut down on the amount of water you waste.

**Check for leaks.** Sometimes you can't see a water leak. Choose a time when you can avoid using any water for a couple of hours. Read your water meter at the beginning of this time period and then again at the end. If the reading has not changed at all, your home should be leak free.

**Stop the drips.** If your faucet drips one time per second, you could waste up to 2,700 gallons of water in a year. A simple washer and a few minutes of your time could save you the water and the expense.

**Air it out.** For less than $5 apiece, you can install aerators with water-flow restrictors on the faucets in your home. These mix air with the water, so you get the same water pressure but use less water. A low-flow shower head works the same way. You can save up to 2.5 gallons of water per minute by adding devices like these.

**Halt the water hog.** Bathrooms claim almost 75 percent of the water used in a home. If you're replacing a toilet, buy a low-volume unit — it uses less than half the water of a conventional toilet. If you're stuck with a "water hog," simply add an inexpensive toilet dam to the tank. It will take up space and keep the tank from filling up with water.

**Keep your toilet in tip-top shape.** Replace any rusted, worn, or bent parts that can cause leaks and constant running. Check for leaks by adding food coloring to the tank. If color appears in the toilet bowl within 30 minutes, you have a leak.

If the problem is the toilet flapper, as it often is, you can replace it with a "short flush" toilet flapper (around $5), which will save as much as 2.5 gallons of water per flush.

**Use clean water twice.** You can save a lot by reusing much of the slightly used or "gray" water in your household. The next time you don't finish your glass of water, pour it into the nearest houseplant instead of the sink. Or while rinsing off fruits or vegetables, catch the water with a bucket, and use it to damp-mop your floor or water your bushes.

**Cure your kitchen of water waste.** Instead of washing dishes under running water, soap them up from a large container in the sink, and rinse quickly under the faucet. Only run your dishwasher when it is completely full.

Use your garbage disposal as little as possible; it takes lots of water to make it work and just adds to sewer waste and cost. Start a compost heap instead, and let veggies and other non-meat food items nourish your garden.

**Run it only when you need to.** Turn off the faucet while you are brushing your teeth or shaving. Instead of thawing frozen meat under running water, put it in the fridge ahead of time. And instead of running the tap until the water is cold, store a bottle in the refrigerator. Then you can treat yourself to a long, cool drink whenever you please.

## Water your lawn for less

Most homeowners use about half their household water on their lawns and gardens. So how can you save on all that water and still keep your yard looking good? Here are a few tips to help stem the tide.

**Time it right.** Water your yard every third day instead of every day. Get out during the cool early morning hours so your lawn gets a good drink, and you lose less to evaporation. You'll also avoid the peak water-use time of 4 p.m. to 9 p.m.

**Monitor your system.** Be sure you are only watering the grass — not the street, sidewalk, or driveway. Reposition sprinklers as necessary so you don't waste water, and turn off the faucet when the ground is saturated.

**Watch the weather.** Don't water on windy days, or you'll just be watering the air or your neighbor's lawn. Buy an inexpensive rain gauge to check your lawn's moisture level so you won't water when you don't need to.

**Let the grass grow.** Adjust your lawn mower to the highest setting so it cuts your grass to a length of about 3 inches. The extra growth helps to shelter and protect the roots so they need less watering.

**Seal it in.** Use a layer of mulch around the base of your bushes and other plants to help seal in moisture. They won't need to be watered as often.

**Use local plants.** Native trees, bushes, and plants often require less water than plants from other areas. Ask your local garden center for these plants and others that are "drought-tolerant" or need less water.

**Change outdoor habits.** Instead of cleaning your driveway with a hose, use a leaf blower or that old standby, a broom. And when you wash your car, use soap and water from a bucket, then rinse briefly with a small stream of water from the hose. Using a nozzle with a shut-off valve is even better.

# FUN AND GAMES FOR LESS

All work and no play makes life a little dull, so go out and have some fun. Whether you enjoy playing games, watching events, or just being outdoors, you can find free and discounted sports and recreation deals.

Take yourself out to a ballgame without taking a lot of money out of your wallet. Learn how to get trading cards, stickers, how-to brochures, catalogs — even a golf putter — at little or no cost.

Explore bargains for boating, savings for skiing, and cost-free camping. Find out the best places to get cheap sporting goods and outdoor gear. It's all here in this chapter. So be a sport, and start saving.

## Camp like a champ

Ever feel like getting away from the noise and traffic of today's fast-paced world? Does breathing fresh air, sleeping under the stars, and enjoying nature seem more your speed? If so, it's time to pack your knapsack and pitch a tent in the great outdoors. And here are some bargain ways to do it.

**Elect to camp on government sites.** Much of the best land for camping and outdoor recreation belongs to the U.S. government. Luckily, you can use most campsites for free or for a low fee.

With more than 80 million acres, the National Park Service has plenty of room to camp. Whether you're looking for nothing more than a remote clearing or a site with an electrical hookup for your RV, you can find it at a National Park. For a complete catalog of publications about the parks, including a map and guide, write to:

National Park Service
Office of Information
P.O. Box 37127
Washington, DC 20013

To ensure that you have a place to camp, you might want to make a reservation. Not all parks require a reservation, but some of the more popular ones do, such as the Great Smoky Mountains National Park. To reserve a campsite at a National Park, write to:

National Park Reservation Service
P.O. Box 1600
Cumberland, MD 21502

Another good source for prime campsites is the National Forest Service, which has about 4,000 campgrounds and 500 cabins. For information about the sites or to make a reservation, write to:

USDA Forest Service
Office of Communications
P.O. Box 96090
Washington, DC 20090
800-280-CAMP

Campgrounds are also available through the Bureau of Land Management, which features national rivers, wilderness areas, and trails. For a recreation guide, write to:

Office of Public Affairs
Bureau of Land Management
U.S. Department of the Interior
18th and C Streets NW
Washington, DC 20240

**Look where you're going.** Write to the National Park Service for free maps of the areas you're planning to camp in. They'll send up to 10 free National Park maps at a time.

National Park Service
Public Inquiries Office
1849 C Street NW, Room 1013
Washington, DC 20240

Another free map called "Outdoors America" highlights all federal recreation land. You'll be amazed at how much land is available. Write to:

Bureau of Land Management
1849 C Street NW, Room LS-406
Washington, DC 20240

If you're going to hike as well as camp, the U.S. Geological Survey can help you avoid getting lost. You can get a detailed map that shows the contours and elevation of the land for $4 plus a $3.50 shipping charge. Before you commit to paying for a map, you might want to send for a free index and catalog of maps available. To order a map or for the free index, write to:

Denver-Earth Science Information Center
P.O. Box 25286
Denver, CO 80225

## Save big in the Yellow Rose State

They say everything's bigger in Texas, and that includes state park savings. Texas offers a "Bluebonnet Pass" that lets qualified people enter its beautiful state parks for free or at a discount.

If you're at least 65 years old or a Texas resident, you are entitled to 50 percent reduced entry to Texas state parks. Anyone who turned 65 before Sept. 1, 1995 is entitled to free entry.

Disabled people getting Social Security disability benefits receive 50 percent off admission to state parks, and U.S. veterans with a 60 percent or greater service-related disability receive free entry. For more information, write or call:

Texas Parks and Wildlife
4200 Smith School Road
Austin, TX 78744
800-792-1112
<www.tpwd.state.tx.us/park>

Texas may be bigger, but your state may offer similar savings. Check with your state's parks and wildlife administration.

# Gear up for savings

Once you decide where you're going to camp, you have to make sure you have the right gear. Several places can help satisfy all your camping needs, but most of them are best reached through the Internet.

Repeat Performance offers used and discounted outdoor gear. They have backpacks, tents, sleeping bags, clothing, and more. The stock is constantly changing, so the best way to keep up is to continually check their Web site at <www.gearmeup.com>. If they don't have what you're looking for, you can even submit a gear request form. You can also contact them by calling 207-879-1410 or writing to:

Repeat Performance Gear
311 Marginal Way
Portland, ME 04101

Recreational Equipment, Inc. (REI) also has many great deals. To request a free catalog, call 800-426-4840. Even more savings are available on the Web site at <www.rei-outlet.com>, which sells camping and outdoor gear at 20- to 80-percent savings. The items are so cheap because they come in discontinued sizes or colors or "no-frills" designs, or they have slight blemishes.

Out In Style.com is a large retail outlet that also sells military surplus goods. To check out their deals, go to their Web site at <www.outin style.com>. The store also offers bonuses, such as a free computer mousepad with every order or a free sweater for any order over $50.

Campmor boasts a large selection of camping and outdoor gear. For a free catalog, call 800-525-4784. You can also check out Campmor on the Web at <www.campmor.com>.

# Gang way for these boating bargains

You love the soothing rocking of the water, the wind in your face, the tranquility of the sea. You even suspect you have salt water in your veins. Even so, when it comes to boating, you might occasionally need a little help.

**Get all the answers.** The United States Coast Guard Office of Boating Safety has set up Infoline, a toll-free number that allows you to ask real people about recreational boating safety.

Just call 800-368-5647 Monday through Friday between 8 a.m. and 4 p.m., and get answers to all your boating-related problems. You can also e-mail your questions to Infoline@mail.rmit.com, or visit the Office of Boating Safety on the Internet at <www.uscgboating.org>. On the Web site, you can view the latest Federal regulations and online publications about boating safety.

**Learn about lifejackets.** In case you need proof that lifejackets save lives, you can get a 64-page booklet of real-life stories about people who survived brushes with death because they were wearing a lifejacket. Send a $2 check or money order (which includes shipping and handling) and a request for "Saved by the Jacket" to:

National Safe Boating Council
P.O. Box 1058
Delaware, OH 43015

**Read all about boating.** Boat owners can benefit from a variety of free publications from Boat/U.S. Among the free items are a sample of *Boat/U.S. Magazine*, which is filled with boating news and consumer tips; a copy of *Seaworthy*, a publication that helps you avoid accidents and injuries while boating; a brochure called *All About Trailering*, which provides tips on everything from how to select a trailer to how to protect your trailer from thieves; and a free catalog.

To request any of these items, call 800-937-2628 (BOAT), or write to:

Boat/U.S. National Headquarters
880 S. Pickett Street
Alexandria, VA 22304

**Save on water-sports gear.** A free water-sports catalog is available from Overton's by calling 800-334-6541. You can also get a free catalog on the Overton's Web site at <www.overtons.com>.

## Sail away with the best bargains

There's no way around it — boating isn't cheap. Buying and maintaining a boat can get expensive real quick, so any discount you find is worth its weight in gold. If you're patient, you can discover great deals out there. Where? In the mail.

Don't traipse all over digging through marinas, attending boat expos, and haggling with reluctant sellers. Send away for these free catalogs to find discounts worth waiting for.

Defender Industries, Inc.
42 Great Neck Road
Waterford, CT 06385
800-628-8225

Defender's free, 350-page catalog will match any price you can find on any boating accessory under the sun. They've been in business since 1938 with no advertising, a sure sign of their customers' satisfaction. See their Web site at <www.DefenderUS.com> for their full line.

E&B Discount Marine
201 Meadow Road
Edison, NJ 08818
(800) 533-5007

In addition to deeply discounted marine products, E&B can help you find people selling the type of boat you want to buy. Write for their free catalog, or check them out online at <www.westmarine.com>.

## Reel in these fishing freebies

Fishing can be a relaxing, peaceful, and exciting way to spend a day. Whether you fish for food or just for sport, you'll be hooked on these free offers.

Planning to restock your lake or pond? Get free help, and possibly even free trout, from the Federal Hatcheries. Write to:

U.S. Department of the Interior
Fish & Wildlife Service
Washington, DC 20240

The same folks also supply a free informational booklet called *Endangered & Threatened Wildlife and Plants*. You can always read it if the fish aren't biting.

Every fisherman can use a few pointers now and then. For some worthwhile tips on how to catch more fish, send 50 cents for a copy of the "Fisherman's Guide" to:

Sheldon's Inc.
Antigo, WI 54409

Finding the right fishing equipment is almost as important as finding the right fishing hole. Why waste precious fishing time going from store to store in search of the right gear at the right price? Shop from the comfort of your own home with these free catalogs.

Bass Pro Shops offers a variety of free catalogs, not only for fishing but also for hunting, camping, and boating. Write to:

Bass Pro Shops
2500 E. Kearney
Springfield, MO 65898

Or you can call 800-227-7776. You can also visit Bass Pro Shops on the Internet at <www.basspro.com>.

To receive a free Orvis Fly-Fishing and Outdoor catalog, call 800-541-3541 or visit the Orvis Web site at <www.orvis.com>.

Internet users will find a free Recreational Fishing Alliance emblem available online. Go to <www.savefish.com> to get yours.

## Grab gear for less

No matter what sport or recreational activity you enjoy, you need some type of equipment. Being active can get expensive pretty fast. Here are some ways to find quality sports equipment at tremendous discounts.

**Save through the government.** One smart way to get discounted gear is through the Department of Defense. The Defense Reutilization and Marketing Service (DRMS) offers surplus sporting equipment, tents, and even clothing at sealed-bid auctions. You'll find these sales in about 70 locations throughout the U.S. For information on local and national sales, write to:

DRMS-LM2
74 North Washington Avenue
Battle Creek, MI 49017
888-352-9333

Ask for the free booklet *How to Buy Surplus Personal Property* from DoD. You can also check out the agency's Web site at <www.drms.dla.mil>.

**Trade it in.** For an easy way to buy gear for less, check out Play It Again Sports. With more than 550 locations in the U.S., Play It Again Sports is a great source for used sporting goods at affordable prices.

You can sell your used equipment there as well, or trade it in towards something a little better. It's terrific for your children or grandchildren who outgrow equipment quickly or lose interest in one sport and move on to another.

To find a Play It Again Sports store near you, check out the store's Web site at <www.playitagainsports.com> or call 800-476-9249.

**Win on the Web.** If you can get on the Internet, you can also check out Overstock.com, which regularly boasts all types of sports and outdoor gear at up to 70 percent off. The site features much more than just sporting goods, too. Just go to <www.overstock.com>.

Another source for sports gear on the Internet is Fogdog.com. It not only features low prices on an overwhelming amount of sporting goods but also gives tips on what to look for when you're buying certain equipment. The site also offers comparison charts of different brands and the option of searching for your product if it's not listed. You'll find it on the Web at <www.fogdog.com>.

## Save with stores that specialize

If you're shopping for a golf club, you don't need to wade through basketballs or baseball bats. You're more likely to find exactly what you want at a store that sells only golf equipment.

So find a shop that specializes in your sport, and save yourself some time and aggravation. Many of the following stores listed offer merchandise at wholesale prices. Some only sell through the Internet so if you're online you'll have even more choices.

**Golf.** Golf Haus provides a free price list of its golf clubs and accessories, which often sell for up to 70 percent off the retail price. Call 517-482-8842 or write to:

Golf Haus
700 N. Pennsylvania
Lansing, MI 48906

More bargains are available at Discount Golf Shops, which showcase new and used equipment. Go to <www.golfsave.com> to view the deals. You can also contact them by calling 800-241-1474 or by writing to:

Discount Golf Shops
1009 Peachtree Parkway North
Peachtree City, GA 30269

The International Golf Outlet features specials, sales, and free gifts with some purchases. Recently, they offered a free personalized cap when you bought golf balls for $19.99. Their Web site at <www. igogolf.com> also gives you access to another site, <www.golfclubtrader. com>, where you can buy, sell, or trade new or used clubs.

For cheap golf balls, try Golfballs.com, which sells at wholesale prices and gives you the option to buy in bulk. Check out their Web site at <www.golfballs.com> or call 800-37-BALLS (800-372-2557) to find the brand of balls you're seeking.

If you want great deals on name brands like Callaway, Taylor Made, Cobra, Titleist, Ping, or Top-Flite, visit the Discount Golf Superstore at <www.golfdiscount.com>. While you're browsing online, you can chat with a customer service representative, either through your computer or by calling toll-free 888-394-4653 or 888-640-4111.

**Billiards.** Mueller Sporting Goods, Inc. sells not only billiards, but also table tennis, darts, and shuffleboard equipment. The company also makes many of the products it sells. For a free catalog, call 800-627-8888 or write to:

Mueller Sporting Goods
4825 So. 16th St.
Lincoln, NE 68512

You can also shop online at <www.mueller-sporting-goods.com>.

**Hunting.** Bowhunters Warehouse, Inc. features bows and arrows, game calls, camouflage, and more for your bow hunting, bow fishing, archery, and hunting needs. For a free catalog, call 800-735-2697 or write to:

Bowhunters Warehouse, Inc.
1045 Ziegler Road
P.O. Box 158
Wellsville, PA 17365

Another free catalog is available from Herter's, which specializes in waterfowling. Just call 800-654-3825.

**Swimming.** World Wide Aquatics offers up to 50 percent savings on swimwear, wet suits, goggles, and bathing caps. For a free 52-page color catalog, call 800-726-1530 or write to:

World Wide Aquatics
10500 University Center Dr., Suite 295
Tampa, FL 33612

**Tennis.** Holabird Sports discounts tennis equipment and also squash and racquetball equipment, athletic shoes, bags, and more. Shop online at <www.holabirdsports.com> or call 410-687-6400 or write:

Holabird Sports
9220 Pulaski Hwy.
Baltimore, MD 21220

# Take yourself out to the ballgame

When it comes to watching your favorite sports, sometimes television just doesn't do the trick. Sure, TV has close-ups and high-tech graphics, but there's still nothing like the sights and sounds of a live game. But who has enough money to attend a game in person? Chances are, if you're a senior, you do.

Most teams offer senior discounts. Plus they often hand out free items, like caps or pennants, if you ask for them. Just contact your favorite team — you might get a cheap seat and a souvenir.

If you're not a senior or your team doesn't offer a discount, you can still find ways to enjoy a ballgame for less.

**Share a seat.** You could split a season ticket with a friend or group of friends. This is a good idea if you plan to attend several games because the per-game cost with a season ticket is usually lower than individual game tickets. Your seats are usually better, too. Your only problem is figuring out who gets the tickets for each game.

**Go down on the farm.** If you don't need major-league names to have major-league fun, you might want to take in a minor-league game. Think of it as your chance to see the stars of the future before the price to see them skyrockets.

For example, single game prices for a Columbus Clippers International League baseball game in 2000 were $7.50 for a box seat, $6 for a reserved seat and $5 for general admission ($4 for students and $3 for seniors). Season tickets cost $310.

Compare that to the price of seeing the Clippers' big league club, the New York Yankees. Individual game tickets in 2000 started at $8 for bleacher seats and ranged all the way to $42.50 for main level box seats. Season tickets began at $648 for reserved bleacher seats and soared to $4,455 for field and loge-level box seats.

So support your local farm team, and enjoy the sights and sounds of live big-league baseball for less.

## 'Fan'tastic team freebies

It's not easy being a sports fan with players constantly demanding more millions, owners raising ticket prices, and teams threatening to relocate if taxpayers don't foot the bill for new stadiums.

But don't give up on your favorite teams. They still care about the fans and are willing to prove it by giving out all kinds of freebies. Most teams will send you a free package of decals, team photos, schedules, and more — just for being a fan.

Send a business-sized self-addressed stamped envelope (SASE) to your favorite team's "Public Relations Fan Mail Dept." requesting their "Fan Mail Items."

Here's a sampling of addresses from Major League Baseball, the National Football League, the National Hockey League, and the National Basketball Association:

## Baseball
New York Yankees
Yankee Stadium
Bronx, NY 10451

Atlanta Braves
P.O. Box 4064
Atlanta, GA 30302

## Football
Dallas Cowboys
PR Dept.
One Cowboys Parkway
Irving, TX 75063

Oakland Raiders
PR Dept.
332 Center St.
El Segunda, CA 90245

## Hockey
Detroit Red Wings
Joe Louis Arena
600 Civic Center Dr.
Detroit, MI 48226

New Jersey Devils
Byrne Meadowlands Arena
P.O. Box 504
E. Rutherford, NJ 07073

## Basketball
Los Angeles Lakers
PR Dept.
P.O. Box 10
Inglewood, CA 90306

Boston Celtics
Attn: Fan Mail Dept.
151 Merrimac St., 5th Floor
Boston, MA 02114

If you don't see your favorite teams listed here, you can contact the following league offices and ask for your team's address.

Major League Baseball
350 Park Ave.
New York, NY 10022

National Basketball Association
645 Fifth Avenue
New York, NY 10022

National Football League
280 Park Ave.
New York, NY 10017
212-450-2500

National Hockey League
75 International Blvd., Suite 300
Rexdale, Ontario Canada M9W 6L9

## Learn the rules of your favorite games

Who says sports have to be physically exhausting? You can learn about a new activity or brush up on the rules of a game you already know just by flipping through these free informational brochures.

For a ringer of a deal that includes a free pamphlet explaining the rules of horseshoe pitching and a diagram showing you how to build a regulation court, send a long self-addressed stamped envelope (SASE) to:

National Horseshoe Pitching Association
1721 San Ramon Way
Santa Rose, CA 95409

To be served a complete guide and rules for table tennis, send 25 cents for postage and handling to:

U.S. Table Tennis Association
Box 815
Orange, CT 06477

Take aim at great deals with these free booklets about archery. Choose from *Archery Made Easy*, *Bow Fishing*, and *Helpful Hints on Archery Shooting*. Write to:

Ben Pearson, Inc.
Pine Bluff, AR 71601

Walk away with important guidelines for hiking from the publication *Hiking Safety*. Send an SASE to:

American Hiking Society
P.O. Box 20160
Washington, DC 20041

## Hit the slopes with skiing specials

You don't have to be a rich mogul to find good ski deals. Whether you enjoy the thrill of racing downhill or the serenity of a scenic cross-country trail, you can find ways to fit skiing into your budget.

How about having someone else keep track of the great deals at the ski slopes? Just order a free copy of *Ski Cheap*, a newsletter for the northeast United States ski areas. It's full of information about which slopes offer free days, $5 days, 2-for-1 days, and much more.

Send a long self-addressed stamped envelope (SASE) to:

Ski Cheap
P.O. Box 429
Chester, VT 05143

Feeling lucky? If you are, and you're online, you can enter a contest to win free lift tickets. Just go to AtPlay on the Web at <www.atplay.com> to register. You'll have to answer a few questions, such as how often you skied last year and where, as well as provide some demographic information. They say the odds are good, so bundle up and cross your fingers.

Military families can take advantage of OpSki, a unit of the Military Sports and Recreation Network. Check out its Web site at <www.opski.com> for discounts on lift tickets as well as other resort bargains.

Al's Ski Barn provides great savings on skis, bindings, and accessories. You can only shop online at <http://untracked.com/cgi-local/cybershop.pl>. For questions, you can call 207-865-0740.

If you'd rather browse for winter sports equipment or clothing in the comfort of your home, send for these free catalogs and brochures. You can start by calling Marker International at 800-453-3862 or writing to:

Marker International
Corporate Offices
P.O. Box 26548
Salt Lake City, UT 84126

You can also request a brochure on the Web at <www.markeri.com>.

To get a cross-country ski catalog, write to:

Eagle River Nordic
P.O. Box 936
Eagle River, WI 54521

Or you can call 800-423-9730 or visit their Web site at <www. ernordic.com>.

If you're looking for ski clothing, call 800-362-4963 for a free 9-page brochure from The North Face.

For a change of pace, you might consider snowshoes. It could be a fun alternative to cross-country skiing. For a 25-page catalog featuring all types of snowshoes, write to:

Tubbs Snowshoe Company
52 River Road
Stowe, VT 05672

You can also call 800-882-2748 or 802-253-7398 for your free catalog. Or visit their Web site at <www.tubbssnowshoes.com>.

## Be a winner with these free offers

Whether you're a diehard sports fanatic or just a casual fan, you always appreciate the chance to get something for nothing. Following are some great free deals for trading cards, sports jewelry, odds and ends, and even a golf putter. Have fun as you explore the wide world of sports freebies.

**Deal yourself in for free trading cards.** Remember the good old days of swapping baseball cards with your pals, the thrill of finding a rare card, or the excitement of watching a promising rookie card grow in value?

Well, you don't have to be a kid to enjoy trading cards — especially when they're free. Here are a few ways to get free cards.

Get 10 free baseball cards from American Promotions. Just send a long self-addressed stamped envelope (SASE) to:

American Promotions
Baseball Card Offer
P.O. Box 1143
Portage, IN 46368-7401

For football or hockey cards, simply substitute "Baseball Card Offer" with "Football Card Offer" or "Hockey Card Offer" in the address.

Score 10 baseball, hockey, or basketball cards. Just specify which sport you want, and send a long SASE plus 50 cents for shipping and handling to:

Danors
5721 Funston Street
Hollywood, FL 33023

Begin a hockey card collection with this starter kit from S&D. You'll receive two hockey cards, two card holders, and a sheet that explains some facts about hockey. Send a long SASE plus 50 cents for shipping and handling to:

S&D
Dept. P
P.O. Box 114
Casey, IL 62420

Keep track of your cards' value and all the national card shows with a free copy of *Trading Cards Magazine*. Send $1 for postage and handling to:

Trading Cards Magazine
8484 Wilshire Blvd., Suite 900-SF
Beverly Hills, CA 90211

**Spruce up your appearance with sports jewelry.** It's not enough just to be a sports fan. You want everyone to know you're one. What better way than with free sports earrings, broaches, and pins? Here's how to get them.

Bag free broaches from Neetstuf. You'll get two broaches shaped like the balls of your favorite sports (choose from baseball, basketball, football, or soccer). Specify which two you want, and send a long SASE plus 50 cents to:

Neetstuf
P.O. Box 353
Rio Grande, NJ 08242

Pin down a free softball pin. Send $1 for shipping and handling to:

ASA/USA Softball
"Free Stuff" Offer
2801 NE 50th Street
Oklahoma City, OK 73111

Earn free earrings from Animal Crackers Sports Fan-atics. Just tell them your favorite sport and whether you want clip-ons or pierced ear-wires. Include $2 for shipping and handling and send to:

Animal Crackers Sports Fan-atics
50 W. Elm Street
Roselle, IL 60172

**Make off with these miscellaneous marvels.** There's no such thing as too much free sports stuff. So enjoy these great odds and ends.

Make a splash with a free U.S. Swimming Team Olympic decal. Send a business-sized SASE to:

United States Swimming, Inc.
Promotions Dept.
1750 East Boulder Street
Colorado Springs, CO 80909

Rev up with a free Motorcycle USA sticker. Send an SASE to:

Motorcycle USA
Attn: Free Sticker
3550 Rogue River Hwy
Grants Pass, OR 97527

Swing for the fences with a free Louisville slugger pen or keychain. Both items feature a major league player's autograph. Send $1 shipping and handling per item to:

H&B Promotions
P.O. Box 35700
Louisville, KY 40232

Beef up on badminton. Get a free packet about the sport plus a free magnet. Send a postcard with your request to:

USA Badminton
Olympic Training Center
One Olympic Plaza
Colorado Springs, CO 80909

**Putt without the green.** Golf can be an expensive sport, with all the clubs, balls, greens fees, and carts. If you're teed off by how much you have to spend to enjoy 18 holes, this offer is for you.

Green Grass Golf is giving away a free putter that normally sells for $69. The offer is only available on the Web. You will have to pay an $18.95 shipping charge. To get a grip on this great deal, go to the Green Grass Golf Web site at <www.greengrassgolf.com>.

# FREE-TIME FREEBIES

Many people complain that they have less and less free time. But when they get some time to themselves — on the weekends, on vacation, or on retirement — they don't know what to do with it.

After reading this chapter, you'll know exactly how to spend your free time, and you'll know how to do it for free. Even if you are an old hand at leisure, you can still learn a thing or two.

Pick up a few new videotapes and music CDs at no cost. Chart your family tree, and discover the secrets of your heritage. Surprise your loved ones with flowers every day — just don't tell them you got them for free. You can even find some cuddly company — a new kitten or puppy — and a veterinarian to care for them, all for free.

So get out there and enjoy your free time. You'll have even more fun when it doesn't cost you anything!

# ENTERTAINMENT

## Three tips for music bargain hunting

The next best thing to free goodies is goodies at a discount. So check out these mail order and Internet opportunities to get listening treats for less.

**Buy used CDs.** Find that classic album you've been looking for at your nearby independent music store. Unlike the typical big-name mall store, a small retailer often carries used compact discs (CDs). They can be good as new but much cheaper — sometimes half off. On top of their cheap prices, these stores usually are much friendlier than those impersonal superstores. Before you buy a used CD from them, though, check out a few things.

★ Make sure the CD inside the case is the one you want. If not, you might get Madonna instead of Willie Nelson.

★ Check the used CD for scratches or nicks. A damaged CD will skip, making listening to it as pleasurable as someone scraping fingernails over a blackboard.

★ Make sure the store guarantees its items even if the CD looks all right. Then you will have no worries no matter what CD you buy.

★ If you cannot find the album you want, browse the store's bargain bins. Many times, a store will have duplicate CDs and will stick the extras in this box.

**Collect a dozen.** You've probably seen advertisements for clubs like BMG Music Service and Columbia House in your favorite magazine or on television. For just the price of shipping and handling, they offer to send you 12 free CDs or tapes.

One of the catches is that you have to buy more music at regular club prices. BMG requires one more purchase, while Columbia House asks that you buy four to six more albums over the course of two years. During that time, they offer deals like two-for-one sales, so it's not hard to meet the requirements.

One other catch with BMG is that they will automatically ship the selection of the month unless you tell them not to. But it's easy to say no by mailing in your response or logging in online.

A good thing about both clubs is that you can quit as soon as you fulfill your obligation. Columbia House even has a similar special for video tapes and DVDs. For information, write to:

Columbia House Music Club
1400 N. Fruitridge Avenue
Terra Haute, IN 47811-1130
800-457-0500
<www.columbiahouse.com>

BMG Music Service
P.O. Box 1958
Indianapolis, IN 46291-0010
317-692-9200
<www.bmgmusicservice.com>

**Be a safe surfer.** With so many shopping sites on the Internet, how can you be sure you've found the best price for a video, DVD, or music album? Go to Mysimon.com, a Web site that allows you to compare prices from all the major online stores. Visit <www.mysimon.com> and see for yourself.

Before clicking on the "buy" button, you might want to stop at FirstLook.com, where you can preview the movies and music of your choice. Go to <www.firstlook.com>.

For one-stop, inexpensive shopping, a few other sites also stand above the rest.

★ For prices that are $1 or more below anyone else's, surf over to <www.cduniverse.com> and <www.cdconnection.com>.

★ The "Internet Superstore" Buy.com sells older but brand-new CDs as low as $3.85. New ones can go for $9.95. Compared to your typical retail price of $17.99, that is nearly a 45-percent savings. Visit <www.buy.com> to take advantage of the bargains.

★ Instead of buying a whole album, just get your favorite song. For as low as 99 cents, you can download it at <www.emusic.com>.

## Wholesale prices with stay-at-home convenience

These wholesale companies cut the costs of shopping for your music and movie needs. And many guarantee your satisfaction and accept returned items.

**Relive the golden age of radio.** Do you ever feel like hearing those old radio shows again? Adventures in Cassettes sells hundreds of tapes of old radio programs like Abbott and Costello, Crime Classics, and Gunsmoke. Just write or call, and ask for their free catalog.

Adventures in Cassettes
5353 Nathan Lane
Plymouth, MN 55442
800-328-0108
<www.aic-radio.com>

**Add some high culture to your music collection.** For classical music buffs, Berkshire Record Outlet is a must. For $2 cash, you can receive their 220-page catalog of vinyls, tapes, and CDs. Write to:

Berkshire Record Outlet
R.R. 1
Lee, MA 01238-9804
<www.berkshirerecoutlet.com>

**Discover a long-lost favorite.** To buy your beloved classic or hard-to-find movie, talk with Video Yesteryear. They have so many movies that it takes two catalogs to list them all. And they offer specials, such as buy three, get one free. The full catalogs are $4.95 and $3.95, but you can get a shorter list for free. Contact:

Video Yesteryear
Box C
Sandy Hook, CT 06482
800-243-0987
<www.yesteryear.com>

Or write to Cable Films and Video for a free catalog and up to 40 percent off classic films from the 1930s and 1940s.

Cable Films and Video
Country Club Station 7171
Kansas City, MO 64113

Here are some other good Web sites to check for video deals:

- ★ <www.ReelUSA.com>
- ★ <www.moviegallery.com>
- ★ <www.bigstar.com>
- ★ <www.blowoutvideo.com>

# Cheap seats can be yours for the asking

Even though enjoying a video or album at home is mighty comfortable, it is nice to see the real thing live once in a while. And it does not have to be expensive or inconvenient to catch a show, a movie, or a concert.

**Arrive late and get the great rate.** Go to the box office just before or after the curtain rises. At many theaters, you can then pay their reduced ticket price for the opera or play you've been wanting to see.

**Get there early.** Stop fretting about how costly movie tickets are these days. Just be the early bird, and go to a matinee or a dinner-time showing. That way you will save a few dollars on each ticket. On top of this discount, most theaters offer a rebate for seniors at any time of the day.

Also keep your eye out for second-run and third-run theaters, where you can catch fairly recent movies for as little as $1.

**Call first, answer questions later.** While you're working around the house or the office, keep the radio on just in case they're giving away free tickets to sporting events, concerts, and other entertainment. Race to the phone and start dialing as soon as the disc jockey announces a contest. If you are the lucky caller, you might get a great prize.

**Usher yourself in for free.** Ask your local theater if they need volunteer ushers. Many times they do, and they will handsomely repay you for the service by letting you watch the show for free.

**Be on your favorite television show.** Many television shows, such as The Tonight Show, Oprah, and The Price is Right, will let you sit in on a live taping for free. If you will be in the Los Angeles or New York area, pick which show you would like to watch. Mail your request to the appropriate network's guest relations department. They will send you a letter in return, which you can bring with you to the studio to exchange for tickets. Contact:

American Broadcasting Companies (ABC)
Guest Relations
7 West 66th Street
New York, NY 10023
Or:
4151 Prospect Avenue
Hollywood, CA 90027

CBS
Guest Relations
524 West 57th Street
New York, NY 10019
Or:
7800 Beverly Boulevard
Los Angeles, CA 90036

National Broadcasting Company (NBC)
Guest Relations
30 Rockefeller Plaza
New York, NY 10020
Or:
3000 West Alameda Avenue
Burbank, CA 91523

## 5 ways to make life all fun and games

Board games and cards are not just for kids. They can be one of the most fun and sometimes most challenging ways to pass time. If you have always wanted to learn a game, look for free books that will teach you the ropes. And if you have been playing a certain game for years, check out these free and discounted supplies that will help you play for years to come.

**Learn to play the classic war game.** From the U.S. Chess Federation you can receive two booklets about playing this challenging board game. For the first pamphlet, *World Chess Championship Play*, send a long, self-addressed, stamped envelope (LSASE) to:

U.S. Chess Federation
Department 68
186 Route 9W
New Windsor, NY 12250

You can get *10 Tips for Winning Chess* by mailing another LSASE to the same address. Just change the "Department" to 17.

Practice your newfound chess talents online at <www.chesslab.com>.

**Master one of the hardest card games.** Once an American fad, bridge has withstood the test of time and is still a popular card game. Various outlets are devoted only to this game, and they usually offer free merchandise catalogs and low-cost supplies. Baron Barclay, for example, sells books, computer software, and playing cards — everything you need to become a better player at up to 50 percent off. For a free catalog, write to:

Baron Barclay Bridge Supplies
3600 Chamberlain Lane, Suite 230
Louisville, KY 40241-1989
800-274-2221
<www.baronbarclay.com>

For supplies for the variation known as duplicate bridge, browse through a free catalog from:

American Contract Bridge League
2990 Airways Boulevard
P.O. Box 161192
Memphis, TN 38116

Read a free newsletter on how to play the game of bridge. You can even send in your own questions and have them answered in the next newsletter. Visit the bridge foundation's Web page at <www.fifthchair.org/news/index.html>. Then practice your skills as much as you want at <www.playbridge.com>.

**Hit the casinos.** After reading these two informative items on playing blackjack, you will want to get to Las Vegas as soon as possible. For your free Blackjack Strategy Card, write to:

Thomas Gaming Services
P.O. Box 1383
Goleta, CA 93116

Or get a free pamphlet by mailing a self-addressed, stamped envelope to:

Winning Blackjack Strategies
S. J. Lee Enterprises
P.O. Box 333-H
Scarsdale, NY 10583

You can also go online to win cash prizes at <www.gamesville.com> and <www.bigprizes.com>.

**Satisfy all your gaming needs.** AreYouGame.com supplies the Web with games and accessories at a discount. They add new stuff to their site daily. You can see for yourself at <www.areyougame.com>. If you do not have access to a computer, you can contact them at 800-471-0641.

**Load up your computer with game treats.** The Internet abounds with free game goodies. At many Web locations you can download all types of programs.

★ Find checkers games at <www.cs.ualberta.ca/~chinook/Software/software.html>.

★ Solitaire, cribbage, euchre, and other card games are free to have at <http://thehouseofcards.com>.

★ Visit <www.yahoo.com> to play cards and board games against the computer or against some other Web surfer.

## A laugh a day keeps the doctor away

If you have been surfing the Internet at all, you probably know it has a ton of funny stuff as well as other handy information. In fact, every day you can receive a free joke, Internet update, movie review, and more.

All you have to do is subscribe to a listserv, which is a list of people who subscribe to a certain service. Here are a few examples of listservs that deliver jokes and reviews to your Internet mailbox.

★ Get unbelievable but true stories about real people. Send your e-mail to <humorousnews@arcamax.com>.

★ How about jokes that will keep your friends in stitches? E-mail <jokes@arcamax.com>.

★ Find out how good (or bad) that new movie is. Get a free daily review from <moviereviews@arcamax.com>.

★ Keep up to date with new Web sites and services with this listserv. E-mail <newsites@arcamax.com>.

To join one of these, just follow these easy steps.

★ Set up an e-mail account if you do not already have one. You can get free unlimited e-mail from Web sites such as Yahoo.com,

Hotmail.com, or AltaVista.com. Type in their Internet addresses, click on "free mail," and follow their simple instructions to open up a new account.

★ Open up a new e-mail letter. Type the name of the listserv you want to join in the "to:" space. Choose one or all of the ones listed.

★ In the subject space of your e-mail, type "subscribe."

★ You should receive your first reply from the listserv that day, along with one each following day.

## Learn the secrets of your personality

A handwriting expert can figure you out just by studying the way you write your name and address. See for yourself by neatly addressing (in cursive) a large envelope to:

GraphoAnalysis
6109 Westridge Avenue
Suite #13
Fort Worth, TX 76116

On another, smaller envelope, write your address. Again, use cursive and take the time to be neat. Stick a postage stamp on it, and place it inside the other envelope. A short time after you mail it off, you should receive the keys to being you. What a neat way to spend a few minutes!

## Find new friends all over the world

Becoming a pen pal is a great way to meet people with your interests and hobbies. You can also get to know a person from a different country or culture. Either way, writing letters to your new friends would be an entertaining way to pass a day. Here are some ways you can become a pen pal.

**Use the mail.** A pen pal service usually costs a few dollars, but it provides hundreds, if not thousands, of names and addresses from around the world. So the more people you meet using the service, the cheaper the service turns out to be.

Started in 1967, International Penfriends is one of the oldest and best pen pal agencies around. They charge $15 to $20 to join, then point you towards pen pals from around the world who share your interests. And they give your address to 14 other members so you get letters welcoming you to their club. For more information, write:

Julie Delbridge
Coordinator
International Penfriends
P.O. Box 1416
East Camberwell Vic 3126
Australia
<www.ozemail.com.au/~penpals>

Student Letter Exchange also has a directory of hundreds of addresses. Their children's service is free, but they charge adults $10.95 to join. Write:

SLE Adult Directory
211 Broadway, Suite 201
Lynbrook, NY 11563
<www.pen-pal.com/adult.phtml>

**Search the Internet.** Look for free pen pal sites on the Internet. Some pen pal services will charge you money, but that does not mean they are any better than the free services. Two of the largest pen pal Web pages are Andy's International Pen pals at <http://andys-penpals.com> and Pen Connection at <http://penconnection.tripod.com>. Both sites can get you to other pen pal locations on the Web. And they let you look for your new friends by age, hobbies, and location.

**Find sites for seniors.** Some pen pal services are designed just for seniors. See Senior Pals at <www.SeniorSTOP.com/SSPals.html>. Or visit Seniors.com at <www.seniors.com/user/registration.html>. Both are free.

# Profit from your free time

One of the best ways to spend your spare time is to give it to others. When you volunteer, you not only brighten another's day, you make yourself feel better, too.

**Serve your country.** Join the National Senior Service Corps, and be a part of the grassroots effort to better America. When you sign up, you can pick how you want to make your local community a better place to live.

★ Become a community volunteer. Work for the neighborhood watch program, direct traffic at your local grammar school, organize fundraisers — do whatever you're good at through the Retired and Senior Volunteer Program.

★ Help a special child through the Foster Grandparent Program. Change the lives of troubled teenagers and needy children. You will be their tutor, mentor, and friend.

★ Come to the rescue of a disabled senior. The Senior Companion Program gives you the chance to assist those who need it most.

To find out more about signing up for one of these programs, call 800-424-8867. Or visit the Corps' Web site at <www.cns.gov/senior>.

**Share your wealth of knowledge.** Sign up for the Service Corps of Retired Executives (SCORE). If you have run a small business, then you have experiences and talents to give to others. Working for SCORE will let you teach today's budding entrepreneurs how to succeed with their company. Call 800-634-0245 for more information, or visit the Web site at <www.score.org>.

**Join the club.** The American Association of Retired Persons (AARP) can point you in the right direction. It will find you the great volunteer opportunity you're looking for and give you a convenient way to meet other seniors. Call 800-424-3410. On the World Wide Web, visit <www.aarp.org>.

# Enjoy a little free culture

Want to treat yourself to a special afternoon at a museum or zoo? Follow these helpful tips, and you won't have to worry about emptying your wallet.

**Look for free exhibits.** To introduce a new exhibit, museums sometimes host a party. The public can usually come for free to see the new artwork and browse the rest of the museum. If you get there early enough, you might get your share of free wine, champagne, and snacks.

## Find yourself by helping others

For many people, retirement is the time of life when you finally can do what you want. Some people travel, and others settle down in Florida or Arizona to bask in the sun.

Not Joe Chafin. After decades of service with IBM, Chafin prefers to spend his well-earned free time at Georgia's Sweetwater Creek State Park. He volunteers at the beautiful nature preserve, right around the corner from his suburban Atlanta home.

Besides maintaining the many miles of Sweetwater's trails, Chafin also builds and writes the signs that dot the park's walking paths. For the thousands of school children that visit the park each year, Chafin's signs tell the forest's fantastic story, from its days as a Native American camping and burial ground to its tragic part in the Civil War.

Why does Chafin do it? Ask him, and you won't find him short on explanations. For one thing, his work at Sweetwater is uplifting, much more so than his old job. "When I worked for all those years," he admits, "I was always fixing something that was broken. That can wear a person down." Volunteering, on the other hand, helps you to "find yourself."

Volunteering also gives Chafin the chance to connect with his 12-year-old grandson, Matt, who has worked with him for the past four years. During that time, Chafin has watched him grow from a shy, unsure child to a self-confident leader.

Chafin has also touched the lives of hundreds of other kids, and he has found many new adult friends with his same interests. And if it wasn't for his volunteer work, he would never have met the "special lady" in his life.

For anyone who wants to feel useful, Chafin suggests to "just look around you." No matter where you are, you can find a way to volunteer that will make you feel better about the world you live in. And if you are still hesitant, remember that you can give as much, or as little, time as you want. Chafin recommends starting slow and always keeping enough time for yourself.

Even though he didn't move to Florida, he still likes to get in a few rounds of golf.

**Seek out specials.** Zoos and museums often have "free days" for seniors, parents, and grandparents. On regular days they also might discount for large groups and offer valuable membership packages. Group rates can run as low as 33 percent less than individual rates.

For a family, membership at a zoo or museum can pay off quickly, too. As a member, you can visit as many times as you like, and the cost to join the club might be the same price as one visit for a big family. So call up your nearby zoo or museum and find out which days are best to go and what specials it has.

To find the address, phone number, and location of museums and zoos, visit ZooWeb at <www.zooweb.com> and MUSEE at <www.musee-online.org>. ZooWeb links its guests to zoos all around the globe and to international environmental groups. You can also get free ZooWeb postcards and computer software. MUSEE gives its guests access to museum Web sites at home and abroad.

## Borrow America's treasures

Thanks to the National Gallery of Art, you can be the proud owner of some of the finest pieces of art the world has ever seen. Regrettably, they'll only be copies — either on slides or video — and you'll only be able to hold onto them for a limited time. The deal is still well worth it though since it is practically free. All you have to do is pay the fourth-class library-rate shipping fee when returning the material to the gallery.

While you have the gallery's slide collections and videotapes, you can impress your friends and family. Maybe you can even start your own art club, or bring the collection to your local elementary school and give a presentation.

Choose from subjects such as ancient art, American art, Baroque and Rococo, sculpture, and Neoclassicism and Romanticism. And you can select how you want to see them — videocassette, slide, book, or even closed-captioned video. Pick as many subjects and formats as you like.

Just make sure to order your copy ahead of time — at least one month — to guarantee you'll get it when you want it. More than a million Americans request these national treasures during the course of a year. To order, or to receive a catalog of available resources, contact:

Department of Education Resources
Extension Programs
National Gallery of Art
Washington, DC 20565
<www.nga.gov/education/education.htm>

# HOBBIES

## A smorgasbord of hobby bargains

If you're interested in starting a hobby, you won't lack for choices. Here are a few to consider that will cost you next to nothing.

**Build your own boat.** If you have ever wanted to build model ships, now's your chance. Across the Pond specializes in this hobby, and they sell their wares at up to one-third the retail cost. For more information, call 781-639-7017, or visit them on the Web at <www.acrossthepond.net>.

**Create beautiful candles.** Stop buying expensive gift-shop candles. Learn how to make new candles from the leftover wax of your old ones. Just send a long, self-addressed, stamped envelope to:

Pourette Candle Supplies
P.O. Box 17056
Seattle, WA 98107

**Make your own clay.** Learn how to use everyday, household ingredients to create modeling clay. Ask for "Play Clay" when you send a postcard to:

Arm & Hammer Consumer Relations
Division of Church & Dwight Company
Princeton, NJ 08543-5297
800-524-1328

**Get the news about free craft paper.** You can get free or really cheap art paper by heading over to your local newspaper and asking for the "end of the roll." If you're lucky, they'll give you their leftovers, which is a lot of paper. You can use it for gift-wrapping, decorating, or just plain drawing and coloring.

You might want to visit your nearest drapery store as well. Their left-over pieces of fabric could come in handy when you work on your next craft project.

**Try your hand at paper-making.** Learn how to make your own paper with things you find around the house. Send for a free pamphlet from:

American Paper Institute
260 Madison Avenue
New York, NY 10016

**Become the master of ceremonies.** Do you want to become the next Houdini or perhaps start your own puppet show? Why not try both? First, order a free magic-for-beginner's videotape. You'll find it online at <www.learnmagic.org>. You pay only $5 for shipping and handling.

Then send for a free, 32-page booklet on *How to Become A Ventriloquist.* It will teach you how to build a puppet and set up your own puppet show. Write to:

The North American Association of Ventriloquists
Box 420
Littleton, CO 80160

# Wholesale prices make crafts affordable

Crafts, like many items, can be bought cheapest from wholesale outlets.

The Artist's Club sells helpful books, project kits, painting supplies, ornaments, and other arts and crafts items at up to 40 percent off retail. They also accept returns for credit or refund. Order a free catalog by writing to:

Artist's Club
P.O. Box 8930
Vancouver, WA 98668-8930
800-845-6507

Circle Craft Supply sells tools and supplies for making beads, jewelry, dolls, ornaments, and many other art projects at up to 40 percent off. They also accept cash-on-delivery (COD) orders. Send $1 for a catalog to:

Circle Craft Supply
P.O. Box 3000
Dover, FL 33527-3000

For 20 to 50 percent off retail prices, Craft Catalog will sell you supplies for almost any craft including sewing, woodworking, quilting, candle making, and lamp making. A catalog costs $2, but shipping and handling is free with orders over $60. Write to:

Craft Catalog
P.O. Box 1069
Reynoldsburg, OH 43068
800-955-5915

When working on art and painting projects, see how much Dick Blick saves you. You can get brushes, paints, and markers for more than half off, satisfaction guaranteed. Get your free catalog at:

Dick Blick Art Materials
P.O. Box 1267
Galesburg, IL 61402-1267
800-828-4548
<www.dickblick.com>

Art Supply Warehouse is another wholesaler that offers painting and art supplies for far less than retail stores. Prices are sometimes more than 75 percent off. For a free catalog, write to:

Art Supply Warehouse
5325 Departure Dr.
Raleigh, NC 27616
800-995-6778
<www.aswexpress.com>

Get all the craft supplies you need, like paints, glues, wooden models, plastic models, display cases, and dioramas. HobbyLinc.com normally offers low prices but has a super discount page as well. Check out the Web site at <www.hobbylinc.com> or call 770-466-2667.

# A bonanza of stamps for practically nothing

Take advantage of these offers, and you'll start one of America's top hobbies with your own instant collection. Stamp collecting — or philately, as the experts call it — is a fun and even money-making way to spend your time. It is educational, too. From studying your stamps, you can learn about American history and the world.

**Learn how to collect.** Stamp collecting can seem complicated, but it does not have to be. Order these free instruction booklets to learn what stamps to look for. Find out how to care for your collection, and discover the best ways to buy new stamps.

For your first lesson, read *How to Collect Stamps.* The free booklet is yours by writing to:

Littleton-Mystic Stamp Company
96 Main Street
Camden, NY 13316

To learn how to get others to join in on the fun, send away for *You Can Start a Stamp Club,* a free brochure from America's leading stamp authority. Mail to:

American Philatelic Society
P.O. Box 8000
State College, PA 16801

The United States Postal Service will send you free booklets on stamps when you write to:

U.S. Postal Service
Consumer Affairs Department
Washington, D.C. 20260

**Start collecting.** Get your collection going, and start learning from experience. To start your world collection, send away for this mixed batch of 20 American and foreign stamps. With $1 for shipping and handling, send your request to:

Williams
P.O. Box 070914
Brooklyn, NY 11207

Get 26 antique stamps that are each 50 to 100 years old. They are worth at least $2 in catalog value, but they will cost you only 50 cents for shipping and handling. You will also receive other stamps on approval, but without any obligation to buy. Write to:

Falcon Stamp Company
072 ST
Falconer, NY 14733

Now order the big load, the one that will keep you busy for weeks. You can get 200 free American stamps. On top of that, they will send you an information kit and price lists. Just send $2 for shipping and handling to:

Mystic Stamp Company
Department 5A378
Camden, NY 13316

## Turn your spare change into a hobby

Coin collecting is a hobby that can add value to your free time. Here are some freebies to help get you started.

**Learn what it's all about.** Beginners should send away for this free introduction to coin collecting. It is a booklet from America's leading coin collecting club. All they ask for is a long, self-addressed, stamped envelope (SASE), mailed with your request to:

American Numismatic Association
Department AS
818 North Cascade Avenue
Colorado Springs, CO 80903
<www.money.org>

**Get weekly updates.** One of coin collecting's top sources of information has an offer that no collector — beginner or expert — should turn down. Get a free copy of *Numismatic News Weekly* by sending your request on a postcard to:

Numismatic News Weekly
Iola, WI 54990

*Numismatic News Weekly* also will send you free guides for figuring out the value of your coins. One is for gold coins, and the other is for silver coins. Both list prices for American and Canadian change.

**Collect all 50 states.** Here's an easy way to collect the new quarters the U.S. mint has produced over the last few years. Get a display board free from the American Numismatic Society. It is giving away official quarter boards that can be used to display the state commemorative quarters. Send $3 for shipping and handling to:

The American Numismatic Society
Attn: Business Office
Broadway at 155th Street
New York, NY 10032
212-234-3130
<www.amnumsoc.org>

# Pocket these low-cost collectibles

People will collect anything on the chance that someday it will be worth something. An old Mickey Mouse pencil holder, for instance, can sell for $75. Or how about a Planters Peanut popgun, which is worth about $220? With that kind of potential, getting collectibles for free is well worth it. And even if their value doesn't skyrocket, they're still fun to have.

**Enjoy a coke token.** Get the gold bottle Coca-Cola key chain. People from all around the world will recognize and appreciate it. Just send $1.75 for shipping and handling to:

Accent Marketing
831 Beacon Street, Suite 296
Newton Center, MA 02159

**Experience the countries of the world.** Some people travel across the globe to collect other countries' flags and money. You don't need to, though, to collect objects from around the world. You can send for these international collectibles from the comfort of your own home.

Use these 3 1/2-inch flag decals to decorate your luggage, car, or anything else. Pick the symbol of your ancestor's country or the flag of almost any other nation. Just send your request, a long, self-addressed stamped envelope (SASE), and $1 for each flag to:

Parker Flags and Pennants
International Decals
5750 Plunkett Street, Suite 5
Hollywood, FL 33023

To decorate your clothing, order this set of eight pins. Each pin has a different country's flag on it. Send a long SASE with two stamps and $1 for shipping and handling to:

Phyllis Goodstein
P.O. Box 912
Levittown, NY 11756-0912

Fill your wallet with genuine foreign money from far-off places like Brazil, China, Argentina, and India. Mail $1 for shipping and handling to:

Foreign Paper Money Collection
The Jolie Company
Box 399
Roslyn Heights, NY 11577

**Don't forget your own country.** You can show off your patriotism with this embroidered American flag patch. With your request, send a long SASE and 50 cents for shipping and handling to:

Pineapple Appeal
Box 197
Owatonna, MN 55060

Let people know you are proud of your state, too. These photo magnets are perfect for your refrigerator and are practically free. And you can pick from all 50 states and Washington, D.C. Get more than one if you want — just send 75 cents for each magnet to:

Hicks Specialties
1308 68th Lane North
Brooklyn Center, MN 55430

**Reach for the stars.** How much would you pay for the addresses of more than 100 celebrities? How about nothing? Just send for this free listing, which even explains how to get the stars to write a signed letter in return. To start collecting famous autographs, write to:

Jim Weaver's Autographs in the Mail
322 Mall Boulevard, #345
Monroeville, PA 15146-2229

**Share your birthday with a celebrity.** For every day of the year, this free calendar lists the celebrities who were born on that date. It also leaves room for you to write in the names of your own personal favorites — children, grandkids, friends. To receive the calendar, send a long SASE to:

Ocotillo Hills Press
P.O. Box 9734-MF
Phoenix, AZ 85068-9734

**Stock up for the holidays.** Families sometimes pass down Christmas tree ornaments from generation to generation. Or some people just love to collect holiday decorations. Either way, get these two for free.

Made from hand-blown glass, wood, or wheat straw, these ornaments are good for Easter, Halloween, or Christmas. You can get yours for only $1, the price of shipping and handling. Normally, they would cost between $3.50 and $8. Contact:

Kaye's Holiday Free Offer
1991 Fays Lane
Sugar Grove, IL 60554

For your Christmas tree, send away for this hand-made angel. Send $2 for shipping and handling with your request to:

Angelic Creations
P.O. Box 4620
Traverse City, MI 49685

# Cheap ways to become a woodworking pro

Build neat handicrafts and toys, or shoot for the big stuff and make cabinets, shelves, chairs, and other useful items. Learning woodworking skills will put you on the path to being a carpentry pro. And these free projects and cheap supplies will take you halfway there.

**Plan your projects for free.** Beginner and expert wood craftsmen should start out their collection of free information with the Rural American Woodworking Pack. Find out about tools, machinery, magazines, and more. Go to <www.nl.freeshop.com/pg003829.htm> to sign up.

To receive a list containing dozens of do-it-yourself woodworking plans, write to:

Western Wood Products Association
Home Craftsman Plan Department
1500 Yeon Building
Portland, OR 97204

You can learn how to build a baseball cap rack, a stand for your television and VCR, and a bedroom organizer, among other things. Two free booklets from Minwax can teach you how. To get *Woodwork Project Plans and Wood Finishing Tips* write to:

Minwax Tips Book Offer
P.O. Box 763
Whippany, NJ 07981-0763

Get a free packet, complete with instructions and color photo, to start a new project. Send $1.50 for shipping and handling to:

Unique Patterns
Route 1, Box 154
Waynesville, MO 65583

**Stock up on cheap supplies and tools.** Get the right equipment for all your projects at these discount mail-order shops.

Do you need heavy-duty tools like drills, sanders, heat guns, and grinders? How about little supplies like hinges, wire fixtures, finishers, and latches? Check out Woodworker's Supply, and you'll find they have it all — at up to 30 percent off. Write or call:

Woodworker's Supply, Inc.
5604 Alameda Place NE
Albuquerque, NM 87113
800-645-9292

Another shop that can supply your woodworking needs:

Woodworker's Hardware
P.O. Box 180
Sauk Rapids, MN 56379
800-383-0130

For expert advice, check out the huge selection of books at Woodworkers' Discount Books. They sell for 20 percent off or more, and they ship for free when you order three or more items. Contact them for a free catalog at:

Woodworkers' Discount Books
735 Sunrise Circle
Woodland Park, CO 80863
800-378-4060
<www.discount-books.com>

---

## Bargain hunting a satisfying hobby

"I have more quilts than I have brains," says Cybelle McAllen of Houston, Texas, jokingly referring to her prized collection of antique quilts. Vintage clothes and fine fabrics are also among the treasures she has gathered, some for just pennies, while digging through racks and bins in charity thrift stores.

For McAllen, thrift-store shopping has developed into an intriguing and stimulating hobby. "It's like anthropology," she says. "You find a wonderful dress, for example, handmade from feed sacks and with pearl buttons. You want to know the story of the person who made it."

McAllen has a particular fondness for antique feed sacks. She paid only 40 cents for one with magnolia blossoms on a pink background, the biggest one she'd ever found. Recently, she realized what a deal she had gotten when she saw quilts made from similar old sacks — carrying really high price tags — at a quilt show.

Sewing is another of McAllen's loves. She often buys completed garments to use as fabric. "Old ball gowns, for example, contain yards and yards of material," she says.

If you, too, love sewing or collecting antique clothing but feel limited by the cost, why not check out the thrift stores where you live? You'll be "in stitches" over the treasures you'll uncover.

# Stained glass for less

Maybe you won't be able to create the incredible works of art that you see in churches and temples. But with free help and discounted supplies, you can design great stained-glass presents and decorations.

**Start with free patterns.** The Internet makes it easy to find lots of ideas for your next stained-glass project. These Web sites have many designs to choose from. Just find one you like, and print it out.

★ Art Glass World offers free patterns and will also point you to the Internet's major stained-glass suppliers. Visit <www.artglassworld. com/pattern.html>.

★ You'll find beautiful stained-glass horse designs at Black Horse Studio. Go to <http://blackhorsestudio.hypermart.net> and click on "free stuff."

**Design with discounted supplies.** Buy your glass, tools, and lamp bases at discount prices. You can find both beginner and advanced supplies in a $2 catalog from:

Warner-Crivellaro Stained Glass Supplies, Inc.
1855 Weaversville Road
Allentown, PA 18103
800-523-4242
<www.warner-criv.com>

For more special prices, a big selection of glass materials, and free pattern ideas, look into a free catalog from:

Stained Glass Warehouse
97 Underwood Road
Asheville, NC 28732
888-616-7792
<www.stainedglasswarehouse.com>

"America's Largest Source for Stained Glass" offers a free catalog and beginners' patterns as well as prices that are up to 50 percent off. Visit them online, call, or write:

Delphi Stained Glass
3380 East Jolly Road
Lansing, MI 48910
800-248-2048
<www.delphiglass.com>

Jana's Stained Glass has given its customers great prices for 23 years. See for yourself by ordering their free 160-page catalog. Visit their Web site at <www.snowcrest.net/janas/request.htm> or write to:

Jana's Stained Glass
1149 Grass Valley Highway
Auburn, CA 95603
530-885-3215

## Turn ordinary paper into works of art

Origami is an ancient Japanese art that is now popular around the world. Discover how to fold paper into swans, butterflies, and all kinds of interesting shapes.

**Learn what it's all about.** Get the free booklet called *Have a Hobby*, which tells you about the origins of origami and other types of paper folding. You will also learn how to fold the paper yourself. Just send a long self-addressed, stamped envelope (SASE) to:

Hobby Industry of America
319 E. 54th St.
Elmwood Park, NJ 07407

From the "world's largest supplier" of origami supplies, get a free lesson in folding. This kit includes instructions on how to make birds, flowers, and other creatures. Along with $1 for shipping and handling, send your request to:

Fascinating Folds
P.O. Box 2820-235
Torrance, CA 90509-2820

**Stock up on free supplies.** Fascinating Folds also sells origami supplies at low prices. You can check their prices and selection by calling 800-968-2418. Or take a look at their Internet homepage at <www.fascinating-folds.com>.

You can get authentic origami paper straight from Japan from the Sadako Project. Not only will you get a sheet of paper, but also a free poster and instructions. Mail an SASE and $1 for shipping and handling to:

The Sadako Project
P.O. Box 67
Santa Cruz, CA 95063
<www.sadako.com>

Collect two bright paper butterflies, and make fancy magnets or even a mobile. To get the paper-folding kit, just send $2 for shipping and handling to:

Woolie Works
6201 E. Huffman Road
Anchorage, AL 99516

## Sewing made free and easy

Sewing and needlepoint are among the most relaxing and creative ways to use your free time. And with these free kits, discounted supplies, and free magazines, needlework will not only be a fun hobby, it will be a cheap one, too.

**Learn from the pros.** For beginners, Crafts Kits offers a set to learn how to cross-stitch and needlepoint. It includes instructions and patterns, all for the price of shipping and handling. Send $1 to:

Craft Kits
P.O. Box 11
Garnerville, NY 10923

If you need advice on how to start sewing, read *Sewing — It's So Soothing*. This booklet is free when you send a long self-addressed, stamped envelope (SASE) to:

American Home Sewing and Craft Association
1375 Broadview
New York, NY 10018

Learn even more about cross-stitch from a free copy of *Cross Country Stitching Magazine*. Find this offer and also a free catalog at <www.cross countryshopping.com/requests.htm>.

**Pattern yourself after an expert.** Send for these free patterns and kits. Then make yourself a winter wardrobe, a pet penguin, and many other neat designs.

Get a free "Honeysuckle Rose" needlepoint design. Mail an SASE, marked with the code "CP15," to:

Just Nan, Inc.
2300 Bethelview Road, Suite 110-402
Cumming, GA 30040-9473

Make either a 9-inch Puffin or a 12-inch Penguin with these designs. Or make both. Send $1.50 postage and handling for each to:

Woolie Works
6201 E. Huffman Road
Anchorage, AL 99516

Brace yourself for the next blizzard. Knit a scarf, mittens, socks, and a sweater. Just send a long SASE to:

Knitting NOW
P.O. Box 353
Norfolk, MA 02056
<http://users.aol.com/knitnow/freepat.html>

Visit <www.janeswool.com> for more free patterns to make hats and mittens, or learn how to design a tote bag at <www.make-it-easy.com>.

Raggedy Andy and Anne never looked so good. Crochet your own Andy and Anne dolls with this free pattern, available when you send in a long SASE and $1 shipping and handling to:

NP Patterns
341 4th Terrace
Egg Harbor, NJ 08215

Get ready for the holidays with home-made ornaments. Send an SASE requesting free instructions for the "Crochet Tree-Trim Pattern" to:

Lorraine Vetter — SR
7924 Soper Hill Road
Everett, WA 98205

**Keep sewing.** Now that you have started the hobby, don't stop. Whenever you run out of free supplies, get these free catalogs full of discounted supplies.

For all types of quilting materials, write to:

Connecting Threads
P.O. Box 8940
Vancouver, WA 98668-8940
800-574-6454

And for yarns at up to 75 percent off, get in touch with:

Smiley's Yarns
92-06 Jamaica Ave.
Woodhaven, NY 11421

## Enjoy beautiful memories for less

Take pictures of your friends and family. Remember your vacations forever. Impress people with your artistic talent. There are many reasons to take up the hobby of photography. Here is one more — free supplies.

**Roll out the free film.** Get two rolls of Kodak film free. Pay only the $2 cost of shipping and handling, a discount of at least 80 percent off the retail price. Write to:

Signature Color Film
5311 Fleming Court
Austin, TX 78744

If you are connected to the World Wide Web, get your first roll of film developed free by requesting a starter kit from <www.photoworks.com>.

**Enjoy the oldies but goodies.** To have a long-lasting supply of cheap film, buy expired film from your local photography store. Put it in your freezer, and bring it out to thaw anytime you need it.

**Take advantage of mail-order discounts.** These mail-order companies get enough business that they can offer you really good prices.

Mystic Color Lab, for instance, sells three rolls of film for only $8.95. They also develop film for 30 percent less than other mail-order companies.

The price is even cheaper when you compare it to shopping mall stores. Plus, they offer free shipping. Get their latest free catalog and information about other specials — like 50 percent off processing and a CD for free Internet uploading — from:

Mystic Color Lab
Mason's Island Road
P.O. Box 144
Mystic, CT 06355-9987
800-367-6061
<www.mysticcolorlab.com>

Get Porter's Camera Store's 128-page catalog for free. It includes everything you need to be a photographer, such as cameras, carrying cases, lenses, and film — all at a discount of up to 67 percent. Contact:

Porter's Camera Store, Inc.
P.O. Box 628
Cedar Falls, IA 50613
800-553-0104
<www.porters.com>

For all digital camera owners, PhotoAccess.com is a must site to visit. They can develop your digital pictures right off your own computer and then mail them to you as prints, on a mug, or even already framed. Get 50 free prints the first time you try them. Go to <www.photoaccess.com> for more details.

**Don't just point and click.** Learn how to take great pictures that you will be proud to frame. Get these free booklets about the art of photography.

Kodak's *Picture-Taking: A Self Teaching Guide* can be requested from:

Eastman Kodak Co.
343 State Street
Rochester, NY 14650

For the booklet *365 Days to Better Pictures*, call 800-599-5929.

Learn to use a 35-mm camera with another free information guide from Kodak. Send a self-addressed label to the above address, but ask for bulletin #AC-1 and add "Department 841" to the address. You can also call 800-242-2424.

Don't forget *Hot Shots with Any Camera*, a 48-page guide that teaches about lighting, flashes, and action photos. Call 800-242-2424.

If you have problems with your Polaroid, find out how to fix it from the people who know — the Polaroid Company. Call the toll-free hotline at 800-343-5000, or mail your problem pictures to:

Polaroid Customer Care Service
784 Memorial Drive
Cambridge, MA 02139

## Free ways to be artistic

Use your hands for other things besides building, knitting, and playing. Express yourself through art and writing.

**Paint like a pro.** When doing crafts, it helps to know how to use paint to shade and highlight. Learn from one of the leaders of the industry — Delta Crafts. Mail a long, self-addressed, stamped envelope (SASE) to:

Delta Ceramcoat Shades of Color
2550 Pellissier Place
Department 1CMC-OL
Whittier, CA 90601
<www.deltacrafts.com>

You can also learn how to enhance your house with decorative painting. For a free manual, send another long SASE to:

The Basics of Decorative Painting
Technique Guide
2550 Pellissier Place
Department 2CMC-OL
Whittier, CA 90601

Also make sure to check out Delta Crafts' Web site for more free tips, discount painting supplies, free patterns, and super offers. On the Internet, surf over to <www.deltacrafts.com>.

**Learn to paint animals.** For only $1.50 for shipping and handling, you can get a free booklet on painting animals. After you have used their lessons to paint your favorite critters, get your paintings graded for free. Send for your free booklet, then send a sample of your work and an SASE. For both, mail to:

Pencil Rider
P.O. Box 242
Venice, IL 62090

On the World Wide Web, you can also find free projects and tips. Try these two pages.

★ Rustoleum gives neat advice on painting furniture and decorating your house on its Internet site at <www.rustoleum.com>.

★ Clapper Communications, publishers of Crafts 'N Things Magazine, hands out free goodies, too. At <www.craftideas.com>, they have projects and patterns you can print or save onto your computer. They put a new idea on their Web site each month, and they store all their old ones in case you missed them.

**Become a better writer.** Good writing is one of the best ways to get a point across. The National Council of Teachers of English will help you teach your children or grandchildren to write better. You might be able to use their free tips, too. Ask for their pamphlet, *How to Help Your Child Become A Better Writer*, and tell them if you want the English or Spanish version. Mail an SASE to:

National Council of Teachers of English
111 Kenyon Road
Urbana, IL 61801

## Toot your horn for less

Make a racket just like when you were young, and learn to play an instrument. It's both fun and creative. With the help of these free information packets and low-cost supplies, you'll soon be tickling the ivories or even tooting your own horn.

**Educate yourself for free.** Get a free copy of *How to Play the Hohner Harmonica*, including lessons and songs. Write to:

M. Hohner, Inc.
P.O. Box 15035
Richmond, VA 23227

While you learn to play, why not let your child or grandchild join the fun? Send away for *How Music Can Bring You Closer to Your Child*. It is free, so simply send your request to:

G. Leblanc Corp.
7019 30th Ave.
Kenosha, WI 53141

Log on to the Internet, and look for LearnAboutMusic.com. It has free articles on topics like learning jazz, tuning your instrument, and playing chords. Visit the site at <www.learnaboutmusic.com/free.html>.

**Order some cheap sheets.** Not the ones you put on your bed, the ones you need to play your instrument. You can buy expensive sheet music at a retail store, or you can get them right from the source. Zephyr Music is one of the world's largest publishers of sheet music. Get their catalog free from:

Zephyr Music Pty. Ltd.
51 Hume Street
Crows Nest, NSW 2065
Australia
<www.ozemail.com.au/~zephyr>

For discounted sheet music, also try Patti Music Company. It specializes in sheet music but also sells other supplies. Some prices are cut by as much as 30 percent. For the $2 cost of postage and handling, you can get a catalog and more information on price specials. (Music teachers get the catalog for free.) Contact:

Patti Music Company
P.O. Box 1514, Department 39
Madison, WI 53701-1514
800-777-2884
<www.pattimusic.com>

Free sheet music is available online at <www.musicaviva.com>. Search the site's collection and see if it has anything you would like. Then download the music to your computer and print it.

**Find low-cost instruments.** Instruments can be expensive to buy, but they don't have to clean out your bank account. Mail-order shops are the key to a low-cost musical hobby.

Musician's Friend, for example, guarantees you the cheapest price anywhere. If you find a lower price than theirs, they will match it, even up to 45 days after you buy the instrument. Get their free catalog from:

Musician's Friend
P.O. Box 4520
Medford, OR 97501
800-776-5173
<www.musiciansfriend.com>

Log on to their Web site, sign up for their free weekly newsletter, and you'll be eligible to win musical gear worth up to $1000.

Interstate Music Supply also claims to match the cheapest prices on the market. For a free catalog, contact:

Interstate Music Supply
P.O. Box 510865
13819 W. National Avenue
New Berlin, WI 53151
800-982-BAND
<www.interstatemusic.com>

# Find your roots for free

Digging up family roots has become the latest hobby craze in the United States. Some of this popularity is because of the Internet, where people can find information quickly and easily. People also look for their ancestors now to help trace illnesses such as heart problems, cancer, and diabetes.

Whether you use the Internet to trace your family history, or rely on old-fashioned means, you'll find plenty of free help.

**Take advantage of free booklets.** Family research can be hard work. It takes patience, time, and luck, but expert advice can help make things easier. The place to start is at the National Archives, home of all Federal records such as census, military, and immigration files.

The free booklet, *Aids for Genealogical Research*, lists important research materials and offers workshop information. It also shows how to order records through the mail from the National Archives. To receive this free pamphlet, write to:

National Archives and Records Administration
Product Development and Distribution Staff (NWCP)
Room G-7
700 Pennsylvania Avenue, NW
Washington, D.C. 20408-0001
800-234-8861
<www.nara.gov>

The Federal Consumer Information Center offers two helpful guides to family history. *My History is America's History* is a poster that will let you know how to save your heritage. It costs 50 cents. The other helpful booklet, *Where to Write for Vital Records*, will point you to state agencies where you can get family documents. To receive both of these, contact:

Consumer Information Center
Department WWW
Pueblo, CO 81009
888-878-3256
<www.pueblo.gsa.gov/misc.htm>

Also write to the Family History Library, the second largest collection of family records in the world. They will send you a free copy of *Discovering Your Family Tree*. Write to:

Family History Library
35 Northwest Temple Street
Salt Lake City, UT 84150

**Know where to look.** The National Archives and the Family History Library are only two places out of many to trace your family history. Try these other locations for help.

★ Local courthouses, newspaper offices, and historical societies. There you might find land deeds, wills, marriage and death announcements, medical records, and leads to other good hunting spots.

★ The National Genealogical Society, which you can call toll-free at 800-346-6044.

★ Friends and family. Once you tell them you're researching your family tree, they might turn out to be a treasure trove of information. Maybe they have old photos or documents hiding in their closet, or maybe they just have a picture-perfect memory.

**Use the Internet.** Because computers can store billions of bits of information in cyberspace, they are almost perfect for family history research. This is probably why family research on the Web is now as popular as sports and finance. One Internet site has been accessed by more than 16 million people. When you try out the Internet's top genealogical sites, you will see why.

★ FamilySearch.org, for example, has more than 600 million names from all over the world saved in its memory banks. And you can search through them for free. On top of this valuable service, they offer top-of-the-line computer programs for free. Keep in mind that these programs normally cost upwards of $40. This site also will give you the location of nearby Mormon Family History Centers, which are libraries set up just for tree-making. Go to <www.familysearch.org>.

★ Visit <www.rootsweb.com>, <www.ancestry.com>, and <www.cyndislist.com>. These are other top Internet sites for researching family history. RootsWeb.com offers thousands of names to look through. And Ancestry.com even allows you to make and save your own family tree at their site. Cyndi'sList.com lists and describes thousands of other useful spots on the Internet.

★ Receive a free daily newsletter full of tips on finding your ancestors. Apply for it at <www.nl.freeshop.com>. Simply click on e-mail newsletters, then scroll down to find Genealogy Tip.

## Spend your free time discovering the past

For all you war buffs, amateur historians, and just curious readers, a lot of reading material is out there that tells the history of everything from the Bill of Rights to ice cream.

**Know your basic inalienable rights.** You can own one of the most important documents in American history — the Bill of Rights. The Founding Fathers wrote it to protect your rights, so find out exactly what they are. For a free copy, write:

Veterans of Foreign Wars
Americanism Department
Broadway at 34th Street
Kansas City, MO 64111

**Become a Civil War expert.** Learn more about one of the greatest times in American history. The Civil War is just as important today as it was 100 years ago so find out more about it with this free Civil War Battlefield Map. It will show you where every battle took place. Just send $1 for shipping and handling to:

Neetstuf
Box 353
Rio Grande, NJ 08242

**Read the tragic story of the American buffalo.** They once roamed the Great Plains by the millions, and now the noble beast struggles to survive. To learn more about its history, write:

U.S. Department of Interior
Fish and Wildlife Service
Washington, DC 20240

**Brush up on American history.** The experts at the Library of Congress created this Web site for all Americans to enjoy. To dig into American history, log on to the Internet and go to <www.americaslibrary.org/cgi-bin/page.cgi>.

**Protect America's monuments.** The National Trust for Historic Preservation needs help to safeguard America's important historic sites and monuments. Start by mailing away for the "Historic Preservation" package from:

National Trust for Historic Preservation
1785 Massachusetts Avenue, NW
Washington, DC 20036

**Discover the real 49ers.** They're not just members of a professional football team. They also were the men and women who joined the Gold Rush. This free brochure will tell you about the miners and cowboys who made the Old West what it was. Write to:

The Gold Information Center
900 Third Avenue
New York, NY 10022

**Learn the history of money.** You can get this free booklet about the story of money. Since Biblical times, people have been spending it, saving it, and worrying about it. Write to:

Coins and Currency Booklet
33 Liberty Street
New York, NY 10045

**Fly with the Wright brothers.** Read about the historic first flight that only lasted 12 seconds but changed the world. To send away for the "Wright Brothers" booklet, write to:

Wright Brothers National Memorial
Route 1, Box 676
Manteo, NC 27954

**Marvel at an ancient civilization.** Send away for these free booklets on Chinese history to:

Chinese Information Service
1230 Avenue of the Americas
New York, NY 10020

**Enjoy some ice cream.** Sorry, you can't get the real thing, but you can get the story of ice cream — for free. Write to:

International Ice Cream Association
1250 H Street NW, Suite 900
Washington, DC 20005

# PARTIES AND GIFTS

## 3 steps to throwing a great, inexpensive bash

**Stock up on supplies.** Glitter and confetti are always fun at a party whether you throw it for children or for your friends. Get one-half ounce of confetti and 14 ounces of glitter for free. All you have to do is send $1 for shipping and handling to:

Tammy
350 W. Lorraine Street, #102
Glendale, CA 91202

**Send away for some fancy swizzle sticks.** They would be great for stirring drinks at your next pool party or tropical get-together. Send $1 for shipping and handling to:

Marlene Monroe
6210 Ridge Manor Drive
Memphis, TN 38115

**Learn from the experts.** If you want to try something different at your next party, check out the Web site <www.greatentertainment.com>. This Internet site offers free party tips and tells you how to organize such gatherings as a dinosaur bash for a child's birthday, a luau, or a retirement roast. It even gives recipe ideas for home-made foods, drinks, and decorations.

**Get ready, get set, go party!** Now that you have some extra supplies and some useful advice, get the party started with lots of decorations.

From 1-800 Party Shop you can buy discounted party packs, which are good for birthdays, Mardi Gras, Halloween, and other event themes. Visit its Web site at <www.1800partyshop.com> for more information and a chance to win a $100 gift certificate. Or call 800-727-8974.

Buy your supplies from Sally Distributors, and gain the expertise of an 80-year-old company. They have everything for your next party in their free 96-page catalog. Get your copy from:

Sally Distributors, Inc.
4100 Quebec Ave. N
Minneapolis, MN 55427
800-472-5597

Paradise Products sells supplies as low as 50 percent off so it's another good company to look at. For a free catalog, write:

Paradise Products, Inc.
P.O. Box 568
El Cerrito, CA 94530-0568

## Say 'I love you' for less

Making your own greeting card is a great (and cheap) way to express yourself. But if you're not really the creative type, you can still say "Happy Birthday" or "I miss you" for less. Try these suggestions for finding free or low-cost greetings.

**Get the Current prices.** As a family-run business that's been open for more than 50 years, Current understands the gift-giving needs of its customers — especially those looking for cards. They offer two-for-one sales and weekly specials as well as regular low prices on card sets. They also sell gifts and gift wrap. For a free catalog, write to:

Current, Inc.
1005 East Woodmen Road
Colorado Springs, CO 80920
800-848-2848
<www.currentcatalog.com>

**Spark a friendship.** One of the best locations for discounted card supplies is Sparks.com with its everyday low prices. First-time customers will get $5 off a $15-plus order. Browse the great selection of cards, and find out more about this special at <www.sparks.com/partners/greater good/greatergood.html>.

**Overload on Internet greetings.** If you use e-mail, you know it is a free and easy way to send people notes. But you might not know about the free postcards and greeting cards available on the Internet. Here are a few Web sites that offer this free service.

★ <www.bluemountain.com>. One of the most popular card sites on the Web.

★ <www.hallmark.com/hmk/Website/hallmark_home.jsp>. Home of one of the world's biggest greetings companies.

★ <www.regards.com>. Greeting cards for any occasion.

★ <www.wegotcards.com>. From wacky to romantic, you'll find just the card you need.

★ <www.zing.com/card>. Personalize your e-cards with your own pictures.

★ <www.mailameal.com>. Postcards with food themes.

★ <www.TABASCO.com/html/po.html>. Cards for those who like spicy foods.

★ <http://mailbits.com/VirtualGifts>. Pictures of the gift you couldn't send — roses, champagne, chocolate.

★ <www.funnygreetings.com>. Wacky animated cartoons and singing cards.

★ <www.senada.com/personal>. Free invitations for parties, showers, and even weddings to send to your friends online.

## Novelty gifts that are sure to please

Wholesale shopping is just as handy for gift buying as it is for entertainment equipment and hobby supplies.

Surprise your favorite child or adult with an off-the-wall gift from American Science and Surplus. This free catalog has a wide selection of gifts, from crock jars, coloring books, and Mexican jumping beans to scientific experiment instructions. They often run sales as well, which can cut prices by up to 60 percent. Contact:

American Science and Surplus
3605 Howard Street
Skokie, IL 60076
847-982-0870
<www.sciplus.com>

Buy educational gifts from the U.S. Toy Company. They offer a free catalog full of gift ideas for young children and even teachers. These include ink stamps, building blocks, bead kits, and art studios — at up to one-third off. For more information, contact:

U.S. Toy Company, Inc.
Constructive Playthings
13201 Arrington Road
Grandview, MO 64030
800-841-6478
<www.constplay.com>

Try the Oriental Trading Company for an odd assortment of novelty gifts. They carry stuff for children and adults, like glass animal figurines, wind chimes, beanbags, and stuffed-animal marionettes. You can get their free catalog and more information on what they offer from:

Oriental Trading Company, Inc.
P.O. Box 3407, Dept. 868
Omaha, NE 68103
800-875-8480
<www.oriental.com>

Don't forget another great present — stickers. Kids love to collect as many as possible, and Stickers 'N' Stuff sells them for a lot less than retail. For a free sample of their wares and a catalog of everything they offer, send $2 for postage and handling to:

Stickers 'N' Stuff
P.O. Box 430
Louisville, CO 80027-0430

Can't decide what to give your child or grandchild? Visit <www.smarterkids.com> for some helpful hints. At this Web site you can search for gifts by the age of the child. Even better, they sell name-brand toys, books, and computer programs at up to 50 percent off. If you find a lower price than SmarterKids.com at a retail store, let them know, and they will actually pay you back 110 percent what you paid them.

---

### Ideas for the perfect present

ThirdAge.com, one of the Web's top sites for seniors, surveyed older men and women for their ideas of the perfect gift. They found that men preferred:

- A nifty gadget.
- A romantic escape.
- Gear for their car.
- Anything for golf, fishing, gardening, or their favorite hobby.
- A candlelight dinner for two.

Women's favorite gifts included:

- A rose on her pillow.
- A hand-made card.
- A night of dancing and dining in a new place.
- Coffee shared in front of the rising (or setting) sun.
- A framed picture of the two of you.

So the next time you're stuck for ideas on that special occasion, try one of these, and you'll be sure to make your sweetheart happy.

---

# Stem the costs of brightening someone's day

Flowers can brighten anyone's day. But if you don't have your own garden, they can become an expensive gift, especially if your special someone likes flowers on a regular basis. To avoid turning your pockets inside-out, try these helpful hints to get flowers at a discount.

**Give away flowers every day.** Next time you go to your local grocery store, have a chat with the florist and ask what the store does with its unsold flowers. Many times a grocery store, and even a florist shop, will just throw away its partially wilted flowers. If you ask them in time, they might give you these flowers for free.

Many types of flowers will stay pretty for days after you bring them home. Carnations, roses, and stargazer lilies last the longest. And when these begin to droop, visit your grocery store again, and get a new batch. That way, you can supply your loved ones with a steady supply of flowers.

**Shop online for savings.** ProFlowers.com is one of the most helpful and inexpensive of the Internet flower dealers. They have a special Web page where you can find bouquets at up to 20 percent off, and part of your money will go to a charity such as the Women's Sports Foundation. Visit them on the Web at <www.proflower.com>.

PCFlowers.com is another leading Internet flower store. With certain purchases, they offer two-for-one deals and free gifts such as ceramic clocks, chocolates, and vases. And if you can't afford real flowers, you can cheer someone up with a free virtual bouquet! Visit their site at <www.pcflowers.com> for more details.

## Smart shipping tips

Mailing gifts does not have to be expensive or difficult anymore. Just try one of these ideas for easier delivery.

- Visit your neighborhood post office where you'll find shipping boxes, tape, and Styrofoam — either free or at low cost. You'll have to put the box together yourself, but you can ship it right from the post office.

- If you don't want to bother with finding a box, wrapping your gift, and taping it all together, then check your local yellow pages for a retail mail and delivery shop. These stores will package your gift for you and ship it off at an affordable price.

- Do-it-yourself shippers can visit <www.smartship.com>. This Web site allows you to compare prices of all major shipping companies for overnight, two-day, and three-day deliveries. It also provides information on getting your package picked up from your house and finding a shipping company's closest office.

# Shower your favorite child with free gifts

Children today might beg for the latest and greatest toy they just saw on television. But there's no need to pay a lot for name-brand toys when you can get these simple gifts for free.

Watch your loved ones roar with excitement when they see this animal watch. Its head is shaped like the face of a cat, dog, mouse, or elephant. The face opens up to reveal a digital clock. Request the face you want, and send $2 for shipping and handling to:

What a Deal!
P.O. Box 850
Huntington Beach, CA 92647

Give your child or grandchild one of the all-time best activities — coloring. Most kids love to spend time with a box of crayons and a coloring book, and yours should enjoy coloring these beautiful and informative pictures of honeybees. Send 60 cents for shipping and handling to:

Dadant & Sons, Inc.
Hamilton, IL 62341

Give your kids a bookmark that looks like a real dollar. Too bad it won't buy them anything but a saved page in their favorite story. For $1 shipping and handling and a long, self-addressed, stamped envelope, you can get two of them from:

Mr. Rainbows
P.O. Box 908
Rio Grande, NJ 08242

Stick them with stickers from their favorite Disney movie. For two sheets, send $1 for shipping and handling to:

Marlene Monroe
6210 Ridge Manor Drive
Memphis, TN 38115

Watch your kids' faces light up when you give them something different to watch other than their typical TV cartoons. You can receive a free "Count with Maisy" video when you send $2.65 for shipping and handling to:

ALFY, Inc.
Attn: Promotions Department
65 Broadway, Suite 601
New York, NY 10006

Send away for these cute pompom teddy bears with pompom noses and bow ties. They can be stuck on the end of a pencil or glued to a magnet. Just send three stamps and your address to:

Teddy Bears
2431 Buck Road
Harrison, MI 48625

Get a free brochure that explains how to buy gifts that are fun and educational for children of all ages and why those gifts are the best for kids. Just write to:

Toy Manufacturers of America
200 Fifth Avenue
New York, NY 10010

## Unique gifts for less

Here are a few gift ideas that will make someone feel extra special — especially those hard-to-buy-for people you know.

**Spread some holiday cheer.** Stock up on gifts from Kaye's Holiday for friends who like holiday ornaments. This company specializes in hand-made ornaments from places like Germany, the Czech Republic, and Poland. But unlike other retail stores, Kaye's sells them at a 20- to 75-percent discount. For more information, contact:

Kaye's Holiday
6N021 Meredith Road
Maple Park, IL 60151
630-365-2224

**Send a "capitol" gift.** How about giving the gift of a flag your Congressman flew over the U.S. Capitol? It's a different way to say you care.

Contact your local representative or senator, and ask if he will fly a flag for your friend's wedding, birthday, anniversary, or other important event. Most will do it, usually for free. Then indicate whether you want the flag sent to your house or your friend's.

Just make sure to ask for this congressional favor way ahead of time so you can have the flag flown on the day you want. You should receive it about a month later.

**Enjoy high-tech discounts.** Buy a unique gadget for that special man in your life. A radio for his shower, a vacuum for his car — you can buy it from the experts in high-tech gifts, Sharper Image. This company always has some gifts on sale — sometimes for more than 50 percent off.

For a look at some of their gift ideas, visit them online at <www.sharperimage.com>. For a free catalog call 800-344-5555. Or check your yellow pages to see if they have a store near you.

## Give a gift that keeps on giving

If you have extra savings, you should consider donating to charity. Not only will you get a break on your taxes, but you will feel better knowing that you made the future better by supporting a cancer research institute, environmental agency, animal abuse watch group, or another worthwhile organization.

**Ask the experts.** Donations can be tricky because you want to make sure you give to a legitimate charity. That's why it's important to get the advice of agencies who check up on various groups. They'll help you spot scams, and they'll also point you in the direction of hard-working, honest charities.

Besides having helpful hints on its Web site at <www.give.org>, the National Charities Information Bureau also sends out a written guide to donating. It updates the *Wise Giving Guide* often. For a free copy, contact:

National Charities Information Bureau
19 Union Square West
New York, NY 10003

The Council of Better Business Bureaus also publishes its own guide to charities. The *Give But Give Wisely* bulletin is available for the cost of a long, self-addressed, stamped envelope from:

Philanthropic Advisory Service
Council of Better Business Bureaus
4200 Wilson Boulevard, Suite 800
Arlington, VA 22203

Or read it on the Internet at <www.bbb.org/pas/give.asp>.

With CharityAmerica.com, you can find the charity that matches your interests. On this Web site at <www.charityamerica.com>, you're allowed to browse through hundreds of organizations by their names or what they do. When you find one you like, the site will tell you how to get in touch with the charity. For more information about this service, visit the Internet page or contact:

CharityAmerica.com
264 North Main St.
Natick, MA 01760
877-KINDACT

**Follow these basic steps.** These hints will come in handy any time you talk on the phone with a charity or receive their information in the mail.

★ Know the exact name of the charity, what it does, and how it goes about meeting its goals. You can find this information by writing the charity for its brochure.

★ Find out how much of your donation actually goes to helping its cause. The National Charities Information Bureau uses 60 percent as an acceptable cut-off.

★ Avoid charities that pressure you to donate or refuse to send out any written information about themselves until you donate.

★ Mail only checks to your chosen charity — not cash.

★ Consider donating to local charities so you can actually see the good your money is doing. Local charities like shelters, boys clubs, and churches might also take non-cash donations such as old clothing, canned food, or your time.

# PETS

## A buffet of free food for your pets

Pet food, vitamins, and treats — find everything you need to keep your animal happy, healthy, and fed. Best of all, it's all free.

**Spoil your dog with this tricky treat.** Famous Fido's dog treats look like people food. Let your dog try them, and he just might believe you're sharing your dinner with him. For a free large sample, send $2.25 for shipping and handling to:

Famous Fido's
1533 W. Devon Ave.
Chicago, IL 60660

**Improve your dog's health.** If your dog has a persistent skin rash or dry, itchy coat, try Improve dog food supplement. Made from fish and other seafood, it is an all-natural powder you add to your dog's chow to heal her skin problems.

For a free sample and information kit, call 800-843-4020, and leave your name and address. Or for faster service, leave an e-mail address. You can also write to:

C.M. Champion, Inc.
P.O. Box 10
West Point, PA 19486

Power Paws is another product you add to your pet's food to make her look and feel better. You can try a free sample by sending a postcard to:

Power Paws Free Sample
Nirmala Enterprise, Inc.
P.O. Box 331
Isle of Palms, SC 29451-0331

Include your name, address, and e-mail address if you have one, as well as your local pet store's name and how you heard about the product.

Believe it or not, you can also give your pet vitamins. Animal Essentials offers samples of two of its pills. One is a soft-gel vitamin, and the other is a multivitamin-herbal supplement. For more information, call 888-463-7748, or visit its Web site at <www.animalessentials.com/samples.html>.

**Give your dog a kiss.** If your dog has bad breath, all the vitamins in the world may not help. Give your dog this free sample of Breath Fresh. Send a long, self-addressed, stamped envelope to:

American Media Group
7300 W. 110th St., Suite 960
Overland Park, KS 66210
<www.breathfresh.com>

**'Tweat' your favorite tweetie bird.** For a sample of Lafeber's Avi-Cakes Gourmet Bird Food, write to:

Lafeber Company
24981 N. 1400 East Road
Cornell, IL 61319

Also try Super Preen, a food supplement that will naturally make your bird's coat prettier and healthier. Send $1 for shipping and handling for a free sample and seven-page brochure from:

RHS Labs
1640 E. Edinger Ave.
Santa Anna, CA 92705

**Help your horse stay healthy.** Try the Select the Best horse food supplement. For a free sample, visit the Web site <www.selectthebest.com/contact/sample.htm>.

**Find those hard-to-find food supplies.** Whether you have a chinchilla, hedgehog, ferret, or any other exotic pet, get the food you need from Brisky Food Products. Try a free sample by calling 800-462-2464.

# Find a free friend

You can avoid one of the most expensive parts of owning a pet — buying it — if you know where to look. Instead of those expensive mall pet stores, try these other places to find a new friend.

★ Check the bulletin boards at your local grocery or department stores. Many people use them to advertise free pets.

★ The classified section of your newspaper usually has ads for free kittens and puppies.

★ One of the best places to find a new pet is your local animal shelter. Not only will the shelter give you a loving companion, but sometimes it even provides free shots for the animal. Spaying and neutering — essential parts of pet care — might come at a discount, too. Call a nearby shelter for more details. The Web site <http://acmepet.petsmart.com/canine/civic/shelter.html> has a state-by-state directory of animal shelters.

# Free goodies for animal lovers

From bumper stickers and postcards to computer art and pet carriers, find free and low-cost gifts for yourself and your favorite pet owner.

**Horse around with these freebies.** To show your love for horses, order this poster and bumper sticker. While you're at it, ask for the free booklet *For an American Quarter Horse.* Just send a postcard with your request and address to:

American Quarter Horse Association
P.O. Box 22
Amarillo, TX 79168

For a free picture and the pamphlet *Tennessee Walking Horse*, send your address to:

Tennessee Walking Horse
Box 286
Lewisburg, TN 37081

**Advertise your pet's presence.** This free decal will come in handy when friends visit unexpectedly or during an emergency. When you place it on your front door, it will notify them that Fido or Fluffy is somewhere in the house. Send a self-addressed, stamped envelope (SASE) to:

Free Decal
St. Hubert's Animal Welfare Center
P.O. Box 159
Madison, NJ 07940
<www.sthuberts.org/scoop/guest.htm>

**Bag this deal.** You can try out the "Doggy-Bag" for free. When you take your dog for a walk, this interesting invention does two jobs for you. It works as a traveling water bowl and as a scoop for your pet's messes. You'll have to see it to believe it. Send an SASE to order your free sample from:

OPC
Doggy-Bag
4020 North Central Park Ave. 3E
Chicago, IL 60618
<www.doggy-bag.com>

**Make your own crate.** If you like to travel with your small dog or cat, you can save a bundle by creating your own pet carrier.

Find two large plastic laundry baskets. Place one on top of the other to form a cage, and attach one side with nuts and bolts. Place a blanket or cardboard on the bottom to cushion your pet's feet. Then put them together, and tie the loose side shut with string.

**Snag these specials.** The World Wide Web offers a lot of deals for pet lovers. Here are some sites to try.

★ Visit <www.thinktreats.heinzpetproducts.com/main.asp> and click on "offers" for a free screen saver, coupons, and more.

★ Find e-mail postcards you can send to all your friends and family at <www.petloves.com/postcards.htm>. Send as many as you like — they're all free.

★ Horse lovers should also visit <www.equizotic.com>. This Web site gives away horse artwork, computer graphics, and pictures.

# Free information for pet owners

Taking care of your pet can be a difficult job. Even if you think you're doing a great job already, why not send for these free information packets to help you do it even better?

**Bone up on pet-sitters.** Don't make vacations even more stressful — leave your favorite pet with someone you can trust. Learn how to choose a good sitter from this free booklet. Send $2 for postage and handling to:

National Association of Professional Sitters
1030 15th Street NW
Suite 870
Washington, DC 20005

**Get free professional advice.** Pet food makers, the American Humane Association, and other helpful groups want you to have these helpful kits.

The Iams Company will give you tips on feeding, house training, and grooming your kitten or puppy. Write to:

The Iams Company
Puppy/Kitten Information Center
Box 1475
Dayton, OH 45401

For more information about caring for your young dog or cat, try Kal Kan's booklet from:

Kal Kan Advisory Service
3386 East 44th St.
P.O. Box 58853
Vernon, CA 90058

Ralston Purina can answer questions about your adult dog. Write for their free brochure at:

Ralston Purina
Dog Food Division
Checkerboard Square
St. Louis, MO 63164

Also from Purina, get a free pet safety kit, a magazine, and a puppy information set. Find all of these and more on their Web site at <www.purina.com>.

Get free advice from the American Humane Association about all your animals — dogs, cats, horses, birds, and fish. Write or call:

American Humane Association
63 Inverness Dr. East
Englewood, CO 80112-5117
800-227-4645
<www.americanhumane.org>

**Learn about natural pet care.** Get a free copy of a book on the benefits of holistic care for your pets, then try a free sample of pet treats. Choose either 7th Heaven Catnip, Fanta-Seeds, or Vita Dreams Daily Greens. Visit <www.halopets.com/feedback.htm> and fill out a quick survey to get your goodies.

**Read up on a dog's life.** Surf over to <www.ifco.com/free.htm> on the Internet, and you can get a free copy of *Dog's Life*, a helpful magazine about dog care.

## Free veterinary care for your pets

A routine trip to the veterinarian for an exam or shot can be expensive, but an emergency operation can really damage your budget. Taking your animal to the vet can be costly because you bear the full brunt of the fees. Unlike people, pets don't have health insurance.

But if you're lucky enough to live near a veterinary school, you may have a way around these costs. Check your local yellow pages, or look on the Web site <www.healthypet.com> for a list of animal hospitals and vet schools for every state.

If you find a vet school near you, call and ask if they offer specials for routine operations such as neutering and spaying, de-clawing, and shots. Some vet schools offer discounted rates — or even free services — for local pet owners.

# Great deals on pet supplies

Don't let your pet take a bite out of your wallet. You can buy food and supplies for much less from these wholesale stores.

With a free 72-page catalog from J-B Wholesale Pet Supplies, you can shop for collars, beds, foods, pens, and much more. J-B Wholesale accepts returns if you are not satisfied, and they allow COD orders. Contact:

J-B Wholesale Pet Supplies, Inc.
5 Raritan Road
Oakland, NJ 07436
<www.jbpet.com>

If you feel comfortable buying from a company owned by veterinarians — who wouldn't — talk to Drs. Foster & Smith, Inc. Their free catalog has everything you could need for your favorite critter, even a toll-free number for free vet advice. Write to:

Drs. Foster & Smith, Inc.
2253 Air Park Road
P.O. Box 100
Rhinelander, WI 54501-0100
800-381-7179
<www.drsfostersmith.com>

Pet Warehouse has so many pet supplies that it needs five catalogs to fit it all. Pick which free catalog you want — dogs and cats, fish, birds, small reptiles and mammals, or ponds. To get one or more of these catalogs, contact:

Pet Warehouse
915 Trumbull Street
Xenia, OH 45385
800-443-1160
<www.petwhse.com>

You'll find prices up to 70 percent off retail in the free catalog of That Fish Place/That Pet Place. And if any other wholesale store beats this discount, the company promises to meet or beat that price. So you might want to check this place last. Contact:

That Fish Place/That Pet Place
237 Centerville Road
Lancaster, PA 17603
800-786-3829
<www.thatpetplace.com>

Omaha Vaccine Company is another store that won't let its prices get beaten. It has a catalog for horses and livestock as well as house pets. Request your free catalog from:

Omaha Vaccine Company
P.O. Box 7228
Omaha, NE 68107
800-367-4444
<www.omahavaccine.com>

## Pets: A boon to your health

Pets can benefit you in any number of ways. Here are seven healthy ones to think about.

- Pets reduce your blood pressure. One scientific study shows that people over 40 with pets have lower pressure than those without them.

- Another study has suggested that people with pets go to the doctor 21 percent less than people without pets.

- Because you have to take care of them, they give you a good reason to take care of yourself.

- Pets cheer you up.

- You get more exercise by walking your pet.

- They're a good way to meet other pet owners and make new friends.

- Best of all, a pet is a friend who's always there for you.

# Freebies for fish fanatics

An aquarium full of fish is a beautiful decoration for your home. And gazing at fish can help calm and relax you when you're feeling stressed. With these free products, you'll be able to enjoy your fish and pay less for their upkeep.

**Sample some fish supplies.** For a wholesale store that sells only discounted fish supplies, look for Daleco Master Breeder Products. Their 120-page catalog is free and full of useful information. Contact them at:

Daleco Master Breeder Products
3556 N. 400 East
Warsaw, IN 46580-7999
800-987-1120
<www.dalecombp.com>

Aquaricare, a company that specializes in fish food and supplies, offers free samples to anyone who asks for them. And when you contact them, make sure to ask for their free catalog of discounted supplies. Visit them online at <www.aquaricare.com>.

**Make your aquarium worry-free.** The Tankminder computer program will assist you with all your aquarium needs. It will keep track of your new and old fish, let you know when to clean your tank, and even diagnose your fish's disease. Try it free for 30 days. Just visit <www.Tankminder.com>.

**"Grow" a water garden.** Give your fish plenty of space. If you have room in your backyard, you can build a pond and fill it with all the fish you could ever want. Learn how to complete this project step by step with the *We Are the Water Garden Experts* brochure. It's free from:

Tetra Pond
3001 Commerce Street
Blacksburg, VA 24060-6671

# LOW-COST HIGH TECH

New technology is changing the face of today's world. Computers, cell phones, digital video players, giant-screen TVs — all these new types of electronics make life easier and more entertaining. But they also make it more expensive.

In this chapter, you will see how you can get the benefits of electronics without the high cost. Learn about the best places to shop for your high-tech toys. Discover new and frugal ways to stock up on computer supplies like printer ink and mouse pads. And believe it or not, learn how to find electronic deals that are absolutely free!

## 4 stops on the road to low prices

When you buy electronics equipment — a television, VCR, stereo, camcorder, camera, or whatever — you should go where you'll find the best prices and the best help. It could save you hundreds of dollars and make you feel more confident about your purchase.

First decide which is most important — convenience, price, or selection. With that information, you can pick the right store for you.

★ **Warehouse clubs.** Not only can you buy bulk food and house supplies at clubs like Costco and Sam's Club, you can find brand-name electronics there, too. These stores typically have the lowest prices. The downside is a limited selection and annual club fees.

★ **Giant retail stores.** Almost every town or city has one, if not more, of a department store chain like Sears or Wal-Mart. Their prices might be slightly higher than warehouse clubs, but their selection is usually much better.

★ **Specialty stores.** At places like Circuit City or Best Buy, you'll find top-of-the-line equipment, but prices may be high on some items. Even with the higher price tags, you still might want to visit one just to talk with their knowledgeable and helpful staff.

★ **Internet and mail-order stores.** These places are quickly becoming the cheapest game in town. With their free catalogs and Web pages, you can easily and quickly compare prices without leaving home. Shipping fees, however, can be a problem. Just keep your eyes peeled for dealers that don't charge them and sites that guarantee safe delivery.

Even after you decide which store is best for you, continue to compare prices. Keep your eye out for sales — especially in the late spring and fall — and don't rush into any purchase. Do your homework first and it will pay off.

## Door-to-door discounts on electronics

You can transform your den into a high-tech entertainment theater without stepping a foot outside. Simply shop for all your home electronics needs from the comfort of your home. Some of the top stores are now online, and many of the country's best mail-order warehouses offer free catalogs.

Crutchfield is one that features audio and video products at 10 to 55 percent off. Even if you don't plan to buy from them, order their free catalog. It not only shows their wares but also serves as an informative guide to buying electronics in general. Contact:

Crutchfield
1 Crutchfield Park
Charlottesville, VA 22906-6020
800-955-9009
<www.crutchfield.com>

Be sure to ask about their "hot specials" and "scratch and dent" deals.

J&R Music World rebates almost everything you could want, like TVs, stereos, speakers, clocks, and cameras. Send away for their free 216-page catalog from:

J&R Music World
59-50 Queens-Midtown Expressway
Maspeth, NY 11378-9896
800-221-8180

For prices as low as half off, take a gander at the catalog from Bennett Brothers. They also offer special gift catalogs. Write, visit, or call:

Bennett Brothers, Inc.
30 E. Adams Street
Chicago, IL 60603
800-621-2626
<www.bennettbrothers.com>

When browsing the World Wide Web for electronics discounts, first try the general shopping sites like <www.buy.com> and <www.mysimon.com>. Then try these electronics specialty stores.

★ <www.800.com>. Their low prices are even lower because they don't charge sales tax. (The main store is in Oregon.) To top off the bargain, they don't charge shipping fees for most purchases, and they guarantee their product for 30 days.

★ <www.1877ftyoutl.com>. The Electronic Factory Outlet also has free shipping and handling, and every order over $25 comes with a free gift. If you want super-low prices, check out their factory-renewed products, which sell at up to 79 percent discount.

★ <www.etronics.com>. Although they charge for shipping, this site has some of the lowest prices around. It also offers free expert advice on setup and accessory equipment, like wires, speakers, and components. Visit the Web site or call 800-323-7669.

To compete with these mail-order and Internet stores, the major retail chains have gone online. Their Web sites are easy to find, and they usually run sales on the Internet. So make sure to check those as well.

## Old-fashioned TV for less

Cable television these days can be costly. Just ordering the most basic channels might run you more than $40 each month. Multiply that by 12, and the yearly cost of cable might surprise you. Satellite systems are no better since they can cost hundreds if not thousands to set up.

Whatever happened to rabbit-eared antennas, VHF, and UHF? They're still out there. People with homes can catch free television signals using a roof antenna. If you live in an apartment, though, you might not be so lucky. You could be trapped into an expensive decision — no TV or cable TV.

Don't lose hope because you do have a third option — powered rabbit ears. This invention sits on your television set and acts as a magnet for TV signals. At a cost of $30 to $80 at most retail electronics stores, these antennas can clear up your fuzzy picture and pull in more channels.

Your best bet is to buy one of the cheaper versions and save the receipt, so you can return it if you are not happy with its performance. Then you can try other brands, always keeping the receipts, until you find one that works well with your set.

## Save thousands on a new computer

If you're ready to dive into computing and the Internet, follow these expert tips, and you may save thousands of dollars.

★ Buying a computer should be as serious as buying any other home appliance. Be as careful as you would when looking for a refrigerator or even a car. Check the Web site <www.pueblo.gsa.gov/cic_text/misc/buy-computer/buycomp.htm> for helpful information on making this important purchase.

★ Figure out what you are going to do with your computer. Will you only send e-mails and occasionally surf the Web? If so, you don't need to spend an extra $1,000 or $2,000 for the latest, fastest model. A lower-end model ($1000 or less) should suit your needs.

★ To make sure you're getting a good computer — at whatever price range — check two key numbers: megabytes (MB) and megahertz (MHz). The higher these numbers the better because that means your computer will work harder and faster. A typical setting for an affordable computer would be 64MB and 500 or higher MHz.

★ If you don't know much about computers, a package deal might be best. Many retailers have all-inclusive deals that land you everything you need — a TV-like screen for your computer, a modem to reach the Internet, and a color printer for all your printing needs.

★ It also helps to load up on free software. Look for computers that come with programs like a word processor, financial planner, and encyclopedia.

Computer prices change constantly, but by following these tips, asking advice from friends and family, and using your own good judgment, you should end up with an excellent computer at a price you can afford.

## Computing the best bargain

Computers have become so popular that you now have many choices on where to buy. You many find that some of the lowest prices are available through the mail and the Internet.

**Mail order your e-mail.** Like many other items, computers can cost less when you buy them from a warehouse or mail-order store.

A company that's been in the business for almost two decades is Computer Discount Warehouse. For a free catalog, write to:

Computer Discount Warehouse
CDW Computer Centers, Inc.
200 North Milwaukee Avenue
Vernon Hills, IL 60061
800-840-4239

Also visit their Web site at <www.cdw.com> for special rebates on all sorts of equipment.

Dartek Computer Supply sells both supplies and computers as low as 60 percent off. Send away for their catalog to:

Dartek Computer Supply Corporation
175 Ambassador Drive
Naperville, IL 60540
888-432-7835

Die-hard Apple fans should talk with MacWarehouse, where you may get what you need for up to 50 percent off. They have a free catalog and give price quotes over the phone. Contact:

MacWarehouse
P.O. Box 3013
1720 Oak Street
Lakewood, NJ 08701-3013
800-397-8508
<www.warehouse.com>

**Use a computer to get a computer.** The Internet is brimming with deals on computer equipment.

MySimon.com is one of the first Internet sites you should stop at. It checks all the major retail stores on the Web, then tells you which sites to go to for the cheapest prices. Check it out at <www.mysimon.com>.

Many of these retail sites — like Outpost.com — offer free delivery and a guarantee on their products. So if your computer is damaged in the mail, you can easily return it. You'll also find computer specials on their Web site at <www.outpost.com>.

**Give your mouse a free home.** The accessories you need for your new computer can really add to the cost. But one thing you don't have to spend money on is a mousepad. All you need to do is visit <www.freemouse pads.com> and fill out a form to receive a free one in the mail.

# Big savings on printer ink

If you print a lot from your computer, you know the hassle of running out of ink. Besides rushing around to find the right printer cartridge, you have to come up with $30 or more to buy a new one.

**Save on new cartridges.** Wholesale mail-order companies offer remarkably low prices to replace your printer's ink container. You can save as much as 90 percent.

Magnolia Ink offers generic cartridges for many name-brand machines. And if their ink fails to look as good as your old ink, they will refund your purchase. For price quotes and more information, contact:

Magnolia Ink
168 Dick Hobby Road
Lucedale, MS 39452
877-464-2934 (toll free)
<www.magnoliaink.com>

Another company, All-Ink, also guarantees its replacement cartridges with a 110-percent refund policy. Get a free copy of All-Ink's monthly bulletin to save even more money. Find out more from:

All-Ink
P.O. Box 50868
Provo, UT 84605-0865
877-491-4465 (toll free)
<www.all-ink.com>

The Ink Store claims to offer the cheapest prices on the Internet. You can see for yourself at:

The Ink Store
P.O. Box 8623
Woodcliff Lake, NJ 07677
<www.theinkstore.com>

**Re-use your cartridges.** It may be cheaper for you to refill your empty cartridges with fresh ink. Several ink dealers now offer kits and bulk quantities of ink to help you recycle old containers and save a lot of money.

The printer stores mentioned above sell refill ink, but the best prices come from the companies that specialize in ink replacement. Mr. Ink Jet offers introductory kits as low as $19.95. These include instructions, tools, and up to 10 refills-worth of ink. You can also buy ink in various amounts ranging from 8 to 64 ounces. Contact them at:

InkJet, Inc.
17742 Hwy 105 West, Suite 1
Montgomery, TX 77356
800-280-3245
<www.inkjetinc.com>

Visit their online site to request a free sample of one of their products or services.

Automation Consulting & Supply sells black ink by the pint (16 ounces) for $21.95. That's about 11 refills at $2 apiece. Although they do not offer beginner kits, their Web site provides free instructions on how to refill your cartridges. This saves you money because you can then buy your tools at the local hardware store for much less. For more information, contact:

Automation Consulting & Supply, Inc.
1980 G Parker Court
Stone Mountain, GA 30087
888-728-2465
<www.oddparts.com/ink>

**Plan ahead to save money.** Buying low-cost ink and printer cartridges are good ways to lower expenses. But follow these tips to spend even less.

★ Set your printer at the lowest quality setting (usually called "draft") when copying everyday documents. For fancier print outs, use the default setting. This way you'll save ink.

★ Put photocopier paper in your printer unless you are printing an official document. It is much cheaper than printer paper.

★ Don't go overboard on ink. Buy as much as you will use in a year or two because ink goes bad. You'll end up throwing out the extra.

★ Check your printer's warranty before you refill your ink cartridges to make sure there's no problem with using a different manufacturer's ink.

If you go through two to four cartridges of ink per year, which is average for today's computer users, these money-saving tips definitely will help.

## Computers: How to log on and learn for free

Computers and the wonders of the Internet are no longer just for teenagers, college kids, and corporate professionals. Today, all age groups are shopping online for bargains, writing e-mails to their loved ones, and finding all kinds of useful information while surfing the Web.

**Try it out first.** If you want to see what the hubbub over the Internet is all about, you don't have to rush out and buy a computer. In many towns across America, local libraries have computers that anyone can freely use.

If you live near a college, you might want to try its library as well. Colleges have a lot of computers with free Internet use. Local residents usually can use these services for free, too.

**See all the sites.** If or when you hop on the Internet, you might feel out of place at first — like a traveler in some faraway land. Just take your time, and slowly get used to wandering around the different Web sites. Use these free guides to help you find your way.

The Federal Consumer Information Center has a brochure called *Site-Seeing on the Internet*. You can receive your free copy from:

Consumer Information Center
Department WWW
Pueblo, CO 81009
888-878-3256

Or read it online at <www.pueblo.gsa.gov/cic_text/misc/site-seeing>.

One of the leading companies of the Internet, Compuserve, offers its own free manual, *Compuserve's How To Get Started Package*. With it, you also get free time to look at the Internet from your own home. Either call 800-848-8199 or write:

Compuserve
5000 Arlington Centre Boulevard
Columbus, OH 43220

**Find a free surfing buddy.** If you want more information about the site you are visiting and a list of other sites like it, try Alexa, a free computer service. Alexa works with your computer's Internet program to make searching the Web much easier. Go to <www.alexa.com> for more information.

**Save with free service.** Sign up for this new computer service that millions of avid Web fans already use. It's called Gator, and it can help you in two ways.

First, when signing up for free services or buying things on the Internet, you usually have to fill out forms. These can get tedious after a while. Gator will fill them out for you automatically. Gator will also lead you to savings at the Web's leading retail shops by giving you coupons just for using the program. Try it out at <www.gator.com>.

## Surf the World Wide Web for free

Before you dismiss the Internet as some newfangled invention, consider all the free stuff you can find on the Web, starting with Internet service itself.

**Take advantage of free specials.** A company that provides an Internet linkup is called an Internet Service Provider (ISP). And like your phone and electric companies, it has the right to charge for its service. Your budget might not be able to handle paying an extra $20 or so per month just to browse the Web.

Don't worry, though, because there are ways to avoid paying this fee.

★ **Save on the start-up.** Big-name Internet service providers such as America Online (AOL), Earthlink, AT&T, and Compuserve often will give you a free trial period. Even smaller ISPs, like your regional phone company, will, too.

★ **Profit from the freedom.** Use this bonus time to find a free Internet provider. There are many to choose from, but the best are Juno.com, AltaVista.com, and NetZero.com. These offer unlimited use of the Web for no charge.

★ **Sign up.** To enroll in a free service, just visit the ISP's Web site. ForAltaVista.com, for instance, it is <www.altavista.com>. Then, look for the button that says "Free Access" or "Free Internet Access." Click on it and follow the directions to set up and save money.

★ **Cancel the other service.** Once you have your free ISP, make sure to let the first ISP know. Do this before your free trial runs out. If you don't, they will begin charging you a fee.

★ **Decide for yourself.** Free Internet service can save you hundreds of dollars a year. With these savings, though, you miss out on some services that the big ISPs provide, such as instant messages, parental controls, and chat rooms. You can pick the services, the no charge, or both. ISPs like AOL offer their features for as low as $8.95 per month, but you can still use your free ISP to connect to the Web.

**Stuff your mailboxes.** Besides free Internet connections, you should explore the world of free e-mail. Set up as many e-mail accounts as you want — they won't cost a penny. Have one just for messages from friends and family and another for business-related notes. Have a third to store your photograph e-mails. Sign up for one more just because you can!

You'll find tons of Web sites offering free e-mail so you can be picky. Sign up with the big names — Yahoo.com, AltaVista.com, Excite.com, Hotmail.com — because they give the biggest mailboxes. Once you start collecting dozens of new e-mails each day from your loved ones, you'll know why it is important to have a roomy mailbox.

**Hit the shopping spots.** This free keyboard is specially designed to make surfing the Web easier. With buttons that send you straight to the hottest shopping spots, it will make you feel like a pro in no time. Even better, you receive free e-mail service, too. Visit <www.swiftboard.com>.

**Soup up your computer.** Internet sites also give you the chance to stock up on free computer programs. Games, financial planners, virus scanners, educational lessons, music players — you can save any or all of these onto your own computer.

Visit these sites for a taste of what you'll find.

★ <www.completelyfreesoftware.com>
★ <http://a524.g.akamai.net/7/524/1239/25/akamai.freeshop.com/pg00042.htm>
★ <www.zdnet.com/downloads>

The Web's free stuff does not stop here. Since the Internet is constantly growing, you'll always have new and different things to take advantage of at no charge. So keep looking.

## 2 deals to speed you along the Internet highway

You may have seen it advertised on television: an unbelievable deal that lets you lease a computer and get free Internet service — all for one monthly fee. And it's true. Today a few companies do offer rental plans for computers.

For example, PeoplePC and Direct Web both offer a package for a personal computer and Internet service for $24.95 per month. For $10 more each month, the package includes a printer, scanner, and larger screen. You just have to pay this price for three years, and then the computer is yours.

This type of deal makes it easy to buy a computer, especially if you don't know your RAM from your ROM. You only have to choose between the simple and the fancy package, but in both cases you get an IBM machine that is Internet ready. You are locked into a three-year contract, though, so make sure you understand exactly what you're getting before you sign on the dotted line.

For more information, call Direct Web at 888-929-2932, or visit their Web site at <www.directweb.com>. Contact PeoplePC at 800-736-7537 or <www.peoplepc.com>.

Another Internet option to consider is WebTV. It turns your TV into a computer, allowing you to surf the Web and e-mail your friends right on your television screen. The machine looks like a VCR and sits on top of your television or entertainment center. You can use the keyboard from your couch.

The WebTV set will cost you around $250, with Internet service costing an additional $21.95 per month. Just remember that you can only use WebTV to surf the Internet or to send e-mail — not for word processing or games. Also, be sure to compare costs. If you buy WebTV and use it for one year at current prices, you will have paid over $500. For three years, you will have paid more than $1,000. Today you can buy a full-fledged computer at both those prices.

You can contact WebTV at 800-469-3288 for all the details. If you have access to a computer, check out their Web site at <www.webtv.com>.

So if you're considering one of these specials, be sure you research them thoroughly, making note of the drawbacks. Depending on what is important to you — ease and convenience, for instance — WebTV or PeoplePC might be the right bet for you. Do your homework first, and you'll end up a satisfied customer.

## High-tech help at no cost

It's only when something goes wrong with your computer that you realize how much you need it. Some people spend hundreds of dollars to have minor glitches repaired. But you don't have to dole out that kind of money. When your computer acts funny, just visit one of these Internet repair shops, where you'll get free advice to straighten out your system.

★ Ask the advice of the volunteers at <www.epeople.com>. One of them will reply within 24 hours with the computer-saving tip you need. Epeople.com even has a page where you describe your dilemma to other Web surfers like yourself.

★ Find a similar page at <www.helponthe.net >. Explain what's wrong with your computer, and receive the help of other Internet travelers.

★ Professional computer experts — called "tekkies" in the Internet world — provide help at <www.experts-exchange.com>. They actually compete to see who can solve your problem, so you are sure to land money-saving help here.

Some computer problems are serious, of course. If these Web helpers don't work, you might need to spend some money. But after visiting these sites, at least you'll have the peace of mind of knowing that repairs were necessary.

# BOOKS AND MAGAZINES

If you are a person who loves to read, you probably get a warm, special feeling when you stroll into a bookstore or library. You know that just beyond those book covers lie fascinating worlds, valuable lessons, and life-changing ideas all waiting to be discovered.

Or maybe you prefer to read magazines. Within their glossy pages, you can get the inside scoop on politics, learn to redecorate your home, check out the latest fashions, or keep up with the next big diet trend. For a true magazine buff, there are never enough issues.

Your passion for reading can certainly enhance your life, but it can also empty your pocketbook. What's a thrifty reader to do? With a little ingenuity and the right information, you can satisfy your love for reading without breaking your budget.

Read on to find clever ways to save on all those wonderful books and magazines you simply can't live without.

## Never pay retail again!

You don't need to walk into a bookstore and pay full, retail price for a book. If you have an envelope and a stamp, a telephone, or a computer, you can get books for less. You can write and request a catalog, or call to get your catalog in the mail even sooner. Most of these companies also have Web sites.

Christian Book Distributors
P.O. Box 7000
Peabody, MA 01961-7000
978-977-5000
<www.christianbook.com>

CBD gives discounts of 25 to 50 percent on Christian books, study guides, calendars, gifts, CDs, and tapes. Shipping cost is $3.50 per order for standard delivery. You may order from their catalog by phone or mail or from their Web site by credit card or by printing your order and mailing it with a check.

Dover Publications
31 East 2nd St.
Mineola, NY 11501
516-294-7000

Dover has catalogs available in several different areas of interest. They reprint older books in an inexpensive, softcover format, as well as printing original works. Their products are amazingly inexpensive and of good quality. With a huge selection of books on art, crafts, and vintage fashion plus collections of non-copyrighted designs, they are a favorite of thrifty artists and craftsmen. They also have wonderful coloring, puzzle, and activity books for children and grandchildren. Shipping and handling is a flat fee of $5 for any size order.

Bargain Book Warehouse
Soda Creek Press
P.O. Box 8515
Ukiah, CA 95482-8515
800-301-7567
<www.1bookstreet.com>

This source for bargain books has a free catalog and a Web site. Discounts begin at 10 to 20 percent and go up to 90 percent. Soda Creek Press also has two other catalogs —"Mysteries by Mail" for mystery novels and "Manderley" for romance novels.

Their Web site is divided into six different "streets," with selections of books in the categories of bargains, mystery, romance, cookbooks, audio (books on tape), and kids. Most bargain books are 40 to 60 percent off, and there is a wide selection of large-print books.

Shipping costs are one low price of $1.99 per order (includes any number of books), and orders of $15 or more are currently shipped free. Write or call for a catalog, or visit their Web site.

Daedalus Books and Music
P.O. Box 6000
Columbia, MD 21045-6000
800-395-2665
<www.daedalus-books.com>

Daedalus Books publishes 12 free catalogs a year, showcasing some fine and unusual books available at big discounts. Most of their books are publishers' overstocks, from which they pick those titles they feel have lasting value. The selection is not quite as wide as some discount book sellers, and quantities are limited, so you need to go ahead and order a book if you see one you like. You can pay by credit card or check, and shipping is one price of $4.95 per order.

Edward R. Hamilton Bookseller
Dept. 5166
Falls Village, CT 06031-5000
<www.hamiltonbook.com>

This company used to do business by mail order only but now has a Web site where you can view the titles and prices of a large selection of books. Whether you order from their catalog or the Web site, you must enclose a written or printed form and a check or money order when you request a book.

Discounts are usually about 30 percent on current best sellers, more on slightly more seasoned choices. Some remainders, publishers' close-outs, and overstocks are up to 80 percent off. Satisfaction is guaranteed. Write for a free catalog or visit their Web site. Shipping costs are $3 per order plus sales tax if you live in Connecticut.

## A sure-fire path to bargain books

Believe it or not, the very books you want to read may be available at bargain-basement prices or even for free. It may just take a little effort on your part to track them down.

**Support your local library.** Libraries are the original bargains for book lovers. They give you access to more books than you could read in a lifetime, and the books are free except for the occasional late fee you might end up paying. Most libraries also have books on tape you can check out if you prefer listening to your books rather than reading them.

These days, many libraries are linked into a network so that if yours doesn't have the book you want, it can get it from another branch. Many also let you keep books longer than the traditional two-week period.

Your local library is also a great place to start if you want your own editions. Most libraries have an annual book sale where you can pick up older gems for just pennies and, at the same time, help replenish the library's stock of bestsellers.

**Check out your neighborhood.** Another good way to get low-cost books is to buy them at garage sales. Most books are priced at under a dollar, and many paperbacks are just 25 cents. If you live in an area with lots of garage sales, a tank of gas and a few dollars could net you months of bargain reading.

If you know something about old books, you may even discover hidden treasure on one of your excursions. One Georgia man recently paid $2.50 for two old books at a garage sale, then sold them to a book dealer the same day for $50.

**Scout the sales.** New books are readily available at discount prices, too. Large bookstore chains, such as Barnes and Noble, B. Dalton Bookseller, and Books-A-Million, usually have bargain book tables within each store. The tables tend to be even more plentiful before the Christmas holidays.

You may not be able to find a specific book on sale or the latest bestseller, but you'll be surprised at the excellent quality and large discounts. Check the sale tables frequently since the selection is driven by the store's excess inventory.

**Look for a creative outlet.** If you happen to live in a town that has one or more publishing companies, check to see if they have company outlets where they sell discounted books. You could find wonderful reading material at a fraction of retail price.

## Join the club for great book prices

Book clubs can be a great way to stock your library for less. If you decide you would like to join one, here are a few popular choices:

**Book-of-the-Month Club** — This is the grandaddy of book clubs, established in 1926, but its books and approach are up-to-the-minute. It even has a Web site. Currently, you can buy five books for $1 each and a sixth book for $4.95. Then you only need to purchase one more in the next year to fulfill your obligation.

You will be sent a brochure about every three weeks (17 times a year) with a "main selection" to accept or reject. This book club does business the old-fashioned way — it sends you the merchandise with an invoice enclosed. You don't have to give out your credit card number or pay in advance.

New and classic hardcover books are normally discounted 30 to 40 percent, with the opportunity to earn points toward bigger discounts. The current free gift for joining is an attaché case to carry your new books. To request a packet of information on joining the club, write to:

Book-of-the-Month Club, Inc.
Customer Service
Camp Hill, PA 17012
E-mail: <www.bomc.com>

**Crafter's Choice** — This club is a subsidiary of Book-of-the-Month Club that is geared to crafters and people who like to sew. When you join Crafter's Choice, you get your first four books for $1 each, plus shipping and handling. You can get another selection for 50 percent off the retail price at the same time and fulfill half of your obligation for the year. Discounts on retail prices are normally up to 25 percent, with special sale discounts up to 50 percent.

The club sends you a letter with a "main selection" about every three weeks. It doesn't have a Web site, but it has a toll-free service for replying or ordering by touch-tone phone.

A recent membership offer included a free tote bag and a chance to win a Bernina sewing machine. The envelope contained a free gift — a plastic stencil in an ivy design that you can use for craft projects. To request a packet of information, write to:

Crafter's Choice Book Club
Customer Service
Camp Hill, PA 17012-0001

**Traveler's Book Club** — Aimed at seasoned travelers, this is a different type of book club. There are no required purchases and no featured selections to accept or reject. If you buy a book, you are a member and will receive mailings for the next year. Trail guides, maps, and travel books are discounted at least 10 percent to as much as 35 percent. You'll find the most popular books as well as the most obscure, and maps "to any location in the world." Write to:

Traveler's Book Club
P.O. Box 191554
Atlanta, GA 31119
<www.mindspring.com/~travbkcl/tbcintro.html>

**Quality Paperback Book Club** — Choose four books for $1 each and a fifth for $2.99. You are not obligated to buy any more books, but you may want to since they publish paperback editions of current hardbacks at discount prices. You don't have to give out your credit card number, and you pay for the books after they arrive. Every three weeks you'll receive a mailing and will need to reply. The address is:

Quality Paperback Book Club
Customer Service
Camp Hill, PA 17012-8845
800-348-7128
<www.qpb.com>

# Books for cheap on the Internet

Buying books online is about as easy as it gets. You sit in front of a computer screen, do a little typing, and the books arrive at your door in a few days. All you need is a computer with an Internet connection. If you don't have one at home, you could go to your local library or borrow a bit of online time from a friend.

Generally, you must use a major credit card to purchase books on the Internet. Most big sites are, by expert accounts, safe to use in this way. But read their security policy first to be sure you are satisfied. Shipping is usually timely, but companies may be a little slower during the Christmas rush.

Here are some Internet booksellers you might want to visit online:

**Amazon Books**
<www.amazon.com>
Customer service: 800-266-7575

Amazon has become a household word among Internet users. Started in 1995, it is the largest of the online booksellers, with more than 13 million customers worldwide. It started out selling only books, but now has expanded into music, videos, gifts, toys, games, electronics, and even an online auction. Amazon.com has a huge inventory of books that you can search by title, author, or subject.

They have a bargain book section with discounts up to 80 percent off retail and groupings of books labeled as under $15, under $10, or under $5. Everyday discounts on books of every description run about 15 percent and up. Shipping costs for books are $3 per shipment plus 99 cents per item.

### BookCloseOuts.com
<www.bookcloseouts.com>
Customer service: 888-402-7273

This Web site has good books at low prices — often including a 50 percent discount or more. You can find current books at discounted prices, but their special "blowout" books are super bargains sold at a fraction of their original retail price. These may be books that sat on bookstore shelves for a while and simply didn't sell. So even though they are technically "new," they may appear a little shopworn when you receive them — good for your own reading, but not suitable as gifts. Books are usually available in small quantities so the site tells you how many they have left of each. Shipping and handling costs vary but are usually $3 to $4.50 in the United States and Canada.

### Books-a-Million.com
<www.booksamillion.com>
800-201-3550

The Books-a-Million chain of large retail bookstores also has an excellent Web site. You get a brief synopsis of each book in the description, as well as the publisher and price. Bargain books can be searched by category. Discounts are from 10 percent to more than 70 percent off retail price. Most discounts are over 50 percent.

You get a larger discount on prices if you join the "Millionaire's Club" for a $5 yearly fee, but the prices are good even if you're not a member. This is what "Club Price" refers to on the Web site. If you click on the name of a book to get more details, you will see the regular discounted price. Standard shipping is $3 per order plus 95 cents per item.

### Kingbooks.com
<www.kingbooks.com>
Customer service: 888-660-6466

More than 1 million book titles can be searched on this Web site by author, title, or subject. Little information is available about each book, aside from price, but available books seem to be current ones. The discount on current titles is about 20 percent. Some books listed are not yet released but will be sent to you when they are published. Standard shipping is $3 per order and 95 cents per item with four to 10 days for delivery.

You can search the site for children's books by grade level. They also have a link to their own Web site for educational books, tapes, and videos at <www.educlick.com>.

### All Books 4 Less.com
<www.allbooks4less.com>
Customer service: 800-231-8932

This Web site guarantees the lowest prices on the Internet, and they certainly appear to be. You can actually compare their book prices to those of Amazon.com or another competitor. If their price isn't the lowest, you can "tell" them how much you will pay for the book.

You'll find very low book prices on this site, some up to 79 percent off retail. They also offer various specials such as discounts on shipping or "buy one, get one for half price." Standard shipping (three to seven days) is $3 per shipment and 95 cents per item.

## Compare and save online

Are you shopping for a book over the Internet? Do you want to save time but still find the best price? You can access online tools that will do exactly what you want — find a book and compare available prices — and do it fast.

These special search engines allow you to type in the name of a book and get cost comparisons from several different online bookstores. You can choose the price of the book and the type and costs of shipping that best meet your needs. Then just click on the deal you choose, and you will be linked to the home page of the online book merchant.

These search engines will help you compare and save:

<www.bestedeal.com>
<www.pricescan.com>
<www.addall.com>
<www.dealpilot.com>

---

## Book clubs — bonanzas or bad news?

Who wouldn't jump at the chance to get four books for 99 cents or a free book and a free gift? The initial deal is always excellent, but that's not what keeps book clubs in business. It's what you do after joining that counts.

Here are some questions you should get answered before you commit to joining a club:

- How long must you remain a member of the club, and how many books do you have to buy during your membership?

- After the introductory offer, how much are books routinely discounted?

- Can you afford to buy the required books within the time specified?

- How much are shipping and handling costs?

- Does the club send you a flyer to notify you of the next "featured" book, or does it automatically send the book?

- How easy is it to decline the featured book if you don't want it?

- How easy is it to return a book if you don't want it? Who pays postage?

---

# A world of free books from the World Wide Web

With a computer and access to the Internet, you can have thousands of books at your fingertips — and all for free!

Online libraries allow you to read books right on the Internet, or you can download them onto a disk (or several disks) and read them at leisure on your home computer. If you like, you can even print them out. But you might want to limit that to really short books, or you could end up spending a fortune to refill your printer ink cartridge.

If you have a computer at home but you don't have Internet access, visit your local library. Take your blank computer disks with you, and ask your librarian to show you how to download a book to your own disks.

Here are three online libraries with an amazing array of electronic "bookshelves" right at your fingertips:

### Project Gutenberg
<http://promo.net/pg>

This first public online library was begun in 1971 when a young man named Michael Hart was given an enormous amount of free computer time to use as he wished. He decided the best use was to establish a library of important books on computer files that could be easily read by anyone with access to a computer.

Project Gutenberg has a search engine that allows you to look for a book by title or by the author's name, or you can browse the extensive list of authors and books. Because of the United States' copyright laws, the PG library consists of works written before 1923. Of course, this includes the Bible, the works of Shakespeare, and a wealth of great books.

### Bartleby.com
<www.bartleby.com>

Named for the character Bartleby the Scrivener in Herman Melville's book of the same name, this online library contains thousands of classic works of fiction, nonfiction, reference, and poetry. The site is easy to use and contains a select group of classic books and collections of poetry and stories by famous authors. It also has a link to Bartlett's Quotations Online.

### The On-Line Books Page
<http://digital.library.upenn.edu/books>

This Web site by digital librarian John Mark Ockerbloom is housed at the University of Pennsylvania Library. It includes more than 10,000 books, listed with their net addresses and access sites. You just click on a link and automatically go to the book of your choice. It may take a couple of minutes to open some of the links, so be patient.

Here you'll find lots of books and documents in specialty areas, such as those that pertain to the Civil War or to women writers through the ages. The archives contain an amazing array of books in foreign languages, from the best known to the most obscure.

## Save big bucks with free online encyclopedia

You can find a mind-boggling array of information on the Internet, but you can't always trust what you read. What if you could look up information on almost any subject and know you could rely on the answer?

Well, look no further. The Encyclopedia Britannica has joined the computer age and is now offering its entire contents online. Information that would cost you as much as $1,250 for a 32-volume set of reference books is available for free on the Internet. Just log on to your computer, and go to <www.britannica.com> to take advantage of this service.

Search on any topic, and you'll come up with the usual research data as well as other Web sites, magazine articles, and books that relate directly to your subject. You can gather all the free information you need and be assured that it's backed up by Britannica's good name. Now that's a deal!

## Free paperbacks for your reading pleasure

Order a book, read it, and exchange it online. You can do all this for free by logging on to a unique Web site called TheBookcart.com.

If you read a lot of paperback books, this site is a gold mine. As a member, you can browse the list of books available from other members and order up to five at a time. If someone requests one of your books, you pay the postage (about $1.13 per book) to send it out. Your account gets credited $1.35 for each book you send, and debited $1.50 when you order. So the program essentially is free except for a 15-cent service charge per book.

Currently, you have to register on the secure site using a credit card, but the company is working on a system that accepts checks. You also may fax in your credit card number if you wish. TheBookcart.com is housed at 222 Saint John St., Suite 144, Portland, ME 04102. For more details and to log on to the book exchange, go to the Web address <www.thebookcart.com>.

## 5 ways to get your favorite magazines for free

Want to get all the magazines you want without paying a penny? Try these strategies:

**Throw a neighborhood magazine swap.** Everyone can bring spare magazines and a snack or covered dish, then exchange good reading to their heart's content.

**Reduce, re-use, recycle.** When you visit your local recycling center, check for magazines you haven't read yet. Take them home, read them, and replace them on your next visit.

**Get a beauty bonus.** If you regularly use a beauty salon, ask the owner to let you have the old magazines when they are replaced. You'll save her the trouble of taking them out in the trash.

**Check with your local library.** They often clean out their periodicals after a specified time, and they can give you the older magazines instead of throwing them away.

**Be a borrower.** Of course, if you don't mind taking the time to go to the library, you can enjoy lots of magazines there for free, along with peace and quiet and a comfortable chair to read in.

## Save up to 90 percent on subscriptions

If you could save $30 off the cover price of a magazine by subscribing through its Web site, you'd probably jump at the chance. But wait — with a little time and effort, you may save even more.

One popular general-interest magazine sells on its own Web site for $12.95 for 13 issues, or about $1 each. That's almost $30 off the cover price of $42 — a great deal. But if you checked five online magazine dealers, you'd find offers of $9.99 for 12 issues (83 cents each) or $9.98 for 13 issues (77 cents each). The dealers beat the magazine's price hands down.

These Internet dealers claim they can save you up to 80 or 90 percent off the cover price of your favorite magazines. To see if you can benefit from these great savings, log on to their Web sites:

<www.enews.com>

<www.magazines.com>

<www.absolutemagazines.com>

<www.magsdirect.com>

<www.mags4sale.com>

It probably would be worth your time to search each of them for the best discount. Just beware of any postage charges added to your subscription price, which could turn your good deal into a bad one. You'll see the extra charge on the subscription form, so be sure to check.

---

### A whale of a sale on magazines

Garage and estate sales can be an excellent source of inexpensive magazines. They are usually a last-ditch effort to find a home for the glossy pages before they go to the trash can.

Stay away from expensive magazine collections billed as "investments," however, unless you really know the market value or they are something you simply must have. Otherwise, you can end up spending too much for "collectibles" that are worthless.

---

# Guaranteed good reading — absolutely free

Many magazines offer their first issue on a free-trial basis. If you don't like the magazine after reading it, you can return the invoice marked "cancel," not pay anything, and keep the issue for free. Here are some no-obligation offers for one or more issues.

**U.S. News and World Report.** If you like to keep informed about news and politics, you might want to try this weekly magazine. Four to six weeks after your request, you should receive four free issues. You will then be offered a subscription of $15 for 22 more issues (80 percent off the cover price).

U.S. News and World Report
P.O. Box 52760
Boulder, CO 80322-2760
800-333-8130
<www.usnews.com/usnews/home.htm>

**Better Homes and Gardens.** For people who enjoy the latest in decorating, building and remodeling, cooking, gardening, and crafts, this magazine is a treasure trove of ideas. They'll give you two years of the magazine for the price of one, so you actually get one year free. The price is $19 ($16 subscription plus $3 shipping).

Better Homes and Gardens Magazine
P.O. Box 37429
Boone, IA 50037-0429
800-374-4244
<www.bhglive.com>

**Travel 50 and Beyond.** Send for a free issue of this travel magazine, and if you like it, you can order three more issues for $9.95, or 37 percent off the cover price. This publication for travelers over 50 features articles on how to save money on travel costs, rental cars, hotels, and tourist attractions.

Travel 50 and Beyond
1502 Augusta Drive, Suite 415
Houston, TX 77057
800-338-4962
<www.travel50andbeyond.com>

**Marco Polo.** This publication bills itself as "the magazine for adventurous travelers over 50." If you're interested in active vacations, this magazine may be just what you're looking for. Contact them for a free issue. If you like it, you can get three more issues for $10.

Marco Polo Publications
1299 Bayshore Blvd., Suite B
Dunedin, FL 34698-4246
727-735-9455
<www.travelroads.com/subscribe/index.asp>

# TREASURE TROVE OF TRAVEL DEALS

Traveling is one of the great joys of life. Unfortunately, it can also be one of the more expensive. Some people believe dream vacations are only for the lucky few with a hefty income or those who don't mind going into debt. That's not necessarily true.

In this chapter, you will find resources you can use to help you save a bundle on your next vacation. There are tips for saving on airline flights, getting free lodging, gaining free admission to national parks and recreation areas, and finding free campsites.

Whether your dream vacation includes lying on the beach, camping in the woods, or visiting a foreign country, this chapter can help you travel for less and enjoy yourself more.

## Be your own travel agent for free

The first step in planning a vacation is deciding where you want to go. Get as much information about your chosen spot as you can. This will eliminate any unpleasant surprises.

If you're going to vacation in the United States, contact the state tourist bureaus. They usually offer free planning guides, vacation kits, or brochures. For a complete list of bureaus and contact information, go to this Internet address: <www.armchair.com/bureau/bur.html>.

Here are a few contacts for the New England states:

★ Connecticut Office of Travel and Tourism: 800-282-6863
★ Maine Office of Tourism: 888-624-6345
★ Massachusetts Office of Travel and Tourism: 800-227-6277
★ New Hampshire Tourism: 800-386-4664
★ Rhode Island Tourism and Travel Center: 800-556-2484
★ Vermont Tourism Department: 800-837-6668
★ Cape Cod Chamber of Commerce: 888-332-2732

★ Greater Boston Convention and Visitors Bureau: 888-733-2678

If you would like to travel to another part of the world but are hesitant about vacationing outside the United States, Hawaii is the place for you. Get everything you need to plan your Hawaiian vacation by contacting the Hawaii Visitors & Convention Bureau. You can order brochures on everything from upcoming events, accommodations, shopping, and attractions to information on Hawaiian businesses, organizations, and education. Call 800 Go Hawaii (464-2924) or visit their Web site at <www.gohawaii.com>.

## How to find the cheapest flights

Flying obviously is the fastest way to travel but also one of the most expensive. It doesn't have to cost you an arm and a leg though. Airline consolidators specialize in selling discounted fares for major airlines, and you can save a bundle by using their services.

Consolidators either buy airline tickets in bulk or have a special agreement with airlines to receive discounted tickets. In the past, consolidators only made their tickets available to travel agents, but many now offer tickets to the general public. Here are a few you may want to try.

★ OneTravel.com sells discounted air tickets, hotel rooms, cruises, and vacation packages. Contact 800-929-2523 or <www.onetrav el.com/index>.

★ EconomyTravel.com specializes in international flights. Contact 888-222-2110 or <www.economytravel.com>.

★ Air Travel Discounts specializes in flights to Europe, Asia, the Middle East, Africa, and India. Contact 800-888-2621 or <www.airtraveldiscounts.com>.

★ 1800FlyCheap offers discounts on advance-purchase tickets. Call 800-359-4683.

★ Cheap Tickets Inc. specializes in selling discount tickets for travel within the United States. Contact 800-672-4327 or <www.mrcheaps.com>.

★ Air4less sells discounted tickets for last minute trips. Contact 800-247-4537 or <www.air-4-less.com>.

★ CheapAirInc. can save you 20 percent on airline tickets for travel to other continents. They also sell tickets for last minute trips to Florida and for flights to small cities. Contact 800-243-2724 or <www.cheapfare.com>.

★ Travel Bargains, once owned by TWA, is one of the largest airline consolidators. Contact 800-247-3273 or <www.1800airfare.com>.

★ Skyauction.com auctions airline tickets, as well as hotel rooms and vacation packages, over the Internet. Check <www.skyauction.com>.

If your travel plans run to the exotic, and Africa is on your list of places to see, try these consolidators for big savings:

Cape to Cairo African Business and Adventure Travel
2761 Unicorn Lane, NW
Washington, DC 20015
800-356-4433
<www.capecairo.com>

Dollar Saver Travel
10630-A Metcalf
Overland Park, KS 66212
913-381-5050
<www.dstravel.com>

Spector Travel of Boston, Inc.
2 Park Plaza
Boston, MA 02116
800-879-2374
<www.spectortravel.com>

If you're willing to travel on short notice, check into 11th Hour Vacations at <www.11thhourvacations.com>. You tell them your interests and desired vacation spots, and they will send you an e-mail when trips matching your description come up. You could save up to 70 percent off regular trip prices.

And for you adventurous types, Priceline.com allows you to set your own ticket price and take the chance they can find it for you. You have to be flexible enough to travel at any time on the dates you choose, and you must pay in advance by credit card. The ticket is non-refundable, so once your offer is accepted, there's no turning back. Check with <www.price line.com> for more information.

## Drive your way to hefty discounts

If you plan to travel by car on your next vacation but don't want to rack up the miles, why not rent one? Many rental companies have large cars and vans that are just perfect for family vacations. Scout around for deals; many companies offer discount rates to seniors or have special weekend rates.

You could also qualify for a discount if you are a member of a particular organization such as the AARP, AAA, or a union. Many also offer discounts through credit card companies. Look for coupons in your credit card statements. Here are some ways you can save when renting from the top companies.

Dollar Rent A Car offers coupons on the Internet. They also have a discount program designed for seniors. The Silver Dollar Club offers 10 percent off most rentals, no charge for additional drivers, and unlimited mileage for those 50 and older. Call 800-800-4000 or visit their Web site at <www.dollarcar.com>.

Alamo has several ways you can save. They offer discount rates to employees of the federal government and military personnel. They also offer summer discounts and weekend specials for everyone. If you make your reservation through the Internet, you will receive up to 20 percent off the retail rental price. They also offer discounts for cars rented in Europe. Call 800-462-5266, or check out their rates on the Web at <www.goalamo.com>.

Hertz car rental company offers discounts to American Automobile Association (AAA) members. They also have coupons for additional discounts in AAA magazines and through AAA clubs. Call 800-654-3131, or visit their Web site at <www.hertz.com>.

Here is a list of the major car rental companies not mentioned previously that may also offer discounts from time to time. Before you make your reservation, ask them what kind of discount programs they offer.

★ Avis: 800-230-4898 or 800-331-1212; <www.avis.com>
★ National: 800-227-7368; <www.nationalcar.com>
★ Budget: 800-527-0700; <www.budget.com>
★ Enterprise: 800-325-8007; <www.enterprise.com>
★ Thrifty: 800-847-4389; <www.thrifty.com>

## Hassle-free deals on car rentals

If you don't find anything to suit your budget with the major car rental companies, you may want to try a consolidator. Car rental consolidators work much like those for airlines and hotels. They rent cars for major car rental companies but at a discount price. The down side is that the majority of them make reservations only through the Internet. Here are some to try.

CarHire4Less claims to have rates discounted up to 30 percent off what the rental companies themselves are charging. The company is in London but books rentals worldwide. You can contact them at <www.carhire4less.co.uk>.

CheapCarRental.com also claims to have prices 30 percent lower than the rates of major car rental companies. They rent vehicles worldwide, including some vehicles you would not expect to see. Their selection includes cars, vans, limousines, heavy trucks, all terrain vehicles, and luxury cars. They can be reached at <www.cheapcarrental.com>.

Car-Rentals-Discounts.com has its Web site set up so you can compare prices of all rental companies before making your reservation. They can be reached at <www.cars-rentals-discounts.com>.

A-thru-Z Discount Car Rentals provides discount car rentals throughout the world. You can pick the class and type of car you would like and the location where you would like to pick it up. Check them out at <http://car-rental.from-a-z.com>.

Apex Internet Car Rentals allows you to make online reservations for cars in the United States and much of Canada, Europe, and Mexico. They make reservations for cars with many of the major car rental companies. You'll find them at <www.soft-links.com/carrentals/carrentals.htm>.

## Take the scenic route and save

Make getting there half the fun. Take a bus or train to your vacation destination and you'll save money and get in some great sightseeing along the way.

If you travel by bus, Greyhound offers a 10 percent discount to seniors 62 and older who join their Greyhound Seniors Club. Membership costs just $5. Non-members receive a 5 percent discount. If you purchase a round-trip ticket at least three days in advance, you can bring along a friend for free. This offer may change at any time, so be sure and ask.

Greyhound buses are air-conditioned, non-smoking, and have reclining seats, tinted windows, and rest rooms on board. Depending on the length of the trip, the bus may make a few stops where you can stretch your legs and buy snacks.

For more information on schedules and fares, call Greyhound at 800-661-8747. Order tickets by calling 800-229-9424. You can also do some research on the Internet at <www.greyhound.com>.

Whether you are going on vacation or to visit family members, a train is a pleasant, interesting, and inexpensive way to travel. Amtrak offers a 15 percent discount to seniors 62 and older. They also offer complete travel packages — sometimes with considerable online discounts. Order brochures and travel planners through their Web site <www.amtrak.com> or call 800-USA-RAIL (872-7245) or 800-654-5748.

## Sleep easy and cheap

Your hotel room will probably be the biggest expense on your next vacation. But getting discounted or even free hotel rooms isn't as difficult as you may think. You just have to know where to look.

The easiest and often most convenient way to find a discounted hotel room is to make your reservation through a hotel consolidator. Much like airline consolidators, they purchase rooms in bulk for a cheaper price — savings they pass on to you. Discounts are often as high as 65 percent. Contact a hotel consolidator when you are traveling to a large city or during a time when hotel rooms are scarce. They will often have rooms when most hotels are sold out.

★ Hotel Reservations Network, one of the largest hotel consolidators, has rooms at 1,600 properties across the United States, Europe, and Canada. They guarantee their low rates and do not charge a fee for their service. You can make reservations by calling 800-964-6835 or by visiting their Internet site at <www.hoteldiscount.com>.

★ Quickbook is another consolidator with rooms in 19 cities. Smaller than Hotel Reservations Network, they also do not charge for their service. Call them at 800-789-9887 or visit <www.quickbook.com>.

Another simple way to get a discount on a hotel room is with coupons. You'll find them in a variety of places. Many credit card companies include them in your statement. Visit <www.roomsaver.com> to print discount coupons for major hotels in the United States from the comfort of your own home. If you do not have a computer, use one at the library or local community college.

A slightly more nerve-wracking way to get discounted hotel rooms is by bidding for them in an auction. Taking this route, however, will often get you an extremely good deal. Certain companies auction hotel rooms, airline tickets, cruises, and even entire vacations. The selection and price range vary but you could save 80 percent off retail value. The only hitch is that you must bid from a computer — another time to take advantage of your library or local community college. Visit <www.bid4vacations.com> or <uBid.com> and see what you can find. Priceline.com is similar since you place a bid for accommodations or other travel arrangements. You'll be more successful if your dates or times are flexible, but you usually have an answer within 15 minutes.

If you're looking for free rooms, it just takes a little more creativity. Some service companies offer free hotel rooms with a trial membership. For example, Preferred HealthPlus offered a free North American Dream Vacation to anyone ordering a 30-day risk-free trial membership in their discount health care program. For one dollar, TravelersAdvantage offered a hotel stay and $700 in American Airlines savings to anyone purchasing a 3-month membership.

You'll find offers such as these in credit card statements, bulk mailings, and newspaper ads. If you are not familiar with the company making the offer, contact the Better Business Bureau before agreeing to any terms.

If you prefer to make reservations the traditional way — by calling the hotel — you can still save money. Many hotels offer discounts to senior travelers, members of AARP or AAA, active duty and retired military, and anyone associated with certain banks or insurance carriers. Just be sure you ask about discounts before you make your reservation.

## Make new friends and stay free around the world

Home exchanging also known as vacation exchanging, is a popular way for the frugal traveler to vacation around the world. It allows you to visit interesting places without having to pay any lodging costs.

The idea is to simply exchange homes for a brief time with someone from another country or another state. You can make arrangements on your own or through a vacation exchange club. If you're planning to travel abroad, you'll have the best luck with an exchange club. Membership in the club includes a directory of people from all parts of the world interested in exchanging homes.

It's safer than it may appear. Before the actual exchange takes place, you talk or write to each other several times. This allows you to back out if you feel uncomfortable with the arrangement. Here are some additional ways to ensure the safety of you and your home.

★ Ask for references. Many swap homes with several different families and former exchangers are great references.

★ Ask about the homeowner's background and profession.

★ Ask for a picture of the house.

★ Put any agreements in writing.

★ Have a friend or neighbor drop in a few times to see how things are going.

In addition to saving the cost of high-priced hotels, home exchanging is also a great way to meet new and interesting people. Here is a list of companies that can help you get started.

Homelink is the largest exchange club. It has more than 11,000 members in over 50 countries. Membership ranges from $50 to $100 a year. They publish five directories annually. You can request free information before joining.

P.O. Box 650
Key West, FL 33041
800-638-3841
<www.swapnow.com>

Landfair Home Exchange Club, in addition to publishing directories, also offers a custom matching service. Membership is $29.95 a year.

54 Landfair Crescent
Scarborough, Ontario
Canada M1J 3A7
800-458-6557
<www.landfair.com>
or
6432 Alemendra St.
Fort Pierce, FL 34951
561-467-0634

Teachers Swap is designed especially for teachers. The similar schedule with long summer breaks allows teachers to more easily exchange with each other. Membership is $45 for the first year and $35 for each following year. You can purchase a directory without listing your home for $55.

P.O. Box 454
Oakdale, NY 11769-0454
516-244-2845

Teacher Trip.com is a free exchange service especially for teachers, retired teachers, or other teaching or administration personnel.

1358 Fair Ave.
Peterborough, Ontario
Canada K9K 2G1
705-749-3437
<www.teachertrip.com>

The Invented City combines the directories of several home exchange clubs from around the world. Membership is $75 a year and includes directories.

41 Sutter Street
Suite 1090
San Francisco, CA 94104
800-788-2489
<www.invented-city.com>

Trading Homes International is similar to Invented City in that they also combine the directories of several home exchange clubs. In fact, the two companies share most of their listings. Membership ranges from $65 to $95 a year. You can look at the directory on the Internet or you can receive the booklets in the mail. Your membership also includes a pamphlet filled with home exchanging tips.

P.O. Box 787
Hermosa Beach, CA 90254
800-877-8723
<www.trading-homes.com>

Worldwide Home Exchange Club specializes in American/British exchanges but has members all over the world. You can receive a membership directory for $31 plus $7 shipping.

P.O. Box 21379
Washington, DC 20009-1379
212-588-5057

The International Home Exchange Network is an Internet-based home exchange club. Potential exchangers make arrangements through e-mail. Membership is just $29.95 a year.

P.O.Box 915253
Longwood, FL 32791
407-862-7211
<www.ihen.com>

Intervac specializes in exchanges to Europe. Membership is $73 for senior citizens.

30 Corte San Fernando
Tiburon, CA 94920
800-756-4663

# Vacation for free in the great outdoors

Camping is a great, and often inexpensive, way for a family or group of friends to spend time in the great outdoors. But long trips, which are increasingly popular among retirees, can often get expensive. You may have a hard time finding a clean and safe campground with reasonable campsite prices. Here are some creative ways to save on your campsite without sacrificing the quality of your vacation.

**Stay at a free campsite.** If you're planning to visit out West and you are computer savvy, check out <www.freecampgrounds.com>. They have a list of campgrounds where you can stay for free or a small donation. The campsites are located from Texas to California. Many are non-traditional campsites such as ranches and wildlife preserves. Each campsite listing includes details on the location and a summary of the campground, often written by those who have stayed at the particular site.

**Volunteer at a national or state park.** Spending a week or even a month volunteering at a state or national park can provide you with a rewarding and adventurous vacation while saving you a bundle on lodging expenses. Often, the park provides volunteers with free campsites with hook ups.

The Volunteers in Parks (VIP) program pairs those with an interest in the outdoors with parks in need of assistance. You could participate in an archeological dig, help maintain and manage national trails, monitor wildlife, or help to restore a building. You can get more information on the VIP program by contacting local parks in your area of interest, by calling the National Park Service at 202-208-6843, or by checking out <www.nps.gov/volunteer/vipguide.htm> on the Internet.

Passport in Time is another volunteer program that will allow you to participate in archeological digs and historic research. Project lengths are anywhere from a weekend to a month. Free campsites with hook ups are often provided. For more information contact:

Passport in Time Clearinghouse
P.O. Box 31315
Tucson, AZ 85751-1313
800-281-9176
<www.volunteeramerica.net/usfs/PIT_Home.htm>

**Try non-traditional campsites.** Many retail stores and restaurants, such as Wal-Mart, Kmart, and Cracker Barrel, allow campers to park their RVs overnight in their parking lots. Flying J Truck Stops also welcome overnight RV parking. No hook ups or dump stations are available, but the sites are free and convenient.

Some stores oppose the practice, however. So, before you settle in for the night, circle the parking lot to see if there are any "No Overnight RV Parking" signs. You should also check in with the manager of the store when you arrive. Often, he will alert security, providing you with not only a free site but a safe one as well.

## Get your free ticket to natural and historic sites

If you are 62 or older, you qualify for the Golden Age Passport. It entitles you to free lifetime entrance to national parks, monuments, historic sites, recreation areas, and national wildlife refuges. You will also get a 50-percent discount on federal services and facilities such as camping sites, boat launching, and parking. Fees charged by private organizations are not covered.

The card costs $10. You must buy it in person and show proof of your age. The passport will admit everyone accompanying you, including friends, if you enter the federal site by car. Otherwise, it only applies to you, your spouse, and your children.

If you're blind or permanently disabled, you're eligible for another special deal called the Golden Access Passport, which provides the same discounts and free entrances.

You'll find the passports at most places they can be used so you don't have to buy them before you leave for your vacation. Look for them at:

★ National Park Service and Forest Service headquarters and regional offices.

★ Forest Service supervisor's offices and most Forest Service ranger station offices.

★ National Park System areas where entrance fees are charged.

★ Bureau of Land Management state and district offices.

★ Tennessee Valley Authority — Land Between the Lakes and recreation areas that charge fees.

★ Fish and Wildlife Service regional offices and national wildlife refuges that charge entrance fees.

★ Bureau of Reclamation — Hoover Dam.

★ U.S. Army Corps of Engineers' project offices.

If you are unsure whether a particular park accepts the cards, call the place you plan on visiting, or contact the National Park Service at:

1849 C Street, NW
Washington, DC 20240
202-208-6843
<www.nps.gov>

## Summer camp isn't just for kids

Do you miss the fun of summer camp? Here is your chance to relive some of those adventures or experience them for the first time. An Elderhostel program is like the summer camp of your childhood in that you have the opportunity to learn, make new friends, and have a very inexpensive vacation. Programs vary from one to several weeks and there's sure to be several to fit your interests.

First, you must understand the difference between a youth hostel and an Elderhostel. A hostel is simply a facility with shared, dormitory-style sleeping accommodations and usually a shared common room and bathroom. Most of these facilities are called youth hostels, but there are no age restrictions and you don't really need a membership to stay. If this sounds like the kind of adventure for you, decide what state or country you want to visit and contact their office of tourism, either by phone or on the Internet. You can also visit these Internet sites devoted to hostelling: <www.hostels.com> or <www.hiayh.org>.

Elderhostel, Inc., on the other hand, is an organization strictly for seniors, offering thousands of affordable educational programs in the United

States and throughout the world. An international network of over 2,000 institutions participates — from universities to national parks, to museums and conference centers. For one to four weeks, you'll attend lectures or discussions and take part in various learning adventures. The best part — no homework, exams, or grades. You can choose your program based on location, type of adventure, or area of interest.

The programs are too numerous to name, but you can raft down the Colorado River, learn to sculpt, climb a mountain, study cultural arts, become part of a service project, travel by train, bicycle, or steamboat. Program fees vary, but cover registration, accommodations, meals, classes, field trips, and limited accident insurance. On average, a six-night program in the United States will cost about $500. Elderhostel Inc. welcomes singles or couples, and accommodations range from dormitories to cabins, lodges, and hotels.

Elderhostel, Inc.
11 Avenue de Lafayette
Boston, MA 02111-1746
877-426-8056
<www.elderhostel.org>

Here are a couple of examples of the kind of inexpensive vacation you can have through Elderhostel, Inc. The Denali Foundation in Alaska, a non-profit education and research organization, sponsors several different programs. Their activities include attending winter carnivals, visiting national parks, riding the Alaska railroad, and studying mining communities. You can take part in nature walks and meet with naturalists, park rangers, and photographers. Contact the foundation by phone, 907-683-2597, or on the Internet, <www.denali.org>.

Study the American Cinema of the 20th Century, Love and Marriage in Shakespeare's Tragedy and Comedy, and Swing with the Big Bands for five nights in the Pennsylvania Pocono Mountains. The resort/convention center offers single and double rooms, indoor and outdoor pools, and lots of other amenities. Sponsored by AGE Inc., this Elderhostel program is truly an adventure in lifelong learning.

The University of Judaism Department of Continuing Education offers several programs based on the Jewish faith through The Schurgin Elderhostel Program.

Elderhostel Office at University of Judaism
15600 Mulholland Dr.
Bel Air, CA 90077
310-440-1535
<www.uj.edu/elderhostel/elder.html>

Canadians over 50 who enjoy new ideas and experiences should find out about Elderhostel Canada. This non-profit, charitable organization provides inexpensive, weeklong programs. You can experience history, culture, wildlife, and recreation throughout the year.

4 Cataraqui St.
Kingston, Ontario
Canada K7K 1Z7
887-426-8056

If you're young, or just young at heart, and really want an adventure, look into a rolling hostel, like the Green Tortoise. About 30 people spend from two days to sometimes a month traveling from one place to another on a large bus. The trip is open to anyone from infants to seniors.

Green Tortoise Adventure Travel
494 Broadway
San Francisco, Ca. 94133
800-TORTOISE (867-8647)
<www.greentortoise.com>

## Plan your vacation over the Internet for free

If you own a computer or have access to one at your library or local college, you can use the Internet to help plan your vacation — for free. There are several Web sites where you can order free brochures, maps, and planning guides for vacation destinations throughout the world.

★ Try <www.travelinformation.com>. They will send you free info on locations throughout the United States, Canada, and Mexico. Choose to receive guides on up to 25 of your favorite vacation spots from their list of over 100. Read detailed information on these areas to decide if a particular place is one you'd like to visit — even before you order the brochures.

★ For something out of the ordinary, visit <//freetravelbrochures. 4all.cc/> and get information on vacations specializing in art, education, sports, and other unique adventures.

★ Desteo offers free travel information for vacation spots in almost every part of the world. You choose an area to visit and the type of trip you're interested in and they will supply you with a list of contacts, maps, travel tips, and anything else you need to make your vacation worry-free. Feel like an exotic fishing trip to Costa Rica? How about a walking tour of some of Europe's medieval castles? However you spell adventure, this site can deliver. Visit <www.desteo.com>.

★ You can also get free travel brochures by checking out <www.web brochures.com> or <www.travelmonthly.com>.

## Pack your bags with extra savings

Luggage allows you to leave home while still taking the necessities of home with you. If you want something that will hold up to the rigors of travel, you can sometimes spend a bundle. But here are some tips on where to find quality luggage at discounted prices or even free.

At BaggageForLess.com you can find luggage at discounted prices and even receive a free travel accessory with a qualifying purchase. Order by phone (877-422-4243) or over the Internet at <www.baggageforless.com>.

Luggage On-line also offers discounts on luggage with a price guarantee. They have a variety of styles and sizes in several price ranges. Occasionally they will have free gifts with a purchase or weekly give-a-ways of free luggage. Call them at 888-958-4424 or find them on the Internet at <www.luggageonline.com>.

Bretts Luggage and Gifts has been selling luggage at discounted prices since 1951. You can order over the phone, by mail, through the Internet, or in person at their Massachusetts store.

423 Boston Post Rd.
Sudbury, MA 01776
888-627-3887

Santa Maria Discount Luggage sells several brands of luggage including Samsonite, Travelpro, and Briggs & Riley. You can order by phone or over the Internet 24 hours a day. If you buy five or more pieces, excluding Travelpro, you'll receive an extra 10 percent off your purchase.

125 E. Betteravia Rd.
Santa Maria, CA 93454
888-832-1201
<www.luggageman.com>

Irv's Luggage Warehouse has a large selection of discounted luggage at their four locations in Illinois. Call 888-300-4787 for more information or shop online at <www.irvs.com>.

Surray also sells quality luggage at discounted prices. They offer free monogramming and free ground shipping on orders of $100 or more. Their selection includes brands such as Tumi, Samsonite, Travelpro, and American Tourister.

125 Broad St.
Red Bank, NJ 07701
732-747-2557
<www.surrayluggage.com>

1st Street Luggage is another discount luggage retailer. Among other brands, they carry Hartmann, Travelpro, Kenneth Cole, Samsonite, Briggs & Riley, and American Tourister. You'll sometimes find special promotions of free merchandise and free or discounted shipping. You can order by phone by calling 845-624-0852 or over the Internet at <www.1stluggage.com>.

Outlet Malls are also a great place to find discounted luggage. Samsonite and American Tourister have outlets in several shopping centers across the country. To find a Samsonite, American Tourister or Lark outlet in your area contact Samsonite at:

Samsonite Corporation
Attn: E-Commerce Manager
91 Main St.
Warren, RI 02885
800-262-8282

You can also check out Outlet Bound at <www.outletbound.com>. This Internet site lists outlet stores throughout the country — including luggage outlets. You can search by state or brand of luggage.

If you're looking for designer luggage but don't want to pay high designer prices try The SNOB, Inc. This consignment shop carries a variety of merchandise including designer luggage.

1930 San Marco Blvd.
Jacksonville, FL 32207
877-590-7662
<//thesnob.net>

Where does lost airport luggage end up? In Scottsboro, Alabama at the Unclaimed Baggage Center. Over one million items of lost or unclaimed baggage and carry-ons wind up in this giant warehouse every year, making it one of the best places to buy discounted luggage. Not only can you buy new or slightly used luggage, but their contents, as well.

Since the instore stock changes almost daily, if you plan to visit the Center you'll have to take your chances on the choices. The Internet online selection is updated daily, but does not list everything available in the store.

Unclaimed Baggage Center
509 West Willow St.
Scottsboro, AL 35768
256-259-1525
<www.unclaimedbaggage.com>

# Get free last-minute items

When traveling, it's often the "little things" that add up. Here are a few you can get for nothing more than the cost of shipping and handling.

**The Airtight Keeper.** This 5-inch pouch will keep your keys, money, and jewelry safe while you're swimming, skiing, jogging, or just sightseeing. Several colors are available. Send a few color choices and $1.50 for shipping and handling to:

Alvin Peters
Dept. ATK-150
P.O. Box 2400
Albany, NY 12220

**Sun Alert Badge.** This badge will help you know if you're spending too much time in the sun. Just place the badge on either your skin or clothing in an area that will get direct sun exposure. The badge will change color when you're in danger of getting burned. Send $2 for shipping and handling to:

Jaye Products
3645 Boca Ciega Dr. #206
Naples, FL 33962

**Mini ID tags.** Use these tags on your luggage, backpack, purse, carry-on, etc. They are about one inch long and come in a variety of colors. Send $1 for shipping and handling to:

Eleanor Curran
Dept. ZMT
530 Leonard St.
Brooklyn, NY 11222

**Hawaiian bumper sticker.** You can get a free bumper sticker and inspirational card by sending a self-addressed stamped envelope to:

Live Aloha
P.O. Box 8578
Honolulu, HI 96830-0578

**Beach set.** If you have children or grandchildren, they will probably need a few "little things" too. This plastic children's set includes a shovel, rake, sand molds, and a bucket or sifter. The pieces range in size from 3 inches to 7 inches. Send $2.75 for shipping and handling to:

McVehil's Mercantile
45 Bayne Ave. Dept. BC
Washington, PA 15301

**Identification wristband.** This waterproof identification band is suitable for children one to 10 years old. There is a place on the underside of the band for you to write any information needed should the child get lost. Send a large self-addressed stamped envelope to:

Practical Parenting
Dept. MT-ID
Deephaven, MN 55391

**Free currency conversion.** If you're going to a foreign country, you should know the exchange rate ahead of time. Although many rates change slightly throughout the day, free Internet service for currency conversion will give you an idea of what to expect. Go to <www.xe.net/ucc/> and type in your information. Within a few minutes, you'll know what your money will be worth on your vacation.

**Free travelers checks.** If you're an American Express Gold or Platinum Card member, you can get free travelers checks. For more information, call 800-721-9768 or visit their Web site at <www.americanexpress.com>.

# LEARN MORE FOR LESS

Gandhi once said, "Live as if you were to die tomorrow. Learn as if you were to live forever." Lifelong learning is essential to aging gracefully. It helps you stay active and keep up with the ever-changing world.

In this chapter, you will find out where to go for the endless supply of free and low cost education resources available to seniors. Included is information on how you can go to college for free, learn to use a computer, and take free classes from the comfort of your own home.

You will also find information on how you can tour the Smithsonian without leaving your home, listen to historically significant speeches and conversations, study the ins and outs of music theory, and learn to speak a second language.

Take classes in a variety of subjects such as art, drama, exercise, and crafts through the many senior centers throughout the country. No matter what your interests, this chapter can help you explore the world through education.

## Get a degree — for free

Is the rising cost of higher education keeping you from going back to school? Many colleges and universities allow senior citizens to attend classes for free. You could receive college credit and even earn a bachelor's or a master's degree.

Here are some examples of colleges and universities throughout the country that have such a program for seniors:

★ New Jersey residents age 62 or older can attend Ramapo College tuition-free. You will receive credit for your course work.

★ In Alabama, both Gadsden State Community College and Jefferson State Community College allow seniors 60 or older to attend classes free of charge. They will also give you college credit for your course work.

★ In Connecticut, Asnuntuck Community College and Central Connecticut State University allow residents 62 and older to attend classes for free and receive college credit.

★ Clackamas Community College and Mount Hood Community College in Oregon both will let you attend classes free and receive college credit if you are 62 or older.

★ If you're at least 62, you could also attend Greenfield Community College in Massachusetts at no cost. You must be a resident of Massachusetts.

★ You can attend University of Colorado at Denver for free if you are a resident, 60 or older. However, you can't receive college credit for the classes.

★ If you're an Iowa senior 65 or older, you may audit classes (no credit received) at Simpson College, located approximately 12 miles south of Des Moines, at no cost. If you want credit for the classes, you can pay just half the regular tuition.

The State Senate in Missouri passed a bill awarding scholarships to residents 65 and older who wish to go back to college. The scholarship will allow you to attend the Missouri college of your choice for free. Although no credit is given for the classes and you must meet the entrance requirements for the school you wish to attend, it's a great opportunity to brush up on your skills and learn some new ones.

Virginia has a similar program. The Virginia Senior Citizens Higher Education Act of 1974 gives seniors the opportunity to attend a Virginia state college or university for free. If you are 60 or older and your income is less than $10,000 a year, you may enroll in courses and receive college credit. Regardless of your income, you may audit classes at no charge.

The majority of states have colleges and universities that will allow you to attend classes for free. Most of them offer the classes on a "space-available" basis, which means you enroll after paying students. Contact the college or university you wish to attend and ask about their policy on senior students.

# Get computer savvy

Every day computers become a bigger part of our lives. With the Internet, you can make travel arrangements, do your shopping, and even attend school from the comfort of your own home. If you're ready to jump on this cyberspace bandwagon, these Web sites can help.

AgeLight lists more than 1,500 computer-learning centers sponsored by many different organizations. The centers offer a variety of classes ranging from beginner to advanced. Contact AgeLight for more information and to find a center near you.

9057 Points Drive NE
Clyde Hill, WA 98004
425-455-8277
<www.agelight.org>

SeniorNet has more than 170 learning centers throughout the country where seniors can learn computer skills. They offer introductory as well as advanced classes. Learn to use a computer to do your taxes, keep track of your finances, or research your family's history. For a center near you, contact SeniorNet at:

121 Second St., 7th Floor
San Francisco, CA 94105
415-495-4990
<www.seniornet.org>

The Central Kansas Library System supports a series of computer training tutorials. Learn everything from how to use a mouse to hardware and software guides to Internet and e-mail help. Visit them at <www.ckls.org/~crippel/computerlab/tutorials>.

Computers Made Easy for Seniors is a free online tutorial with links to sites designed for seniors. Use the site to get information about health related topics, look up an old friend, find out what's happening in the senior community, and even create your own homepage. Find the classes listed at <www.csuchico.edu/~csu/seniors/computing.html>.

Sheclicks.com is a Web site aimed at women. Find free tips on using computers, keeping your computer running smoothly, and easier ways to get to your favorite web sites. Visit them at <www.sheclicks.com>.

# Learn to say 'free' in a new language

Learning a foreign language can be fun. Whether your goal is to become fluent in a second language or to just learn the basics for conversation, there are several free online resources.

Transparent.com: The Internet Language Community is a great place to start. They have developed a free online program that is both fun and effective. Their program allows you to approach the language of your choice in two ways. You can learn one word at a time with the Word-of-the-Day or you can pick up the pace with the dual-language newsletter.

The Word-of-the-Day is given alone and used in a sentence. If you're not sure of the pronunciation, you can hear the word or sentence spoken by a native.

The free monthly newsletter contains information on the history, holidays, customs, and slang expressions in the area where your chosen language is spoken. The newsletter is in English as well as the language you choose so you can practice your skills.

You can also send cards through the Internet in the language you are learning. Find Transparent.com: The Internet Language Community at <www.transparent.com>.

International Language Development is another free online resource for learning French, German, Japanese, Korean, Russian, and Spanish. In addition to learning the language, you can also learn the cooking styles of cultures that speak your chosen language and take virtual tours through some major cities. You can even chat online in your chosen language to test your skills. Visit International Language Development at <www.ild.com>.

If you're not ready to learn an entire second language but need a translation of a word, phrase, or Web site address, try FreeTranslation.com. You can have information translated into English from another language or from English to another language. Go online at <www.freetranslation.com>.

Dictionary.com at <www.dictionary.com> is another free Web site that can quickly translate words or phrases. They have 12 different translation combinations such as English to Portuguese and German to French.

# Explore the arts online

With technology at the center of so much of our world, you may feel the arts are sometimes left behind. If you want a little culture with your Internet, here are some ways to have both for free.

**Music.** Music enthusiasts, both experienced and beginners, will want to visit <www.musictheory.halifax.ns.ca> to take a free 26-lesson online course in music theory. Included in each lesson are an instruction sheet, a quiz, and an answer sheet. You don't have to register, just follow the lessons at your leisure.

You can also find a complete glossary of music terms at <www.hnh.com> by exploring their Learning Zone.

**Literature.** The Great Books Foundation is a nonprofit educational organization you can visit online at <www.greatbooks.com> or call at 800-222-5870. Through Great Books, you can read and discuss important works of literature. Start your own Great Books discussion group, order copies of books, receive a newsletter, and take part in special events. They even have a Junior Great Books program.

The Write Page is an online newsletter offering information on authors and books in a variety of genres, from science fiction to romance to murder mysteries to poetry and non-fiction. They also provide links for writers. Visit them at <www.writepage.com>.

**History.** History buffs will want to visit *History and Politics Out Loud* at <www.hpol.org>. You can listen to historical speeches and recordings such as Martin Luther King's "I have a dream" address and the original tape recordings that uncovered Richard Nixon's involvement in Watergate.

If you have always wanted to visit The Smithsonian but have yet to make it to Washington, D.C., your troubles are over. You can now tour many of the historical collections of The Smithsonian right from your home. The institution's Web site now includes pictures, brief descriptions, and historical significance of items. Visit <www.si.edu> to begin your journey.

Take a virtual stroll through The Library of Congress' Performing Arts Reading Room. Start at <www.lcweb.loc.gov/rr> and choose the Performing Arts link. From there, you can visit all avenues of art and history. Look at photos, view documents and maps, or listen to audio recordings from the

American Memory Sound Recording Collections. Hear band music from the Civil War era or folk music from the '30s.

If you're a fan of the music of the Civil War, you should visit <www.civilwarmusic.net>. It's filled with interesting facts about the music of the period, lyrics, photographs, and the origins of many of its songs.

**Art.** If great works of art thrill you, see them all without leaving home. Visit these Web sites for images and information on paintings, sculpture, jewelry, photographs, etc. and the artists who created them.

★ ArtMuseum.net is an Internet-based museum experience presented by Intel Corporation. Visit it at <www.artmuseum.net>.

★ The Art Museum Network at <www.amn.org> is the official website of the world's leading art museums.

★ Artcyclopedia at <www.artcyclopedia.com> allows you to visit art museums around the world, search for works by artist, title, medium, or subject, and view a monthly featured work with plenty of background information.

★ The Smithsonian American Art Museum at <www.nmaa.si.edu> offers a tour of collections and exhibits as well as a link to American Art worldwide.

## Learn from home for free

If you'd like to learn the latest exercises, expand your computer skills, manage your money, make a quilt, or discover your creative writing potential, just turn on your computer. The Internet is quickly becoming an outlet for free classes on just about every subject you can imagine. You're bound to find a class you can take at home — and it might even be free.

Third Age, an organization aimed at seniors, offers several free online classes taught through e-mail. Twice a week you will receive an e-mail with your assignments, which will include links to reading material, quizzes, and tests. Each class has a tutor, also a senior, to answer questions via e-mail should you get stuck. You can also join a study group with your fellow classmates through group e-mails.

Begin classes whenever you like and work at your own pace. Since there is no set meeting place or time for the class, you can work on your assignments when it is convenient for you. For more information or to register for a class, contact Third Age at <www.thirdage.com/learning/>.

Another good site to check out is Computers Made Easy for Seniors, offering information and resources for improving your computer skills. The Web site includes a glossary of Internet terms as well as links to free tutorials and instructional sites. Go to <www.csuchico.edu/~csu/seniors/computing.html>.

Learnfree.com, at <www.learnfree.com>, offers a variety of free online classes designed for seniors. Here are just a few.

★ **Napkin folding.** Add some flare to your next family gathering or dinner party with cloth napkins folded into the shape of flowers. This course provides step-by-step instructions on a well-known napkin-folding technique.

★ **Fitness for seniors.** Low-impact aerobics is a main ingredient in staying healthy. This course gives you tips on getting started and preventing injury and illness. You will also find testimonials from fellow seniors who have benefited from an aerobics program.

★ **Introduction to piano scales.** If you have always wanted to learn to play the piano but never had the chance or if you just want to brush up on your skills, look into this course. Beginners can start by learning the names of the notes and then move onto learning scales. If you're more advanced, you can jump right into the introduction to playing scales.

★ **Introduction to potted plants.** Add flowers and greenery to a walkway, a front porch, or a balcony. This course covers everything from pot type, color, and size to the best ways to plant your flowers. Once you've completed your project, you can move on to the Caring for Plants course.

★ **Swing dance for seniors.** Swing dance is making a comeback. If you're a little rusty and need a refresher course, you're in luck. This course covers the fundamentals to the fancy on the lindy, the jitterbug, and more.

# YARD AND GARDEN 'GIVEAWAYS'

Gardening is a hobby enjoyed by millions, and manufacturers know it. You could spend your children's inheritance on books, tools, plants, advice, and maintenance.

But growing beautiful things shouldn't be expensive. You can make your yard the envy of the neighborhood without spending a lot of money. For one thing, many companies want to give you free samples. Seed samples are especially nice because they continue to produce year after year. And the explosion of information on the Internet has been a bonanza to gardeners seeking free horticultural advice.

So keep your kids in the will and take advantage of some of these cost-saving offers and ideas. Once you realize how easy it is to garden inexpensively, the grass will start to seem greener on your side of the fence.

## Grow your groceries and save

Do you find yourself complaining every week about the high prices at the grocery store? And how about all those added ingredients that no one can pronounce? Fight back! Start growing your own food. You can buy seeds for pennies and get lots of healthy food for your family in return. With these free vegetable and herb catalogs, you'll want to get started right away.

**Seed Savers Exchange.** Don't like new-fangled things? Plant the way the pioneers did. Try these "heirloom" seeds for vegetables, herbs, and flowers. These seeds have been lovingly saved through generations of growing, without any scientific tinkering. You can have their free catalog by going online to <www.seedsavers.org>, or by writing to:

Seed Savers Exchange
3076 North Winn Road
Decorah, IA 52101

**Burpee.** One of the best-known seed companies, they offer a free catalog of their vegetables, herbs, and flowers. Call them at 800-888-1447, or go to their online site at <www.burpee.com> where you can request a catalog or place an order. Burpee frequently gives free flower and vegetable seed packets with orders.

**Stokes Seeds.** This company sells seeds to home gardeners and commercial growers, and has the largest "test garden" in North America. It's actually a working farm where they test their new varieties before selling them. Stokes Seeds has a Web site with a "tips" section, and newsletters that you can read online. You can order their free catalog online at <www.stokeseeds.com>, or write to:

Stokes Seeds
P.O. Box 548
Buffalo, NY 14240-0548

**Park Seed.** This company has been in business since 1868 selling seeds for flowers, vegetables, plants, shrubs, and trees. You can request a catalog with more than 2,000 items by visiting their Web site at <www.parkseed.com>. It's best to order a catalog in early winter before they run out. You can contact them at:

Park Seed
1 Parkton Avenue
Greenwood, SC 29647-0001
800-845-3369
E-mail: info@parkseed.com

**Johnny's Selected Seeds.** Located in Albion, Maine, this company sells vegetable seeds, herb seeds for cooking and medicine, and flower seeds. Their 1,200-item, full-color catalog is available to you at no charge. The catalog is also available online on their Web site at <www.johnnyseeds.com> where you can also get gardening tips and find out about new products. Write to:

Johnny's Selected Seeds
Foss Hill Road
Albion, ME 04910

If you have a computer with an Internet connection and are interested in growing organic foods, there are several companies that specialize in these seeds.

**Seeds of Change.** This seed company says that everything it sells is 100 percent organic. They also have a variety of seeds that have been handed down over many generations. You could grow vegetables exactly like your great-great grandparents did. There is also a free E-newsletter if you have e-mail. For more information and a free online catalog, go to <www.seedsofchange.com>.

**The Natural Gardening Company.** This all-natural company claims to be the first certified organic, mail-order seedling nursery in the country. For more than 11 years, they have been selling vegetable, herb, and flower seeds — tomatoes being their specialty. The company is online at <www.naturalgardening.com>, where you can find all sorts of useful information about gardening without using harmful chemicals.

---

### Find treasure in another's trash

Do you want a whole collection of gardening tools without having to pay retail prices? Start watching your newspaper for estate sales and auctions.

Sometimes people inherit what they think is a garage full of junk, when really they have hundreds of dollars worth of gardening tools. Often at auctions there is a flurry of bidding for things like furniture and collectibles. By the time the auctioneer gets around to the stuff in the garage, many people have left or spent their money.

You might get boxes of perfectly useful tools for a couple of dollars if you're patient. And who knows, you might find that someone hid a fortune in the gardening gloves you just bought for pennies.

---

# Seed your garden for free

Let's face it — companies want you to buy their products, and organizations want you to join. Sometimes these people are so eager to have you as a customer or member that they'll give you free samples with no obligation to buy anything. The following companies and organizations want to give you free seeds for your garden. Why not take them up on it?

**New Jersey Championship Tomatoes.** Want to grow the biggest tomatoes on the block? This company promises to send rare and select champion tomato seeds if you send them a self-addressed, stamped envelope and $1 for shipping and handling. They mail all seeds during the first week of December. Write to:

New Jersey Championship Tomato Weigh-In
Box 123
Monmouth Beach, NJ 07750

**Just for teachers.** If you or someone you know is a teacher, this could be the perfect project for October. Teachers can get a free pack of pumpkin seeds and instructions for growing pumpkins in the classroom. Send an SASE and $1 for shipping and handling to:

Pumpkin Seed Offer
Pumpkin Circle Project
P.O. Box 67
Santa Cruz, CA 95063

**Trees Again.** This non-profit organization has a mission. They want to replant the forests and meadows of this country with the trees and flowers that were originally here. They will send you handmade, recycled paper that contains tree and/or wildflower seeds for you to plant. Instructions are included. All they ask is that you make a $1 or more contribution and send a legal-sized SASE to:

Free Seeds
c/o Trees Again
726 Mountain Meadows Drive
Golden, CO 80403

**Butterfly Club of America.** If you plant these, they will come. The butterfly club of America wants to give you free seeds for a nectar-rich flower garden that will attract butterflies to your yard. Plant a garden that will create a haven for these beautiful creatures. Send an SASE (two stamps) to:

Butterfly Club of America
Box 629
Burgin, KY 40310

# 'Wooden shoe' like these free catalogs?

You would pay a lot of money for a book of high-quality color photos of beautiful flowers. But you can find plenty of great color catalogs for free. Here are some eye-catching catalogs that are practically works of art. All of these companies sell flowers from Holland, especially tulip bulbs, one of nature's best ideas. There is no obligation to buy anything.

**Breck's Dutch Bulbs.** This company sells tulips, daffodils, hyacinths, irises, wildflowers and more. Breck's guarantees your satisfaction, or you can return your order for a full refund or exchange. And if you order before fall planting time (July 31 is the cutoff each year), you can get up to 50 percent off the retail price of your order. Breck's, a strictly mail-order company, is now also online for your viewing pleasure.

To get your free color catalog, simply call 800-806-1972 or visit their Web site at <www.brecks.com>.

**Dutch Gardens.** Escape the winter blahs with beautiful photos of tulips from Holland. Dutch Gardens offers a Spring Planting Catalog and a Fall Planting Catalog, both free of charge. They also have a Web site with an online catalog and delightful information such as "The History of the Tulip," and, of course, lovely pictures of flowers, flowers, flowers.

For a free catalog, contact them at:

Dutch Gardens
725 Vassar Ave.
P.O. Box 2037
Lakewood, NJ 08701
800-818-3861
<www.dutchgardens.com>

**John Scheepers, Inc.** For more than 90 years, John Scheepers has supplied gardeners with tulips, narcissi, lilies, amaryllis, and rare and unusual Dutch bulbs. Their prices are competitively low, and they offer volume discounts. You can have their 76-page catalog, complete with 500 color photos, for free. The catalog, called *Beauty from Bulbs*, offers 700 varieties of gorgeous flowers for your garden.

To request your free catalog, go online to <www.johnscheepers.com> and click on "Request a Catalog." Or write to:

John Scheepers, Inc.
23 Tulip Drive
Bantam, CT 06750

**Van Dyck's.** You guessed it — another fabulous and free catalog featuring color photos of flowers from Holland. Van Dyck's offers a 100-page catalog of irises, crocuses, tulips, daffodils, and many others. These people are determined to keep their prices the lowest in the industry. If you see a lower price in any other consumer catalog, they want you to let them know. They will cheerfully refund you the difference. They do have a Web site, and it's full of good gardening information, an online catalog, and more beautiful pictures. If you are stumped by a gardening problem, you can click on "Ask Jan" and fire off a question for owner Jan Van Dyck. Of course there is no charge for the advice.

For your free catalog, call 800-248-2852, or visit their Web site at <www.vandycks.com>.

## Add roses to your coffee table

Do you love roses? These free catalogs will brighten your mailbox and your day as you see old favorites and new creations in the world of roses.

**Jackson & Perkins.** These people know roses. They've been in the rose business for over 125 years, and they are constantly developing new varieties and winning awards. You can have a free copy of their 56-page color catalog, which includes not just roses, but also tools, gardener's clothing, greenhouses, storage sheds, and more. Like many mail-order companies, Jackson & Perkins is also now online. If you are a Web-surfing bargain hunter, you can go to their Web site and click on "Yard Sale" to find great discounts on out-of-season merchandise.

To order your free catalog, go online to <www.jacksonandperkins.com> or call 800-292-4769.

**Nor'East Miniature Roses.** What could be cuter than a rose? Why, a miniature rose, of course. Nor'East specializes in these tiny beauties, growing many of them in their greenhouses in Rowley, Massachusetts. You can

have a free color catalog of all the latest varieties of miniatures by visiting their Web site at <www.noreast-miniroses.com > or writing to:

Nor'East Miniature Roses, Inc.
P.O. Box 307
Rowley, MA 01969

## Dig these free gardening catalogs

Here are some good discount catalogs that you can order free of charge. You won't have to pay full price for gardening equipment, landscaping plants, or decorations for your yard. You could even use these catalogs to get ideas and plan for things you want to do in the future.

**Northern Tool.** Northern Tool wants to save you money on lawn and garden equipment. They also sell power tools, generators, pressure washers, and much more. For a free catalog, check online at <www.NorthernTool.com>, or call 800-427-0417.

**A. M. Leonard.** This company has been providing gardening tools and supplies for professionals since 1885. Now their catalog and discounts are available to you. The catalog also includes special gifts for gardeners. To order a free catalog, go to their Web site at <www.amleonard.com>, or contact them at:

A.M. Leonard, Inc.
241 Fox Drive
Piqua, OH 45356-0816
800-543-8955

**Stark Brothers.** You can spruce up your lawn and save money on food by planting fruit trees. Stark Brothers, in business since 1816, specializes in fruit and nut trees. They would like to send you their catalog for free and give you a $5 discount coupon towards your first order. You can contact them at:

Stark Brothers Nurseries & Orchards Co.
P.O. Box 510
Louisiana, MO 63353-0510
800-775-6415

Want to put some pizzazz in your yard? Try adding a sculpture or a colorful bird feeder. If you're the creative type, these catalogs could be great inspiration for your own designs and artwork.

**Design Toscano.** This stuff isn't cheap, but it sure is fun to look at. Design Toscano offers a free catalog of their great sculptures, gargoyles, fountains, stone benches, and more. They even have outdoor wall art. For a free catalog, visit their Web site at <www.designtoscano.com>, or call 800-525-0733, extension 2017.

## Teatime for your English garden

Have you always wanted an English country garden to relax in at the end of the day? Now you can plan that garden with the help of a native English woman. Lady Sarah Seymour would like to send you her free catalog, *Seymour's Selected Seeds*. The catalog is filled with English flower seeds and ideas for arranging your garden. Her American staff is in Sussex, Virginia, but the flowers are all English varieties. She also has a lovely Web site complete with gardening tips and great pictures of English gardens. You can get a free catalog by going online at <www.seymourseedusa.com> or by writing to:

Seymour's Selected Seeds
P.O. Box 1346
Sussex, VA 23884-0346

What could be more appropriate than taking tea in your English country garden? How about making tea *for* your garden?

Plantamins, Inc. would like to send you a sample of PlanTea, a specialty fertilizer for all your indoor and outdoor plants. PlanTea is an organic fertilizer in a tea bag that you brew just like real tea. Once the water has cooled, it can be poured directly on your plants. It is made from kelp, rock phosphate, fish bone meal, greensand, yarrow, vegetable powders, herbs, and other ingredients, and is safe around children and pets. PlanTea will never burn your plants the way some synthetic fertilizers do. For your sample, send $2 to:

Plantamins, Inc.
P.O. Box 1980
Kodiak, AK 99615-1980

# Create a critter haven without cost

Want your yard to be the neighborhood hangout for birds and other wildlife? You can attract creatures great and small with these free instructions on building birdhouses and wildlife habitats. And once they start visiting regularly, you can use the free guides to identify your new friends.

**Make a wildlife habitat.** With all the home and commercial construction going on in our country, animals are literally dying for a place to live. Welcome them back home by setting aside a portion of your yard as a natural habitat. You can make your yard comfortable for critters with simple things like branches and plants. For more information, send for the free brochure *Make it Natural* by writing to:

National Wildlife Federation
1412 16th St. NW
Washington, DC 20036

**Build your own birdhouses.** Do you love those adorable birdhouses you see in stores and magazines, but don't want to take out a second mortgage to buy them? Make your own with leftover wood and other scrap material. This 32-page brochure will show you all you need to know to build birdhouses and identify the birds that start calling your place home. Ask for *Home for the Birds* by writing to:

Consumer Information Center
Dept. 572X
Pueblo, CO 81009

**Learn how to attract feathered friends.** Need tenants for your new birdhouses? The Hyde Bird Feeder Company wants to send you a free brochure on how to attract birds. Of course, they want to sell you one of their bird feeders, but there is no obligation to buy one. Ask for *How to Attract Birds* by writing to:

Hyde Bird Feeder Company
56 Felton St.
Waltham, MA 02254

**Discover the names of your flying visitors.** It would be rude to entertain guests without finding out their names. You could spend a lot of money on fancy bird books, but why bother? Dunecraft, the maker of the only bird feeder endorsed by the Audubon Society, wants to send you a free bird-watching catalog. Call 800-593-5656.

Have interesting birds using your yard as a pit stop? Find out about migrating birds by requesting a free pamphlet on that subject from:

Office of Migratory Bird Management
U.S. Fish and Wildlife Service
4401 N. Fairfax Drive, Suite 634
Arlington, VA 22203

---

### Recycle a gardening book

Don't pay retail for a gardening book without checking this Web site first. Gail's Books at <www.gailsbooks.com> is run by Gail Sanders in Richland, Washington. She sells used books on a variety of subjects, including gardening. Just go to the Web site and click on "Home and Garden" for a current list of books. Gail includes a full description of the book, including its condition and price. She may have one copy or several of a particular title.

For example, *The Garden Book* by John Brookes is a 288-page, hardcover book with a dust jacket, published by Crown in 1986. It's in very good condition and is listed for $15.

---

# Grow green and save greenbacks

Do you try to reduce, reuse, and recycle whenever you can? Organic gardening should save you money because of its emphasis on using natural solutions. For example, did you know that ladybugs will eat aphids? You can plant certain herbs like fennel, dill, and parsley to attract ladybugs to your garden. The ladybugs should take care of the aphid problem, and you can still use the herbs you planted.

If you have Internet access, you can visit the Web site of Terra Viva Organics at <www.tvorganics.com>. This Canadian company specializes in organic growing. They offer free growing advice, a free monthly newsletter, and lots of tips for a healthier garden. You can also order products like sticky insect traps that you can use instead of pesticides. There is no obligation to buy anything, and you can even access a newsletter archive to see articles from months past.

If you are thinking about composting, but not sure you want to invest in equipment, this offer is for you. The manufacturer of the Compos-Tumbler compost bin claims its product can turn food, garden, and lawn waste into useful compost in just 14 days. In fact, they are so confident of their product that they're willing to let you use it free for a full year. For more information, call 800-880-2345.

## Make your own worm bin

You've heard of composting — piling up organic garbage and turning it once in a while to create fertilizer. It's a good way to recycle your trash, but it can take several months for the process to be completed.

Redworms, also called compost or manure worms, will process your organic material quickly and efficiently. They quite simply eat and excrete all the organic material in their path, leaving behind "castings" which are their waste material. The castings of redworms are better than other types of compost because the worms create more nutrients per square inch of soil as they eat their way through it.

This type of composting is called "vermicomposting," and it can be done in a compost bin made of wood or plastic. Your little workers can live inside or out, just as long as the temperature doesn't get higher than 85 degrees or lower than 32 degrees. Generally, you can expect to process one pound of your garbage per week for every square foot of surface area.

★ **Be creative and thrifty.** To get started, you'll need a bin. Although you can use wood or plastic, wood is often preferred because the plastic tends to "sweat" once the temperature in the box starts to heat up. Worms aren't fussy about architecture, so recycle whatever you can. You can use an old bureau drawer or an old crate for your worm bin. A box about 8 to 12 inches deep is best. Put some holes in the sides of the bin, near the bottom, so some air can get in.

★ **Make a comfy bed.** Worms need bedding for their home. Start by putting a couple inches of gravel in the bottom of the bin for drainage. You can use shredded cardboard or newspaper, dried, crumbled leaves, sawdust, or aged manure. Don't use colored newspaper or shredded magazines because the dyes in the print are poison for the worms. Dampen your bedding with some water, and mix in some plain old dirt to make your worms feel more at home.

★ **Add worms.** You can find redworms at your local bait shop, or at an organic nursery. Be sure to get redworms, since other types of worms will not work. One pound of worms should be enough to process about a pound of garbage per week. If you know your worms, you can often find redworms in aged manure piles. Just be sure they're the right type of worms. Cover the worms you've added with a few inches of your bedding material. Worms work best in the dark.

★ **Feed them regularly.** Your worms can eat fruit and vegetable scraps, including all peels, coffee grounds, tea bags, and crushed eggshells. Add half an inch of food and mix it with the top layer of soil once or twice a week. About half a pound of food for every pound of worms is about right. After feeding, be sure to cover them over again with bedding material like shredded newspaper.

★ **Harvest your fertilizer.** Your fertilizer will be ready to harvest in about three months. You'll know because your compost will look more like dirt than food and paper. Simply move the dirt over to one side, and add new bedding in the space you created. Toss in some new food for the worms, and the worms will automatically move to that side to eat. After about 10 days, all the worms should have made the move, and you can remove your fertilizer from the other side.

The idea of having a "worm farm" may seem strange, but redworms are really all around us working anyway. If you've ever turned over a rock and seen small, red, squirming things, you've probably already met some. And if you've ever encountered "red wigglers" at the bait and tackle shop, you've definitely made their acquaintance.

Why not put redworms to work for you? You'll be helping to save the local landfill, making chemical-free food for your garden, and saving yourself a bundle on fertilizer.

# Put the government to work in your yard

Do you ever wonder what your tax money is used for? Fortunately, not all of it goes toward $800 hammers for the Pentagon. Believe it or not, entire departments of government employees are paid to help you with your yard.

**National Resources Conservation Service.** This government department exists to help people conserve, improve, and sustain this country's natural resources. This includes your yard, whether it's the size of Rhode Island or the size of a postage stamp.

The NRCS offers free, detailed brochures on subjects such as tree planting, pest management, backyard ponds, composting, terracing — even creating a wildlife habitat in your backyard. For more information contact:

Natural Resources Conservation Service
Attn: Conservation Communications Staff
P.O. Box 2890
Washington, DC 20013
888-LANDCARE
<www.nhq.nrcs.usda.gov/CCS/Backyard.html>

**United States Department of Agriculture.** Abraham Lincoln founded the USDA in 1862 at a time when 90 percent of Americans were farmers. Now that only 2 percent of us are farmers, the USDA is still hard at work helping Americans grow things.

Over the years, the USDA has built up quite an arsenal of information about how to grow things, and all of it is free. The USDA Web site features a huge database with thousands of horticultural topics. You can learn about slug control, dividing bulbs, and building a butterfly garden. In addition, there are thousands of pictures of the plants and plant-eating critters they describe. You can access this amazing resource at <www.usda.gov/news/garden.htm>.

**State Extension Service.** Before you call a landscaping company to help you with a gardening project, check out this excellent, free service. This government-funded program puts experts in each county or section of each state to help local people with horticultural problems.

The extension services are usually run in cooperation with state universities, so you have access to the latest agricultural research. Usually these local programs have a few full-time employees and several people who volunteer to help local gardeners and farmers. The universities even train local people to become Master Gardeners, experts who volunteer their time to answer your gardening questions.

You can find your local extension service by contacting the nearest state university and asking about the extension service program. If you have Internet access, you can use an online nationwide directory. Go to <www.reeusda.gov>.

**U.S. Botanic Garden.** Established by Congress in 1820, this stands as the country's oldest botanic garden. The U.S. Botanic Garden's free services include a plant hotline and an educational program. For more information, go online at <www.aoc.gov> or contact the garden at:

U.S. Botanic Garden
245 First Street SW
Washington, DC 20024
202-225-8333

# Set your sites on free gardening info online

Maybe you've tried to surf the Web for information about gardening, but instead of finding a few good sites, a tidal wave of information flooded your computer screen. Don't despair. Here are some of the best sites for free expert information on horticulture.

**Become a garden wizard.** Go to Burpee, one of the most trusted names in gardening, for gardening information you can trust. At <www.burpee.com>, you'll find all sorts of resources to help make your thumb green.

Sign up for Burpee's e-mail newsletter, and receive helpful tips and other gardening secrets. Or consult the "Garden Wizard," which recommends the perfect plant for you. Just answer a few multiple-choice questions such as how much sun it will get, when you want it to bloom, and how big a plant you want, and the "Garden Wizard" will match you with a fruit, vegetable, flower, or ornamental plant.

If you want a little more information, you can attend Burpee's online "Garden School." This lets you learn everything you need to know about vegetables, annuals, and perennials. You'll even take an occasional pop quiz to spark your memory. And Burpee's site never gets old, because it offers a gardening tip of the day.

**Follow this guide.** Another super site for gardening is Garden Guides at <www.gardenguides.com/forms/search>. Type in any plant name in Garden Guide's search engine, and chances are you'll come up with all the information you need.

You'll find a huge index of articles that are broken into categories such as Design, Flower Gardening, Food From the Garden, Roses, and State Flowers. There is even a section called "Tours" which takes you on informative walks through famous gardens. The pictures are so good you can almost smell the flowers.

Also, you can send for free newsletters on subjects like perennial gardening, growing herbs, and vegetable gardening. All this in one Web site.

**Go to garden school.** Next time you're out surfing the net, check out Etera's Web site at <www.etera.com>. You enter your ZIP code for a list of stores near you, then click on which store you want to explore. Each store's site is divided into three main sections: Shop, Garden Club, and Garden School. Click on Shop to go window-shopping for gardening supplies. There is no obligation to buy.

Click on Garden Club for lots of interesting stuff for gardeners. You can sign up for Etera's free newsletter, or log on to a free online forum for gardeners. Check out the Web pages of other green thumbs, or send a free electronic card with vivid flower scenes. You can even download beautiful gardening screensavers for your computer. And all of it's free to you.

Garden School is Etera's technical information on gardening. It features dozens of instructional articles on topics such as laying a flagstone path, forcing bulbs, and aerating your lawn. Stumped by a gardening problem in your yard? Send an e-mail to one of Etera's gardening experts. They will cheerfully answer your questions, and there is no fee for any of these services.

What are you waiting for? Surf's up for free gardening advice.

# INDEX

# I

# J

# L

# M